THE SUMERIAN ROOTS OF THE AMERICAN PREAMBLE

Richard:
Thanks for having
me have an expert puts
a book together. Very
best to Uoa—
Jim [illegible]

THE SUMERIAN ROOTS OF THE AMERICAN PREAMBLE

James T. McGuire

Illustrations by Cecilia McGuire

LEP

Lough Erne Press

1994

THE SUMERIAN ROOTS OF THE AMERICAN PREAMBLE

Text design: Richard Jones

Printed in the United States of America

ISBN 0-9640880-0-2

Library of Congress Catalog Card Number 93-081291

DUST THOU ART NOT

The Prologue

Created from clay,
Ignited by his god,
The Sumerian took the base
Unlit material of his own being,
Inscribed on it a dream.
Then, fire quenched,
He became, once again,
Part of the very substance
That made his dream
Immortal.

The Prologue to the Law Code of Lipit-Ishtar (1934-1924 B.C.) sets out the purposes of the Sumerian king's administration and resembles, in form and substance, the Preamble to the Constitution of the United States more closely than any document produced during the centuries that separate the two.

"Mankind are so much the same, in all times and places, that history informs us of nothing new or strange in this particular. Its chief use is only to discover the constant and universal principles of human nature."

David Hume, *Essays*

Anatolian fertility goddess: terra cotta, height: 6.5 inches (ca. 6th century B.C.)

To Patricia

And to Milly and Samuel Kramer

CONTENTS

APPENDIX

MAPS AND ILLUSTRATIONS

Maps

Illustrations

ABBREVIATIONS

The following abbreviations have been used herein:

ABL	*Assyrian and Babylonian Letters belonging to the Kouyunjik Collection(s) of the British Museum,* by R.F. Harper (Chicago, 1892-1914).
ANET	*Ancient Near Eastern Texts Relating to the Old Testament,* 3rd. ed., ed. James B. Pritchard, (Princeton: Princeton Univ. Press, 1969).
AR	M. Schorr, *Altbabylonische Rechtsurkunden* (Leipzig: J.C. Hinrichs'sche Buchhandlung, 1913).
BWL	W.G. Lambert, *Babylonian Wisdom Literature,* (Oxford: Clarendon Press, 1960).
CH	Code of Hammurabi
HL	Hittite Laws
JAOS	*Journal of the American Oriental Society* (New Haven, 1843).
JCS	*Journal of Cuneiform Studies* (New Haven, 1947).
JNES	*Journal of Near Eastern Studies* (Chicago, 1942).
JSS	*Journal of Semitic Studies* (Manchester, 1956).
LE	Laws of Eshnunna
LI	Laws of Lipit-Ishtar
LU	Laws of Ur-Nammu
MAL	Middle Assyrian Laws
NG	Adam Falkenstein, *Die neusumerischen Gerichtsurkunden* (Munchen: Verlag der Bayerischen Akademie der Wissenschaften, 1956).
RSL	Rhodian Sea-Law
RSV	*Revised Standard Version of the New Oxford Annotated Bible* (Oxford, 1973).
U.C.C.	Uniform Commercial Code (U.L.A.).

FOREWORD

This book by James T. McGuire is an outstanding example of a humanistic research project that began as a rather hopeless visionary quest for a solution to an enigmatic literary-historical puzzle, and ended up with a series of findings and discoveries that open up a vast new area of comparative inquiry into the evolution and development of Western man's political concepts and legal practices.

Struck by the rather bizarre coincidence that the wording of the Preamble to the American Constitution was almost identical with that of the Prologue to the Sumerian document commonly known as the Lipit-Istar Law Code, inscribed with a reed stylus on clay tablets in the first half of the twentieth century B.C., McGuire began searching for some explanation of this striking correspondence between two documents separated so far in time and space, whose authors came from such different cultural backgrounds and horizons. Could there be some overlooked, unrecognized link between the two, and if so, what might be its nature and character?

To resolve this rather fascinating problem, it was obviously essential (1) to have some idea of the origin of the wording of the Preamble to the Constitution; (2) to probe and analyze the Sumerian ethical, political, and legal ground and setting of the Lipit-Istar Law Code; (3) to have a reasonably comprehensive understanding of the evolution and development of Western man's political views and legal thought and practice during the well-nigh four millennia that elapsed between the days of the Sumerian authors of the Lipit-Istar Code and the days of the Founding Fathers responsible for the wording of the Preamble to the Constitution.

Beginning therefore with an overview of the more significant theories relating to the sources of the Preamble that had been proposed by modern legal scholars, McGuire concluded that none of these were cogent and convincing. Neither the New England Confederation of 1643, nor the various state constitutions adopted after the American colonies renounced their allegiance to Great Britain, nor the venerable Swiss Constitution of 1291, could be reasonably considered as sources for the wording of the Preamble to the American Constitution, and certainly not for the literary form in which it was enshrined. Nor did the stylistic format of the Preamble have any recognizable counterpart in any of the numerous and variant constitutions presently current throughout the world.

McGuire next turned to an investigation of the ancient Sumerian laws and legal practices to see if he could uncover the background for the wording of the Prologue to the Lipit-Istar Law Code. It was in the course of this highly specialized, original investigation that he discovered, identified, and analyzed quite a number of parallels between the ancient Sumerian laws and legal practices, and their modern Anglo-American counterparts: laws and practices relating to mayhem, conversion, bailment, suretyship, contracts, foreclosures, burglary, murder and false imprisonment. Virtually none of these parallels had hitherto been recognized and evaluated by any cuneiformist or by any contemporary legal historian.

Having thus established a "mirror-image" between Sumerian law and Anglo-American law corresponding in a way to the Preamble-Prologue "mirror-image," McGuire next turned to an examination of the ethical, political, and legal ideas which were current in Colonial America, and with which some of the authors of the Preamble were undoubtedly imbued, and found that these had been profoundly influenced by the two books most cherished and valued in the Western world throughout the centuries: Plato's Republic and the Hebrew Bible. But these two impressive and inspiring works, time-honored though they were, had obviously not been created in a vacuum—the views, thoughts and insights expressed in them must have had precursors and forerunners in the ancient world. He therefore delved deeply into a study of the possible and probable interconnection, interrelation, and intercommunication between the Greeks, Hebrews, Persians, and Babylonians of the first millennium B.C., and realized that not a few of the ethical, political and legal concepts found in the Republic and the Bible had been absorbed, assimilated, and adapted from Babylonian sources, which in turn went back to Sumerian origins.

This was especially true of the ideas relating to the purposes and goals of an effectively functioning organized state, and it is not surprising therefore that though written down millennia apart, the Preamble to the American Constitution and the Prologue to a Sumerian Law Code made use of a similar vocabulary to formulate their aims and goals: the establishment of justice, the ensuring of domestic tranquility; protection from foreign enemies; the promotion of the welfare and well-being of all the people. What is rather astonishing however is how and why the two documents came to summarize their ethical and political purposes in almost identical grammatical, syntactical literary turns of speech, a "mystery" that remains unresolved.

While, therefore, McGuire failed to find a solution for the enigma that sparked his researches, he has succeeded in providing us with a book that is of fundamental significance for political and legal history. His imaginative insights into the circuitous and labyrinthine channels by which Sumerian political and legal concepts may have penetrated and influenced Western man over the millennia will help to illuminate much that is dark and obscure about the role of cultural diffusion in the history of civilization. And the surprising discovery of a considerable number of specific, concrete, significant parallels between Sumerian and Anglo-American law will inaugurate an aspect of legal research that may well revolutionize the study of the history of law and legal practice, both ancient and modern.

Samuel Noah Kramer
Curator Emeritus of the Tablet Collection, University Museum
Clark Research Professor (Emeritus) of Assyriology, University of Pennsylvania

I

THE MYSTERY OF THE PREAMBLE

Introduction

When I was a boy making my way through the New York City public school system, I was taught in the eighth grade by a wonderful and formidable lady, a Miss Lunning. She had many novel ideas. On the first day of school, for instance, she required each of her students to sand and varnish his or her desk. On the following day, everyone began the term with a pristine and very personalized writing surface. She made us sit, listen to, and learn the titles and composers of many exotic and bewildering musical selections; amongst them the "Quartet" from *Rigoletto* by Verdi, the "Sextette" from *Lucia* by Donizetti, the "Habanera" from *Carmen* by Bizet. She insisted upon a hardy regimen of rote learning. We memorized passages from Shakespeare, Milton, and Coleridge, the beginning of the Declaration of Independence, at least as far as "Governments are instituted among men, deriving their just powers from the consent of the governed," and, of course, the Preamble to the United States Constitution. Its phrases resounded in our minds: "establish justice," "ensure domestic tranquility," "provide a common defense," "promote the general welfare," "secure the blessings of liberty."

One night many years later, after I had finished Professor Samuel Noah Kramer's fine book *The Sumerians* and was leafing through the Appendixes, I came across the Prologue to the Law Code of Lipit-Ishtar, a Sumerian king of the twentieth century B.C. Immediately an impression of the sterling Miss Lunning took form before me, and I thought, "My Lord, this is the Preamble to the United States Constitution!" So close was the apparent correspondence between Prologue and Preamble in grammatical structure and in the content and sequence of their objectives that I wrote to Professor Kramer inquiring whether the similarity had ever been noted or commented upon. His response, though gracious, was basically the command, "Be specific!"

At the time, I was about to retire as general counsel of a San Francisco corporation specializing in inventory and accounts receivable financing. I was not then, and am not now, a historian. Nevertheless, intrigued by the curious similarity that marked two documents emanating from such disparate cultures, drafted so many years apart, I decided to attempt to find some reasonable theory to account for the phenomenon.

It appeared to be generally accepted that the Preamble had been adapted from earlier political writings of Colonial America, an explanation, for reasons discussed below, not completely convincing. The Prologue's origins, surprisingly, were not difficult to trace. The image of a powerful, just, and benevolent king, capable of realizing the goals of the Prologue and charged by his gods with a duty to do so, was a commonplace of Sumerian hymnology.

Was there, then, a connection between the culture of ancient Sumer and the civilization being founded on the shores of the American continent? Indeed there was, that link, or series of links, being the endless reiteration by intervening generations of the Prologue's objectives. The cry for security, justice, and welfare, traditional goals of the modern state and the substance of both Prologue and Preamble, arises everywhere throughout the religious, political, philosophical, and legal writings of the Sumerians, Akkadians, Hittites, Hebrews, Persians, Greeks, Western Europeans, and Colonial Americans.

Halfway through recorded history, Greek-Ionian philosophers explained how man and the state had come to be; Plato peopled his commonwealth with professionals trained in the art of government; and Aristotle elaborated the services the state is to provide if it is to be self-sufficient. The progress and adaptation of this Greek speculation through the interval which separates Greece flourishing from the American Revolution is the history of Western theoretical statecraft.

But Socrates was not the first to ask what a state is, or what a statesman. The very first laws of Sumer make it clear that men of the third millennium B.C. had already learned how human beings, living in a group, should conduct themselves. They had identified the admirable qualities men always hope to find in their leaders, and they had reached agreement, endorsed by subsequent ages, as to the goals an ideal state might be expected to achieve. When the Sumerians invented a process for memorializing their thought, they and their successors gave voice to those ideas constantly, in their poetry, their prayer, and their laws, during the twenty-two centuries that passed before the Greeks learned how to write with their new Phoenician letters.

No one can tell, with any degree of certainty, how much of the brilliant Greek work-product represents borrowings from the East. Numerous parallels drawn throughout this book demonstrate how similar were beliefs and practices of the ancient Near East and ideas associated with Greek scholars and statesmen who traveled there or were reputed to have done so before Plato's time. Some measure of their understanding was surely based upon Mesopotamian ideas. Many of the provisions included by Plato in his dialogue the *Laws* are so similar in form and content to those of Hammurabi that it is difficult to conclude they did not derive, ultimately, from a Babylonian source. The Greek form *Ean tis* ("If a man"), used liberally by Plato in the *Laws*, is identical with the usual beginning of all ancient Near Eastern laws, including Hammurabi's. Is it possible that Plato knew of Hammurabi's Code?

Scholars agree the Persian king Darius fashioned his Ordinance of Good Regulations (ca. 520 B.C.) on Hammurabi's Code (ca. 1765 B.C.), using Babylonian priests for help with the translation. Plato and other Greeks knew of and admired the laws of the Persian king. Might they also have known the source from which those laws were taken? If Darius's Ordinance, which has since been lost, contained the substance of the prologue and epilogue to Hammurabi's work, the divine attributes of wisdom, power, and benevolence always claimed for Mesopotamian rulers by their poets, and the concept of a blessed state those qualities portend, passed without pause through Hammurabi's masterpiece into the political philosophy of Greece.

The form used to express the purposes of Preamble and Prologue poses a special and vexing problem. That form is too explicit and too profound to be passed over as merely coincidental; yet I have been unable to uncover any intermediate writing that resembles the manner in which the Prologue presents its goals as precisely as does that of the Preamble.

The Preamble

WE THE PEOPLE of the United States, in Order to form a more perfect Union, establish Justice, insure domestic Tranquility, provide for the common defence, promote the general Welfare and secure the Blessings of Liberty to ourselves and our Posterity, do ordain and establish this CONSTITUTION for the United States of America.

The English "preamble" comes from the Latin *prae-ambulare,* meaning "to walk before." "Prologue" is from the Greek *pro-logos,* a "speech before." Both terms describe introductory statements and are frequently used interchangeably. A preamble more often than not precedes a formal document or statute. A prologue usually introduces a dramatic performance or discourse and is often cast in poetic form. Some introductions to the legal compilations of ancient Mesopotamian kings were originally recited as poetry and are called prologues. Presenting formal codes of law, they might as well have been called preambles.

The single sentence of the American Preamble has acquired a great prestige. Distinguished writers hold it to be an intellectual achievement of the first order. Edward S. Corwin, an expert on American constitutional theory, asks, "Where could a better statement be found of the wider objectives sought by good government?" Another constitutional scholar, David K. Watson, exclaims, "It is doubtful if history affords a finer expression of governmental purpose and a more philosophical conception of national desire." Catherine Drinker Bowen, known for her carefully researched historical accounts, says, "The seven verbs rolled out: to form, establish, ensure, provide, promote, secure, ordain. One might challenge the centuries to better these verbs."[1]

These tributes are well deserved. Nevertheless, America's early settlers were not the first to set forth the objectives of good government expressed in the Preamble. The quest for a government possessing the wisdom to establish justice, the power to maintain order within, to defend against aggression from without, and the goodness to provide the necessities of life for its people began in the most ancient days. The scribe of a Sumerian king, in fact, recorded the purposes of the Preamble for the first time on a clay tablet almost four thousand years ago.

The Prologue

In 1929, fragments of four clay tablets recovered from the ancient Sumerian center of legal learning at Nippur by the 1889-1900 University of Pennsylvania expedition were taken from storage at the University Museum. They were to be catalogued together with almost three thousand other tablets and fragments and placed with other archives from Nippur. A decade later, Dr. Samuel N. Kramer, making a brief survey of the Nippur collection for literary material, noted that the four pieces contained segments of laws. Shortly thereafter, Francis Rue Steele also noted the pieces and proposed to publish them. In the course of transliteration and translation, the four fragments were ingeniously and painstakingly matched. When compared with previously published documents, it became apparent that these were no random segments of Sumerian laws, but that all four fragments came from one large tablet of a code that antedated the famous collection of Hammurabi's Laws by almost two centuries. The excitement that must have gripped those dedicated researchers when they realized the true significance of their project is barely hinted at in Steele's reserved report: "Sections of a prologue and an epilogue also came to light indicating that the text was actually a code of laws; and, finally, the name of the codifier, Lipit-Ishtar, was deciphered."[2]

The partial reconstruction of the Lipit-Ishtar tablet indicates it measured roughly nine by eleven inches, contained around twelve hundred lines of text, of which about four hundred could be restored. Of these, approximately one hundred lines are devoted to a Prologue to the legal corpus. The Prologue told why the great gods of Sumer called Lipit-Ishtar to the princeship of the land:

. . . when An (and) Enlil had called Lipit-Ishtar—Lipit-Ishtar, the wise shepherd, whose name had been pronounced by Nunamnir—to the princeship of the land in order to establish justice in the land, to banish complaints, to turn back enmity (and) rebellion by the force of arms, (and) to bring well-being to the Sumerians and Akkadians, then I, Lipit-Ishtar. . . procured . . . the freedom of . . . the sons and daughters of Sumer and Akkad upon whom . . . slaveship . . . had been imposed.[3]

When the objectives of the regime instituted by the Sumerian king in 1934 B.C. are matched, phrase by phrase, against the goals of the nation planned by the Founding Fathers of the United States in 1787 A.D., the similarity between the two becomes immediately apparent:

Preamble	**Prologue**
In order to	
(1) *form a more perfect union*	
(2) *establish justice*	(1) *establish justice in the land*
(3) *ensure domestic tranquility*	(2) *banish complaints*
(4) *provide for the common defense*	(3) *turn back enmity (and) rebellion by the force of arms*
(5) *promote the general welfare*	(4) *bring well-being to the Sumerians and Akkadians*
(6) *secure the blessings of Liberty to ourselves and our Posterity.*	(5) *I . . . procured . . . the freedom of . . . the sons and daughters of Sumer and Akkad.*

The second and fifth objectives of the Preamble correspond to their Sumerian counterparts in this translation of the Prologue; the third and fourth address the issue of the state's internal and external security, as do the second and third objects of the Prologue; the Preamble's sixth object looks to the freedom of the existing and future peoples of the land, as does the fifth object of the Prologue, although expressed there as an accomplishment rather than as a purpose.

If the Preamble had employed a familiar, traditional, or even recognizable form for setting out the purposes of the United States Constitution, tracing that form back through intervening centuries would have been interesting and useful. The fact is, however, that both the Preamble, written in 1787, and the Prologue, written nearly four thousand years earlier, express their objectives in an unparalleled fashion. Each sets out what have become traditional goals of benign and effective government by incorporating a series of mutually dependent infinitive clauses dealing with justice, internal order, defense against external aggression, the welfare of the people, and freedom—and in that same order. No modern document, independently prepared, employs a similar form.

A survey completed in 1949 indicated that the world's two and a quarter billion human beings were organized into approximately eighty-three political entities that were accorded, for most purposes, sovereign national status.[4] Of these, seventy-three nations, nearly ninety percent, had adopted written constitutions, fifty-one being less than twenty-five years old. The United States had the oldest of all written constitutions then in force. A close reading of these seventy-three constitutions reveals that forty-two contain no preamble at all. Seven nations with historical ties to the United States when their constitutions were written—Argentina, China, Korea, Liberia, Paraguay, Philippines, and Cuba—adopted preambles that are substantially in the United States mode and appear to be merely derivative. Argentina, Paraguay, and Liberia modeled their constitutions expressly after that of the United States.

The preambles of the twenty-four remaining constitutions display no pattern that would justify comparison with the arrangement of the Preamble, no combination of objectives, no sequence of purposes. Despite a cry from all corners of the earth for liberty, justice, welfare, happiness, and freedom, the preambles of these nations express purposes differing so widely and in styles so diverse that they cannot justifiably be likened to the Preamble of the United States. With the single exception of Liberia, the phrase "in order to establish justice" appears in none of the foreign constitutions nor in any constitution of the thirteen original American states.

How, then, did the framers of the United States Constitution manage to duplicate a passage as old and extraordinary as the Prologue? The problem is compounded because authorship of the Preamble itself is almost as great a mystery as that of the Prologue. The following are the circumstances that led to the composition of the Preamble.

The Writing of the Preamble in 1787

Many Americans were convinced, by the close of 1786, that the existing government formed by the Articles of Confederation was inadequate to cope with the challenges faced by the allied states. Internal rebellion, economic dislocation, financial instability, parochial legislation, border disputes, a foreign presence on American soil, and impotence in foreign affairs all threatened the existence of the Confederation, and with it, the idea that men might successfully govern themselves. The necessity for dealing effectively with those issues and a host of other injustices enumerated by James Madison caused Congress to call for a Federal Convention to be held in Philadelphia on May 14, 1787, in order to "render the Constitution of the Federal Government adequate to the exigencies of the Union."

The Congressional call had anticipated no more than a revision of the Articles of Confederation, but to those members of the Convention whose views were eventually to prevail, the magnitude of the crises facing the Confederation necessitated the formation of a truly national government. Accordingly, on August 6, a Committee of Detail, chaired by John Rutledge of South Carolina, to whom the responsibility for preparing a constitution establishing a national government had been assigned, submitted a report that ultimately became the Constitution of the United States. Its preamble read:

We the people of the States of New Hampshire, Massachusetts, Rhode Island and Providence Plantations, Connecticut, New-York, New-Jersey, Pennsylvania, Delaware, Maryland, Virginia, North Carolina, South Carolina and Georgia, do ordain, declare and establish the following Constitution for the Government of Ourselves and Our Posterity.

This report was based upon the "Virginia Plan" introduced on May 29 by Governor Edmund Randolph as a series of fifteen resolutions addressed to reform of the Confederation. Randolph wrote that a preamble seemed proper, but "not for the purpose of designating the ends of government and human polities—This . . . display of theory, howsoever proper in the first formations of state government, is unfit here."[5]

On August 7, the Convention unanimously accepted the preamble thus reported by the Committee of Detail. For a month afterward, the delegates studied and debated provisions of the proposed constitution. On Saturday, September 8, 1787, the Convention appointed a committee of five "to revise the style of and arrange the articles which had been agreed to by the House." This Committee of Style and Arrangement consisted of Dr. William Samuel Johnson of Connecticut, Alexander Hamilton of New York, Gouverneur Morris of Pennsylvania, James Madison of Virginia, and Rufus King of Massachusetts.

On Monday, September 10, after debate, the House referred a revised draft of the Constitution, still bearing the preamble of August 6, to the Committee of Style. It adjourned Tuesday's session because the Committee's awaited report had not been received. On Wednesday, September 12, the Honorable Mr. Johnson reported in at the Secretary's table a refurbished draft of the Constitution. It contained a completely new preamble, the compact sentence which now graces that document. Although inconsistent with Randolph's belief that a preamble framed as a statement of philosophic purpose was inappropriate, a view unanimously approved by the House a month earlier, on Thursday, September 13, the House accepted the new Preamble without further comment or debate.

There has been a continuing debate, however, over the specific authorship of the Preamble:

> *Who had composed it, whether it was phrased by one or through the joint efforts of all has never been ascertained. . . . Champions of the memory of one and another of these men have been at great pains to seek proof that their idol was the author of the preamble. Their efforts have borne no more definite fruit than that of the Shakespeare-Bacon controversy.*[6]

Gouverneur Morris later claimed that he had written the Constitution and James Madison acknowledged that Morris had, indeed, "given finish" to its style and arrangement.

The significance of the dispute as to which member of the Committee of Style and Arrangement deserves credit for drafting the Preamble has probably been overstressed. The Preamble's purposes were well known to educated Colonial Americans. They had studied the Bible, classical and contemporary literature, and the history of constitutions; they had participated in philosophical speculation and listened to the endless sermons of the day describing the nature of an ideal state and the attributes of a just ruler. Any one of the Committee's learned participants was capable of producing a similar version of the Preamble that would have been readily accepted by the Convention.[7]

Suggested Sources of the Preamble

Constitutional scholars usually attribute the Preamble's origins to two Colonial documents, as David Watson has done: "We find the earliest antecedent of the preamble, almost a century and a half before the adoption of the Constitution, in the second article of the New England Confederation of 1643. . . . We also find a distinct outline of it in the Articles of Confederation."[8]

The colonies of New England, Massachusetts, New Plymouth, Connecticut, and New Haven formed The New England Confederation of 1643 in order to settle boundary disputes and secure its members against incursions of the Indians, French, and Dutch. Article 2 of that agreement provided:

The said United Colonies, for themselves and their posterities do jointly and severally, hereby enter into a firm and perpetual league of friendship and amity, for offense and defense, mutual advice and succor, upon all just occasions, both for preserving and propagating the truths and liberties of the gospel, and for their own mutual safety and welfare.

In 1777, Congress accepted Articles of Confederation based upon a plan John Dickinson proposed in 1776. By March 1, 1781, all states had ratified those Articles, of which Article III provided:

The said states hereby severally enter into a firm league of friendship with each other, for their common defense, the security of their Liberties, and their mutual and general welfare.[9]

Similarities between the New England agreement of 1643 and the Articles of Confederation accepted by Congress one hundred and thirty-four years later are readily apparent. The subscribers of both documents enter into "firm league[s] of friendship" and commit themselves to their common defense, the securing of their liberties, and their mutual welfare.

Neither of these compacts, however, addresses the necessity for establishing justice or maintaining domestic tranquility, purposes having to do with the internal administration of the colonies. The omission is understandable, for both firm leagues were founded by sovereign constituents, and an avowed purpose to maintain internal order or establish justice would have implied a relinquishment of sovereignty to a single authority, a result not intended. Many Colonials were for this reason wary of the likely result of giving literal effect to the aims of the Preamble. In 1788 an Anti-Federalist writer "Brutus" (Robert Yates?) warned of the Preamble's "principal ends and designs":

Now, to make a union of this kind perfect, it is necessary to abolish all inferior governments and to give to the general one compleat legislative, executive and judicial powers to every purpose . . . its spirit is to subvert and abolish all the powers of state government and to embrace every object to which any government extends.[10]

These early American confederations by their very nature could not have supplied all objects of the Preamble, however much the phraseology in which they expressed three of those objects—security, liberty, and welfare—might have guided the draftsman of the Preamble. Nor are those three objects truly comparable. As used by the confederations, they represented immediate, tactical advantages independent confederates hoped to obtain by contract, through their firm and perpetual leagues of friendship. The Preamble's intent is broader and more spiritual: the creation of an ideal state on earth through the realization of goals men have always turned to in framing ideal forms of government.

The State Constitutions

When the American colonies renounced their allegiance to Great Britain in 1776, each new state retained its "sovereignty, freedom and independence," as Article II of the Articles of Confederation expressly provided, and each adopted its own plan to establish the structure and character of its government. By the time the federal Constitution was ratified in 1790, all states had adopted their own constitutions except Rhode Island and Connecticut, who continued under their colonial charters into the nineteenth century. Historians frequently refer to these state constitutions as possible sources for the language of the Preamble.

Of these new state plans, only the Massachusetts document drafted by John Adams contained a preamble designated as such. It provided that the end of government was

to secure the existence of the body-politic, to protect it, and to furnish the individuals who compose it, with the power of enjoying, in safety and tranquillity, their natural right, and the blessings of life. . . . The body politic is formed by a voluntary association of individuals; it is a social compact, by which the whole people covenants with each citizen, and each citizen with the whole people, that all shall be governed by certain laws for the common good. It is the duty of the people, therefore, . . . to provide for an equitable mode of making laws, as well as for an impartial interpretation, and a faithful execution of them; that every man may, at all times, find his security in them.

Here, in John Adams's explanation of social compact theory, all purposes of the Preamble appear, if not its very language. The obligation to establish justice is implicit in the requirement that the people provide an "equitable mode of making laws" and arrange for their impartial interpretation and faithful execution; the safety, tranquility, and common good of the people are made explicit ends.

Responding to his own question as to what are the proper ends of the modern state, a professor of political science recently wrote:

Traditionally, they are held to be security, liberty, justice and welfare. Security includes the protection of life, limb and property against disorderly elements within or enemy attack without it. . . . Perhaps some persons might question the inclusion of liberty among the ends of the state.[11]

The Preamble's recital of the perennial and unquestioned goals of good government—security, justice, and welfare—reflected the classical curriculum and scriptural tradition in which the Founding Fathers were well schooled. A covenant signed on October 21, 1620, by Pilgrim leaders who had entered Cape Cod harbor aboard the Mayflower two days before proclaimed the same objectives:

In the name of God, Amen! We whose names are underwritten, the loyal subjects of our dread sovereign Lord, King James . . . do by these presents, solemnly and mutually, in the presence of God and of one another covenant and combine ourselves together into a civil body politic, for our better ordering and preservation . . . and by virtue hereof to enact, constitute and frame just and equal laws, ordinances, acts, constitutions and offices from time to time as shall be thought most meet and convenient for the general good of the colony.

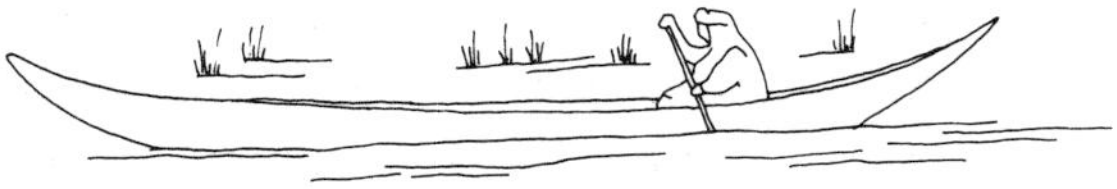

Explanations most frequently given for the origin of the Preamble have done no more than take the language for several of its purposes out of context from earlier historical documents and cite those documents as sources. Omitting all reference to the necessity for establishing justice and maintaining domestic tranquility, such explanations are neither definitive nor persuasive.

The purposes of the Preamble were in fact the goals of an ancient well-ordered Mesopotamian city. Recast in a theology of the eighteenth century A.D., those same goals defined the Kingdom of God conceived by the zealous, predominantly Protestant students of Holy Scripture who gathered in Philadelphia in 1787 to write a constitution for their new nation. With the exception of Lipit-Ishtar's Prologue, no independently prepared document, contemporary or ancient, repeats the form used by those pious Americans to express the purposes of the Preamble. The true and unresolved question posed by the phrasing of the Preamble's objectives is how a declaration of national purpose so singular in form came to resemble the prologue to one of the first law codes ever written.

So remote are the cultures from which Preamble and Prologue arose that it would be futile to seek an immediate common source or parallel development. Nor can there be any question of a direct influence by Mesopotamian authority on American legislators. It was not until the middle of the nineteenth century A.D. that the interpretation of cuneiform writing gained substantial momentum through the heroic efforts of H. C. Rawlinson and the scholarly contributions of Edward Hincks and Jules Oppert. French archaeologists discovered the stele bearing the Code of Hammurabi in the winter of 1901-2, and research has brought to light the earlier Laws of Ur-Nammu, Eshnunna, and Lipit-Ishtar only within the last few years.

In attempting to better understand the surprising correlation of Preamble and Prologue we must initially inquire whether any justifiable basis exists for comparing the two documents. Are the concepts embodied in the phrases of the Preamble truly comparable to the translated purposes of the Prologue, or are those ideas the fruits of different and irreconcilable species? Must we attribute a surface likeness to chance and agree that a Sumerian chimpanzee given a reed stylus and enough clay would eventually duplicate the entire United States Constitution? Or is it possible that the cultures which produced both introductory passages shared basic moral and political values that account for the similarity? To begin to answer these questions, we must examine the concepts and wording of the Prologue against the background of the Sumerian society emerging from the mists of protohistory forty centuries ago.

---

[1] Edward S. Corwin, "Constitutions and Constitutional Theory," in *American Constitutional Theory,* eds. Altheus T. Mason and Gerald Garvey (New York: Harper & Row, Publishers, 1964), 107-8; David K. Watson, *The Constitution of the United States,* vol. I (Chicago: Callaghan & Co., 1910), 105; Catherine Drinker Bowen, *Miracle at Philadelphia* (Boston: Atlantic, Little, Brown, 1966), 241.

[2] Francis Rue Steele, "The Code of Lipit-Ishtar," *American Journal of Archaeology*, 52 (1948): 425. Steele expressed his gratitude for the assistance of Dr. S. N. Kramer and Dr. E. A. Speiser in the translation and publication of Lipit-Ishtar's Code.

[3] Samuel Noah Kramer, *The Sumerians—Their History, Culture, and Character* (Chicago: Univ. of Chicago Press, 1963), 336.

[4] Amos J. Peaslee, *Constitutions of Nations*, Rev. 3rd ed. (The Hague: M. Nijhoff, 1956), 3.

[5] *The Records of the Federal Convention of 1787*, ed. Max Farrand, vol. II (New Haven: Yale Univ. Press, 1911), 137.

[6] Robert J. Peaslee, Chief Justice New Hampshire Supreme Court, "Our National Constitution: The Preamble," *Boston University Law Review*, 9 (Jan. 1929): 22.

[7] William Pierce, a delegate from Georgia, wrote a series of sketches of his fellow delegates to the Federal Convention. His appraisals of the members of the Committee of Style and Arrangement are set out in Exhibit J of the Appendix.

[8] Watson, *The Constitution*, 89. See also Joseph Story, *Commentaries on the Constitution of the United States*, 5th ed., vol. I (Boston: Little, Brown, 1891), sect. 461; David Hutchison, *Foundations of the Constitution* (Secaucus, N.J.: University Books, 1975), 12ff.; and Charles A. Beard, *The Republic* (New York: Viking Press, 1943), 108, where he says of the general welfare clause, "But the committee did not have to go up into the sky for the words. They were in the old Articles of Confederation."

[9] Benjamin Franklin had submitted a similar draft of Articles of Confederation to Congress a year earlier. See *Secret Journals*, vol. I (Washington D.C.: Congressional publication, 1821).

[10] *New York Journal*, vol. 12, Feb. 7, 1788.

[11] J. Ronald Pennock, "The Obligation to Obey the Law and the Ends of the State," in *Law and Philosophy*, a report of the sixth annual meeting of the New York Institute of Philosophy, ed. Sidney Hook (New York: N.Y. Univ. Press, 1964), 79.

ANCIENT MESOPOTAMIA

II

SUMER AND THE VERY FIRST LAWS

Sumer

Scarcely more than a century ago, the existence of Sumer was unknown, and to this day the origin of its people remains uncertain. Settled perhaps as early as the sixth millennium B.C. in the delta region of southern Mesopotamia, where the Euphrates and Tigris flow into the Persian Gulf, the land was subject to periodic assault by desert-wandering tribes of the west and to invasion by the warlike mountain peoples of north and east.

Despite the constant threat of external aggression, the Sumerians soon began to establish a civilization in the marshlands lining their principal rivers. With little more than sun, water, and mud, they provided for their material needs, constructed houses of sun-dried brick and tools of baked clay; built dams, dikes, and channels to control the flow of water, initiating what was to be an extensive irrigation system. They cultivated the rich soil, grew wheat, barley, and vegetables, planted herbs, date palms, fruit trees and vines. The Sumerians herded sheep, goats, donkeys, and oxen, took fish from the seas, fish eggs from the canebrake,

Sumerian workers shown on the so-called Royal Standard of Ur (ca. 2600 B.C.), a wooden box decorated with shell figures on a field of lapis lazuli.

and snared birds. They manufactured a distinctive pottery, traded for wood to build with, acquired metals and precious stones, which they worked, cut, and polished with great skill.

The resourceful settlers of Sumer consolidated their early social organizations into larger political associations. A dozen or so city-states emerged—walled cities enclosing a stepped tower, or ziggurat, upon which the city-god dwelled, and at lower levels, numerous temples, administrative buildings, and the palace of the earthly ruler—the entire complex supported by surrounding villages, farms, and pastures. The Sumerians paid taxes, bought and sold property, and taught themselves to write in order to keep track of their assets. Early in the third millennium B.C., trained scribes were already drafting deeds and bills of sale to record the transfer of title to houses, lots, and slaves.

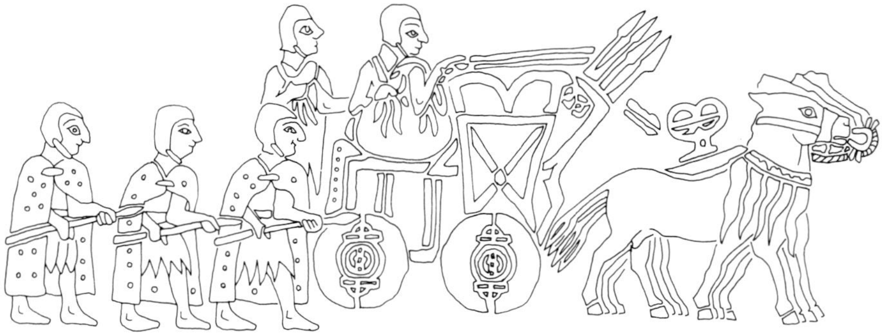

The reverse of the Royal Standard depicts the fighters responsible for the security of the city.

The Sumerians formed military units to defend their cities when necessary and to attack others when propitious. With fighting imminent, they chose a commander to lead their armies and granted him extraordinary, but temporary, powers. Their soldiers fought on foot, in tight phalanxes, armed with long spears, behind a wall of large rectangular shields. Their leaders organized workers into specialized groups according to function and placed them under the supervision of respected overseers. These groups were available to support the military.

Halfway through the third millennium, a king of Lagash recorded the measures he instituted and the abuses he curtailed in order to restore justice and the "freedom" of his beleaguered people. This is the famous "reform document" of Urukagina, the first written acknowledgment by any ruler that he had a responsibility to establish justice and provide for the well-being of his subjects.[1]

Sumerian society evolved about a recognizable morality. Sometime before the twenty-second century B.C., its priests had warned the "black-headed" people they could not kill, rob, rape, commit adultery, swear falsely, or deprive one another of their freedom with impunity. Those elementary prohibitions provided a foundation for the Sumerian concept of justice and the way of life it produced.

Utu, Sumerian Sun-god and god of Justice, holding his emblematic pruning saw.

In 2350 B.C., forces from the city of Agade led by the great Sargon descended from the north and subdued most of Sumer. Although the Akkadians were able to maintain control for the next century and a half, toward the end of the millennium a resurgence of Sumerian economic and political might centered about the city of Ur. A final burst of prosperity and creative achievement distinguished the reign of its king, Ur-Nammu (2112-2095 B.C.), founder of Ur's celebrated Third Dynasty. Estimates of Ur's population at this time range from twenty-four to three hundred and sixty thousand. The lowest estimate would place the total number of Ur's inhabitants midway between New York's population (ca. eighteen thousand) and Philadelphia's (ca. thirty thousand) at the time of the American Revolution.

The burgeoning civilizations of Sumer and Colonial America faced challenges that were similar in many ways. Both peoples sought to establish footholds in lands posing awesome natural obstacles: in America, a vast and unexplored wilderness; in Sumer, a plain wracked by seasonal drought and the flooding of two rivers that caused widespread destruction when not controlled. Both communities confronted alien and sometimes threatening peoples. The sustenance and eventual wealth of both derived from the soil; both employed slaves, but slaveship under the ancient regime was less hopeless. Both considered themselves a chosen people and were destined to produce great new societies organized about their religious beliefs. One brought civilization to the Old World, the other to the New.

The American settlers enjoyed a great advantage, however, in that many of the most elementary devices, forms, and technologies they took for granted had to be conceived or developed from the very beginning by the Sumerians. An appliance as basic as the wheel, for example, which bore the weight of the workman's cart, the soldier's caisson, and the philosopher's carriage in America, first appeared on the toys of Sumerian children in the fourth millennium B.C. Pillars like those of Greek temple porticoes that adorned public buildings, colleges, and churches in the American colonies had Sumerian prototypes in columns constructed of bundled reeds, packed with mud, and covered with glazed tiles. The arches and vaults of cathedrals the Colonists had left behind in European capitals were similar to architectural forms developed in Sumer. The dome shape of Thomas Jefferson's Monticello first appeared on the huts and tombs of Sumer's inhabitants.

Clocks that intrigued Jefferson marked time according to a sexagesimal system conceived by Sumerian mathematicians. The "orrery" of Philadelphia's David Rittenhouse, a mechanism run by clockwork that showed the movement of the planets around the sun, a technical marvel of the time, would have interested the Sumerians, who were first to record their astronomical observations. It would also have fascinated their successors, those astute students of the skies, the diviners of Babylon, who correctly identified Jupiter as the largest planet and associated it with Marduk, the ruler of their gods. A professor of physics has recently suggested that in order to arrive at Jupiter's distance from the earth and to compare that result with corresponding data for other planets, the Babylonians must not only have had a telescope (a rock crystal lens has, in fact, been found) but a "reasonable theory for the estimation of planetary distances" as well.[2]

Paul Revere, a talented goldsmith and sometime dentist, fashioned dinner services, urns, goblets, jewels, medallions, and cross-keys of the highest quality for members of the Masonic lodge to which he belonged. Revere practiced a craft mastered in Sumer, where gold, silver, and copper had been worked in the fourth millennium. The renowned Assyriologist Cyrus H. Gordon says of the treasures unearthed from the royal tombs of Ur, "In the field of metallurgy, the Sumerians are unsurpassed in antiquity, while in the arts of the goldsmith and gem cutters, the Sumerians are second to none in all history."[3]

Writing, the process of representing thought by means of symbols inscribed on tangible surfaces, fully exploited by the Founding Fathers in recording the imperishable sentiments of the Declaration of Independence and setting out the structure of their new republic, had begun with Sumer's cuneiform script, prepared almost fifty centuries before. Cuneiform writing (Latin, *cuneus,* "wedge") was a method of impressing signs, pictures, syllables, and eventually words into a moist clay tablet with a wedge-shaped stylus.

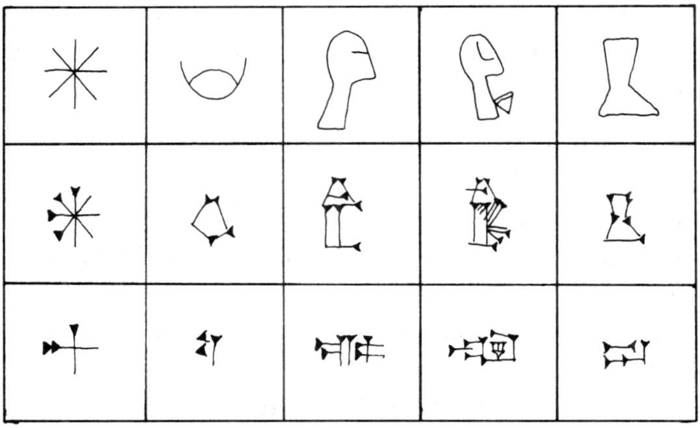

Evolution of cuneiform writing from the third and second to the first millennium B.C. The star, upper left, represents "heaven," "god"; next to it the sun rising between the mountains to the east, "day"; the human head, "man"; food before the man's head, "eat"; the foot, "stand" or "walk."

Devout American patriots encountered ideas first expressed in Sumerian literature when they read the Creation and Flood stories of the Bible. The literary works of ancient Greece, a major element in the educational process of pre-Revolutionary America, contained numerous parallels between the qualities admired in its heroes and traditional virtues of the kings of Sumer.

It is highly unlikely that their American counterparts could have matched the writing skills or mathematical accomplishments of Sumerian students. In Colonial America, public grammar schools emphasized the study of Latin and Greek grammar. Vocational, or "useful," education came by way of private tutor. In 1728, the Bostonian Caleb Philips offered to teach a system of shorthand, a "way of Joining 3,4,5, and 6 words in one and every sentence."[4] Presumably, an American stenographer who applied himself to Philips' method might have hoped to attain a proficiency comparable to that attained by the proverbial Sumerian scribe in his *edubba* ("tablet house," or "school")—"A scribe whose hand moves as fast as his mouth, that's a scribe for you."[5] It is probable that America's first students could not have matched the precise numerical competence of the Sumerian, whose school tablets reveal an understanding of advanced mathematics, geometric and algebraic problems and solutions. It was not until after the Revolution that Harvard required candidates for admission to possess an elementary knowledge of addition and subtraction.

For all its brilliant men of letters, Colonial America produced no poetry to match the stark originality, charm, and emotional appeal of the Sumerian. The magnificent opening lines of the Sumerian poem "The *Huluppu*-Tree," from *Inanna, Queen of Heaven and Earth*, describe the very beginnings:

> *In the first days, in the very first days,*
> *In the first nights, in the very first nights,*
> *In the first years, in the very first years,*
> *In the first days when everything needed was brought into being,*
> *In the first days when everything needed was properly nourished,*
> *When bread was baked in the shrines of the land,*
> *When bread was tasted in the homes of the land,*
> *When heaven had moved away from earth,*
> *And earth had separated from heaven,*
> *And the name of man was fixed.*[6]

Bread baked in the shrines of Sumer was made from a barley meal, for barley was the principal cereal crop produced in the ancient Near East. Later, Homer repeatedly distinguished civilized mortal men from the gods, from less highly developed peoples, and from giants by their dependence upon and enjoyment of baked bread, the "blessed pride of the barley" (*Iliad* XI:630). When American classicists read of Greek emigrants who settled "far away from men who eat bread" (*Odyssey*, VI:8), of Odysseus seeking "what men, eaters of bread, might live here in this country" (ibid., IX:89), and of a monstrous wonder "not like a man, an eater of bread" (ibid., IX:190-1), they were encountering a criterion of ancient Sumerian lineage for fixing civilized man's time and place in the cosmos.[7]

Inanna's poem also introduced one of the three elementary purposes of an ideal state. In recalling the first days "when everything needed was brought into being" and "properly nourished," when "bread was baked in the shrines" and "tasted in the homes of the land," the Sumerian poet described a blessed state that had already achieved, through divine dispensation, a principal goal of the Prologue: the care and feeding of its people. It was the same purpose expressed in the general welfare provision of the Preamble: the nourishment sought by pious founders of the American commonwealth when they prayed to God for their daily bread.[8]

The Very First Laws

The Sumerian "revival" that took place in the twenty-second century B.C. produced the world's first written law "Code," a collection of some thirty provisions.[9] Underscoring the cogency of one jurist's observation that the more archaic the code, the more full and minute its penal provisions, Ur-Nammu's compilation was almost exclusively penal in nature.

A fragment of the stele of Ur-Nammu (2112-2095 B.C.) excavated at Ur, showing the king receiving instructions from the Moon-god Nanna, tutelary deity of Ur. The god holds a measuring rod and plumb line—the symbols of justice.

It was followed by a body of fifty-nine Akkadian laws from Eshnunna, a city situated northeast of Babylon that flourished after the downfall of Ur. In 1934 B.C., a king named Lipit-Ishtar assumed sovereignty over Isin, a Sumerian city in lower Mesopotamia. He was the fifth ruler in a dynasty that was to prevail through the first two centuries of the second millennium. Lipit-Ishtar sponsored the third law code presently known, a code that contained a prologue, a text of thirty-seven laws, and an epilogue, a form similar to that adopted by Hammurabi two centuries later.

Before these early codes were compiled, however, the very first laws were spoken by judges who sat at the city and temple gates. Tablets recording their decisions, inscribed and filed toward the end of the third millennium, have been unearthed throughout the Near East. They include approximately two hundred and fifty neo-Sumerian entries, dating from 2050-1950 B.C., frustratingly brief and often reconstructed with difficulty from fragmented tablets. As Adam Falkenstein's comprehensive study makes clear, these neo-Sumerian legal documents are records of court proceedings, trials, entries of judgments, judicial settlements, and simple court authentications.[10] Numerous other more detailed trial court records from the dynasty of Hammurabi have also been recovered, some of which contain the verbatim testimony of witnesses reported more fully than in the short Sumerian entries. Such court decisions often provided precedents for the laws that appeared in later compilations, or codes.

The legal codes of ancient Mesopotamia (i.e., Sumer and Hammurabi's Babylon), and to a greater extent the decisions of its judges, display a familiarity with a range of legal conceptions and substantive issues that can only evoke astonishment in one coming upon them for the first time. The system of judicial process was surprisingly advanced. In many cases, the ideas, forms, and procedures utilized in the Near East during the opening centuries of the second millennium do not appear in Anglo-American jurisprudence until the modern era. Sixteenth-century England, for instance, resolved land-title disputes with the battle axe (wielded frequently by professional or falsely sworn champions), an option not abolished until the nineteenth century. In Mesopotamia, litigants brought such disputes to judges of probity, who listened to the testimony of witnesses, read the relevant documents, and reviewed the records of the land-registry office when necessary before reaching their decisions.[11]

The Sumerian father who entered into a contract for the marriage of his daughter to the son of another man went to court seeking specific performance of the contract when her proposed father-in-law tried to breach the agreement (NG #14).[12] The Babylonian banker who possessed no interest in funds held by him and claimed by two contestants agreed to pay the money to the successful party in the suit when the court reached its decision—the course open to the stakeholder in a modern interpleader action.[13] The very essence of Hammurabi's 53rd law, the affirmative duty of a land-occupier to maintain his property so as not to cause injury to others, considered a late development in Western legal history, was again argued in a leading California case decided in 1966.[14] The Sumerian who wished to pay a debt addressed a written order to his grain warehouseman, directing him to pay the requisite number of bushels of barley to his creditor; this system of finance using commodities as a medium still prevailed in the American colonies of the eighteenth century A.D. The wrongful assertion of dominion over the personal property of another, a "conversion," may occur, according to today's legal texts, in five distinct ways, all of which may be found in cases decided and many in laws enacted before the close of the eighteenth century B.C.

Today's penal statutes define precisely many of the sins of the over-reaching sons and daughters of Sumer and Akkad.[15]

One series of third-millennium reports demonstrates how capably Sumerian judges disposed of difficult issues that arose from the ingenious financial arrangements devised by their countrymen. In 2032 B.C., a Sumerian court entered a judgment in favor of a man named Urenki, who had purchased a slave three years before from one Langa. Langa retained possession of the slave at the time of sale. The court awarded Urenki fourteen shekels, the price of the slave, and eighteen shekels in addition as a "rental" for his use during the three-year period. Urenki's return on the monies he advanced, therefore, was in excess of forty percent per annum (NG #204a).

Urenki's suit was not an anomaly. In at least three other recorded decisions, the seller retained possession of the slave at the time of sale and was later successfully sued by the buyer for rentals due. These cases demonstrate that by this early date, the inhabitants of Sumer, with their remarkable precocity in matters of finance, were already using legal fictions to accomplish their economic ends. The parties appear to have been avoiding interest limitations on loans of silver, for these "sale and lease-back" transactions, based upon the same financing technique used recently in the sale and lease-back of the Bank of America building in San Francisco, enabled the buyer-lender to realize a return twice the amount of the statutory limit.[16]

An unexpected parallel also exists between the inalienable rights claimed by American Revolutionaries and those protected as fundamental by the lawmakers of Sumer. When American Colonists declared their independence from Great Britain in 1776, they justified their action by charging that the British Parliament and the King himself had violated fundamental rights the Colonists shared with all mankind. John Locke had defined those rights as "Life, Liberty and Estate."[17] Colonial patriots reduced the scope of Locke's "Estate" and incorporated his basic rights in their rallying cry for "Life, Liberty and Property." The Declaration of Rights adopted by the first Congress in 1774 maintained the Colonists were entitled to "Life, liberty and property." The Virginia Declaration of Rights, published in May 1776, proclaimed that all men had certain rights, "namely the enjoyment of life and liberty with the means of acquiring and possessing property."

Modified in the Declaration of Independence, where the "pursuit of happiness" replaced "property" as an inalienable right, the right to life, liberty, and property was incorporated in the Constitution's Amendment V: "No person shall be . . . deprived of life, liberty or property, without due process of law" and repeated, in the 14th Amendment (1868), as a specific limitation upon state power.

In the twenty-second century B.C., the lawmakers of Sumer guaranteed their version of those same fundamental rights. A highly damaged tablet (Si 277) has been recovered from the ancient city of

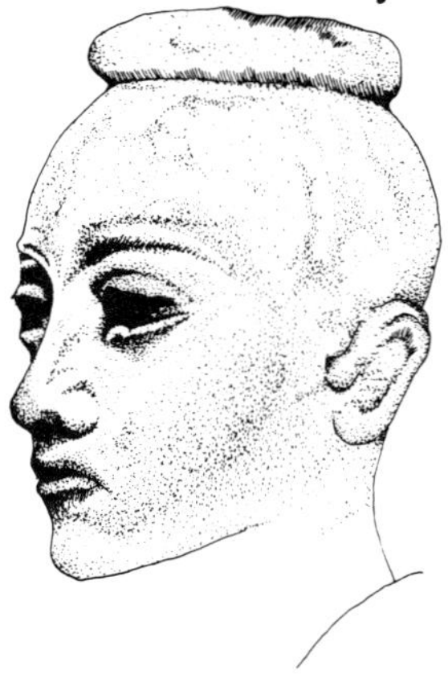

Head of Ur-Nammu from a copper statuette

Sippar, once a rich trading center in lower Mesopotamia. In 1979, Professor J. van Dijk identified the tablet, stored then in the Archaeological Museum of Istanbul, as part of the Law Code of Ur-Nammu. Van Dijk's identification of Si 277 was a discovery of major importance, for it made possible the elimination of other lacunae in prior texts and also disclosed the first six laws of Ur-Nammu, which had theretofore been missing.

The first law of Si 277 reads:

> *That day, if a man commits a murder, that man is to be killed.*

The second:

> *If a man commits a robbery, he will be killed.*

The third:

> *If a man is wrongfully bereaving a person of his freedom,*
> *that man must sit in prison (and) must pay 15 shekels of silver.*[18]

The first three laws of the first law code ever committed to writing, therefore, condemned the "crimes" of murder, robbery, and false imprisonment, offenses that would have deprived an individual of his right to life, property, or liberty.

In the ancient Near East, law did not originate with the human ruler; it was conceived as having descended from a cosmic, metadivine source. The Mesopotamian king was merely a trustee, whose duty it was to give effect to the laws on earth. Since the king was "answerable to powers outside himself," the king's subjects were "automatically protected against autocracy," and the individual had "the comfort and assurance of certain inalienable rights."[19] Despite the warning of an ancient axiom that if the king failed to do justice, his people would rebel and lay waste his kingdom, there is no evidence that deprivation of those fundamental rights ever caused the peoples of the Near East to rise up against the royal authority as American Colonists did against Great Britain.

High officials of the state, however, were not always immune to process. In the first year of the reign of the Sumerian Ibbi-Sin (2028 B.C.), the farmer Sage instituted an action against the grand vizier and City Prince, Irnanna, claiming that Irnanna had confiscated Sage's slave six years before. The court ordered Irnanna to return the slave and pay a rental for his services during the six-year period (NG #67). Perhaps we should not place too broad a reading upon the authority of this case, for Falkenstein perceptively asks whether it does not indicate that the fortunes of the once powerful Irnanna were in decline at the time of Ibbi-Sin's ascension.

A series of tablets from Nuzi, an Assyrian town of the fifteenth and fourteenth centuries B.C., also records the prosecution of a lawsuit filed by the citizens of the community against "His Excellency, the Lord Mayor," Kushiharbe. They charged that the Mayor had committed many now familiar misdeeds, including acceptance of bribes, cattle theft, kidnapping, stealing wood, using workers from public projects for his own purposes, and illicit relations with a young lady. Gordon suggests the case indicates these ancient communities could liberate themselves from tyrannical rule by appealing to courts of law, but it is also possible that Kushiharbe and his codefendants were prosecuted, as Irnanna had been, only after they lost political support.[20]

Rights incident to life, property, and liberty, however, were freely asserted by the general population of the Near East and were adjudicated in the earliest courts of law.

Life

Proponents and opponents of capital punishment today maintain a furious dialogue as to which places a higher value on the sanctity of human life. The Assembly at Nippur stated its view in unmistakable terms after a murder trial in Isin about 1900 B.C., when it condemned three men to death for killing the son of a *nishakku*-priest. The Assembly also condemned the wife of the murdered man, for she "did not open her mouth" when the murderers admitted their crime to her. "As men who have killed a man, they are not (fit to be) alive; those three males and that woman should be killed in front of the (official) chair of [*their victim*]."[21]

Another murder case indicates that Sumerian courts required a murderer to compensate the next of kin of his victim. In this case, the judges convicted a man named Kuli of killing Babamu, the musician. When Kuli in turn had been killed (the cause of his death not given), his estate, wife, and daughters were awarded to the sons of Babamu (NG #41).

In 1758 A.D., a Continental jurist reminded Colonial America that in an early state of nature, an individual's inalienable right to life included the right to defend himself against those who unjustly threatened him with harm. He maintained that "every man has a right to protect himself from injury, and by force to provide for his own security, against those who unjustly attack him. For this purpose, he may, when injured, inflict a punishment on the aggressor."[22] A Sumerian report of the late third millennium B.C. brings the reader as close to the Colonial's presumed state of nature as he is ever likely to get. There, the defendant Guzani entered a plea of self-defense in another Sumerian prosecution for homicide. Guzani had killed Kali and attempted to justify his action by claiming that "Kali struck me first with this pincer (?)" (NG #202). The incomplete report fails to indicate what weight the court accorded this plea of first resort by a defendant who claimed a right to take the life of another in order to save his own.

Property

Many delegates to the Federal Convention believed that protection of property was the sole or primary purpose of government. Others, Gouverneur Morris amongst them, placed the protection of property ahead of liberty as the noblest object of society. The Sumerian's sense of property was no less keen. When he first devised a system of writing, he was motivated by no irresistible compulsion to sing the praises of his gods nor to pose the everlasting philosophical questions; his prosaic aim was to keep track of his worldly goods, his revenues, livestock, utensils, and other possessions. Consistently, deprivation of property took precedence over deprivation of liberty in Ur-Nammu's catalogue of offenses and called for a capital penalty; the deprivation of liberty brought only fine and imprisonment.

Sumerian judges scrupulously guarded property rights and provided compensation to victims of robberies if the criminal was not apprehended. In an early Sumerian proceeding, Urmes, a fisherman, robbed Sulgilugal, another fisherman, and fled. The court awarded Urmes' wife, daughter, and slave to Sulgilugal (NG #42). The 23rd and 24th of the Laws of Hammurabi (ca. 1765 B.C.) later required that if a robber was not apprehended, the city and the mayor were to compensate the victim for whatever was taken and to pay one shekel of silver to his kinfolk if he was killed. In 1965, California became the first in the United States to enact legislation, considerably less generous than Hammurabi's, providing compensation to victims of crime.

By the middle of the eighteenth century B.C., Akkadian jurists had arrived at a concept of community property similar to the law of California and seven other states today. The general theory of the community property system, which came to the United States from Spain, holds that property acquired during marriage by the labor or skill of husband or wife belongs to both. Section 5110 of the Civil Code of California sets forth the general rule of that state. After listing certain exceptions irrelevant here, it provides that community property encompasses "all real property situated in this state and all personal property wherever situated, acquired during the marriage by a married person while domiciled in this state." Sections 5107 and 5108 of the same code provide that all property of the wife or husband owned before marriage and that acquired afterwards by gift, bequest, devise, or descent, with the rents, issues, and profits thereof, is separate property.

Draftsmen of Hammurabi's Code adopted the basic theory that property acquired by one or both spouses during marriage should be shared equally between them, at least under the special circumstances of Sections 176 and 176a. The wife's dowry in those sections was treated as separate property, as are gifts under current statutes. Section 176 provided that if a slave married the daughter of a free man and the couple acquired goods after they had set up a household, upon death of the slave, the wife took back her dowry, and whatever they had acquired after marriage was divided in two, the slave's owner taking one half, the wife taking the other half for her children. Under 176a, if the freeman's daughter had no dowry, whatever the couple acquired after marriage was divided and distributed in the same manner.

Liberty

The right protected by Ur-Nammu's third law—that a man not be wrongfully deprived of his freedom—was, by its terms, effective only against the actions of his neighbors. Presumably the Sumerian had no defense against the actions of the ultimate legislator—the crown. Nevertheless, the law provides an additional parallel to the American experience, for, as Corwin has written, "Many of the rights which the Constitution of the United States protects at this moment against legislative power were first protected by the common law against one's neighbors."[23]

The courts of Ur's Third Dynasty were remarkably liberal in making their scales available to those of minimal social and political standing. They listened with great patience to the cries of the enslaved who called for their freedom. In Falkenstein's collection of reports, slaves instituted sixteen suits challenging their status; one slave brought three actions over the course of fifteen years. It is a melancholy fact that no slave ever succeeded in gaining his freedom, but the mere commencement of the suits indicates the suppliants had reason to believe their claims would be considered with some degree of objectivity, and none was fined or punished for bringing frivolous actions. In at least two cases, slaves who had been freed by their masters successfully defended actions brought by heirs of their former owners, challenging their new status (NG #186, #205).

Legal historians, students of jurisprudence, and Orientalists themselves have largely ignored the remarkable corpus of early cuneiform literature, the "priceless records of pre-classical law."[24] If the Assyriologists' claim that these records are beyond price requires confirmation, we need only refer to the fragmented text of tablet Si 277. It indicates that the first of the Sumerian law codes, drafted almost a thousand years before Moses descended from the Mount, anticipated four of the six commandments (as enumerated by John Calvin) of the second table of the Decalogue. A fifth commandment was part of an unwritten Eastern tradition; the sixth appears in a document from Babylon dating from the mid-second millennium B.C.

The cuneiform legal literature of the ancient Near East merits institutional study. These are the records Sir Henry Maine dreamed of, 130 years ago, when he wrote:

> *If by any means we can determine the early forms of jural conceptions, they will be invaluable to us. These rudimentary ideas are to the jurist what the primary crusts of the earth are to the geologist. They contain, potentially, all the forms in which law has subsequently exhibited itself.*[25]

Indeed, no comprehensive understanding of man, his nature, concepts, laws, and institutions is possible that does not include an appreciation of the contents of the cuneiform literature. How strange, if not perverse, that theories and assumptions based upon tenuous, post-Homeric evidence still circulate, while the written eyewitness accounts and recorded voices of the most ancient documented civilizations, expressing ideas already far from rudimentary, are ignored.

When Justice Holmes observed that "the life of the law has not been logic; it has been experience," he set no limit on place or time.[26] If Holmes's intention was less far-reaching, his dictum nevertheless helps explain the similarity between the laws of the ancient East and those of the recent West. No abstract philosophic formulation, poetic invention, or priestly instruction accounted for the first laws of Mesopotamia. Those laws and the procedures instituted to implement them were carefully measured responses to the immediate exigencies of their time. The laws were forged and tempered in the heated exchanges of litigated dispute; their smiths were highly intelligent jurists who drew upon their own experience and weighed that of their predecessors in reaching their decisions. If the laws of the ancient Near East resemble those of later civilizations, it is because they represent the most practical and effective means reasonable men have been able to devise to cope with tensions and conflicts that constantly recur in organized society.

Their experience also taught the sensible men of ancient Mesopotamia that a state worth saving must nurture, protect, and ensure to its citizens the elemental rights of life, liberty, and property. Later they expressed their understanding in their poetry, songs, hymns, and in the introductions to their law codes.

Let us return then to the earlier comparison of Prologue and Preamble to consider in more depth how the ancient concepts of justice, security, and welfare came to be and how closely they resemble the modern.

---

[1] A tablet discovered several years ago indicates this King's name was Uru-inim-gina. References herein will nevertheless be made in the older form, Urukagina.

[2] A. Kyrala, "Speculations on Babylonian Telescopes, Planetary Distances and Sizes," *Sumer*, 28 (1972): 21.

[3] Cyrus H. Gordon, *The Ancient Near East* (New York: W.W. Norton, 1965), 27.

[4] Robert Middlekauff, *Ancients and Axioms* (New Haven: Yale Univ. Press, 1963).

[5] Kramer, *The Sumerians*, 226.

[6] Diane Wolkstein and Samuel N. Kramer, *Inanna, Queen of Heaven and Earth* (New York: Harper Colophon Books, 1983), 4.

[7] The Homer quotations throughout are taken from *The Iliad of Homer*, trans. Richmond Lattimore (Chicago: Univ.of Chicago Press, 1951), and *The Odyssey of Homer*, trans. Richmond Lattimore (New York: Harper & Row, 1965).

[8] It is probable that the bread referred to by Matthew in the Lord's Prayer was made from barley, the principal bread plant of the Near East, Greece, Rome, and Western Europe at

least until the Renaissance. Barley was brought from Europe to the new colonies of America and grown there, although Americans made their bread most often from wheat, corn, or buckwheat. A special spiritual or religious significance has accompanied the spread of barley, perhaps because of its availability or its use in beer and whiskey making. In the Greek Eleusinian ritual, initiates walked in a procession from Athens to Eleusis, abstaining from food and drink in a ceremony that has been compared to making the Stations of the Cross. The Greek pilgrims broke their fast finally in a communion-like taking of barley water and cakes. In 1984, a two-thousand-year-old, remarkably well-preserved body was found in an English peat bog; the contents of the stomach included bits of a blackened barley bread, "carefully burned," suggesting that the sacrificial victim had been chosen by lot before being ritually slaughtered (Anne Ross and Don Robins, *The Life and Death of a Druid Prince* [New York: Simon & Schuster, A Touchstone Book, 1989], 14).

[9] Although often called "Codes," the Mesopotamian law codes fall short of satisfying the definition of a Western code as a "complete, self-contained, internally consistent, systematically arranged set of legal concepts, principles and rules" (Harold J. Berman, "The Origins of Western Legal Sciences," *Harvard Law Review*, 90 [1977]: 904).

[10] Adam Falkenstein, *Die neusumerischen Gerichtsurkunden*, (Munchen: Verlag der Bayerischen Akademie der Wissenschaften, 1956), hereafter cited as NG in the text.

[11] Five short, specific parallels between the laws of the ancient East and those of the modern West are set out in the Appendix, Exhibit A, "Legal Parallels Ancient and Modern."

[12] When damages at law for breach of contract are inadequate, Courts of Equity will at times require the defendant to perform specifically what he has agreed to do. Courts are reluctant, for obvious reasons, to compel perfomance of a contract requiring personal services. This Sumerian Court, in causing the marriage contract to be performed, was not so constrained. Its action speaks to the authority, power, and prestige of Sumerian judges.

[13] C.H.W. Johns, *Babylonian and Assyrian Laws, Letters and Contracts* (Edinburgh: T. & T. Clark, 1904), 109.

[14] Hayashi vs. Alameda County Flood Control, 167 CA 2nd. 584; 334 P.2. 1048. See Appendix, Exhibit B, "The Negligent Sumerian—Misfeasant and Nonfeasant" (195).

[15] Numerous Sumerian transgressions against personal property are compared to analogous sections of the California Penal Code in the Appendix, Exhibit C, "The Earliest Laws of Conversion."

[16] See Appendix, Exhibit D, "The Sale and Lease-back of Sumerian Slaves."

[17] John Locke, *Of Civil Government* (New York: Cambridge Univ. Press, 1960), 87.

[18] Fatma Yildiz, "Animadversiones—A Tablet of Codex Ur-Nammu from Sippar," *Orientalia*, 50 (1981): 87. [Pontificium Institutum Biblicum, Rome, Italy.] Si 277 also makes it probable that the Laws of Ur-Nammu were actually promulgated by his son, Shulgi; the "Law Code of Ur-Nammu" designation will nevertheless be continued throughout this text.

[19] E.A. Speiser, "Cuneiform Law and the History of Civilization," *Proceedings of the American Philosophical Society*, 107 (Dec. 1963): 536.

[20] Gordon, *The Ancient Near East*, 113.

[21] *Ancient Near Eastern Texts Relating to the Old Testament*, ed. James B. Pritchard, 3rd ed. (Princeton: Princeton Univ. Press, 1969), 542, hereafter cited in the text as ANET.

[22] Emerich de Vattel, *The Law of Nations* (London: G.G. and J. Robinson, Paternoster-Row, 1797), Bk. I, sect. 169. Subsequent citations in the text (Ch. VI) are from this edition.

[23] Edward S. Corwin, "The 'Higher Law' Background of American Constitutional Law," *Harvard Law Review*, 42 (1928): 170.

[24] E.A. Speiser, "Early Law and Civilization," *Canadian Bar Review*, 31 (1953): 863.

[25] Sir Henry Sumner Maine, *Ancient Law* (New York: Dorset Press, 1986), 2.

[26] Oliver Wendell Holmes, Jr., *The Common Law* (Boston: Little, Brown and Company, 1963), 5.

III

JUSTICE, SECURITY, AND WELFARE IN SUMER AND AKKAD

The Structure of the Prologue

In the Prologue, Lipit-Ishtar claims that he procured the "freedom" of the sons and daughters of Sumer and Akkad. The Sumerian word for freedom is *amargi,* which appears for the first time in the middle of the twenty-fourth century B.C., in the so-called "reform document" of Urukagina. *Amargi* means, literally, "return to the mother." How the idea of freedom evolved from its literal meaning has not been fully explained. As used by Urukagina, *amargi* described the release of the people from the oppressive taxation and outright extortions of palace and temple officials. The prologue to the Laws of Ur-Nammu repeats the word: *ama-ar-gi-bi hu-mu-gar*—"Verily, I established their freedom," and Lipit-Ishtar used *amargi* to describe his unshackling of Sumerian cities from a "slaveship" that had been imposed upon them, presumably by invading Elamites who brought about the destruction of the Third Dynasty of Ur.

Although parallels may be drawn between aspects of the Sumerian and Colonial American concepts of freedom, the term *amargi* carried with it no sense of an individual's right to choose a ruler or participate directly in the political process as the American concept of liberty did. There was a fundamental difference between the two as well; the Sumerian's freedom was a grant from the temporal ruler, the American's came from a higher power. As John Milton expressed it:

> *Our Liberty is not Caesar's. It is a blessing we have received from God himself. It is what we are born to. To lay this at Caesar's feet, which we do not derive from him, which we are not beholden to him for, were an unworthy action, and degrading of our very nature.*[1]

The first, second, third, and fourth objectives of the Prologue, however, are the essence of the Preamble, as the following literal reading from the Sumerian indicates. A change has been made in line 30, in accordance with an article by Dr. Samuel Kramer entitled "The Ur-Nammu

Law Code: Who Was Its Author?" Steele's account translated the term *giš-tukul gi-gi-dè* as "to turn back enmity and rebellion by the force of arms." Dr. Kramer advised that the probable phrase is *éba gi-gi-dè* "to return enmity and violence into their house."

25. *níg-si-sá*
26. *kalam-ma gá-gá-dè*
    "to establish justice in the land"

27. *I. An. UTU*
28. *ka-ta* ku_6*lam-e-dè*
    Lit. "to wipe out complaints from the mouth"

29. *níg-erím níg-á-zi*
30. *é-ba* gi_4-gi_4*-dè*
    Lit. "to return enmity and violence into their house"

31. *ki-en-gi ki-uri*
32. *kuš-ba dùg-gi-dè*
    Lit. "of the Sumerians and Akkadians to make good their bodies."

Theophile J. Meek translates a passage from the Code of Hammurabi similar to lines 31-32 as "to promote the welfare of the people" (lit. "to make good the flesh of the people") (ANET, 64).

The series of infinitive phrases used by Preamble and Prologue to express their objectives and enunciate the fundamental purposes of good government provides an explicit parallel. In Sumerian, the infinitive is frequently formed by the addition of *dè* to the verb root and is used, as in English, to express purpose. In lines 26, 28, 30, and 32 of the Prologue, *dè* has been affixed to the verb roots, *gá, e, gi,* and *gi*. The repetition of every other line ending develops a cadence that, recited or chanted, might have been even more stirring than the rhythm of the Preamble. The Prologue in fact was originally written as poetry, in a traditional Sumerian mode.

Lines of Sumerian poetry, when combined, form distichs, or couplets; the couplets joined form a quatrain, or stanza of four lines. The pattern is apparent in the eight discrete lines of the Prologue (25-32 above). Consecutive lines are combined as necessary to complete the phrases, forming four distichs. Thus the objectives of the Prologue are set out in two quatrains.

Sumerian writers often employed a poetic device to produce tensions in their compositions by setting a line, or elements of a line, against a predecessor. The second provided a balance, contrast, or parallel to the corresponding line or element of the first. Sumerian poets wove the parallels into patterns of great complexity. They often matched a positive verb (P), one that posits, promotes, or accepts, against a negative (N), one that removes, banishes, or rejects. Typical are lines 8-10 of "The *Huluppu*-Tree," a poem of Inanna, the Sumerian goddess of heaven and earth:

8. (N) *When heaven had moved away from earth,*
9. (N) *And earth had separated from heaven,*
10. (P) *And the name of man was fixed;*[2]

If lines 25-32 of the Prologue are combined into distichs, the verbs produce the following parallelisms:

25-26 (P) *to establish justice in the land*
27-28 (N) *to wipe out* [banish] *complaints from the mouth*
29-30 (N) *to return enmity and violence into their house*
31-32 (P) *to make good the bodies* [promote the welfare] *of the Sumerians and Akkadians.*

The Prologue's negative verbs convey a sense of rejection or banishment of that which is evil or threatens harm; its positive verbs approve and put in place the good and desirable. The subtle thrust and parry of the Sumerian form contrasts sharply with the Preamble's battery of positive verbs fired in rapid sequence like cannon shot. Lipit-Ishtar might well have responded to Catherine Drinker Bowen's challenge to the centuries.

By the end of the third millennium B.C., the poets of Sumer as well as its lawmakers had come to recognize that justice, security, and welfare were necessary attributes of an ideal kingship. Three hymns glorifying the great Shulgi (2094-2047 B.C.) extolled the king throughout for his "extraordinary wisdom; his implementation of justice and equity in the land." Their royal hymns often described Sumerian kings as

> *the ideal type of rulers, who uphold social and religious order in the land, who protect the borders of Mesopotamia from the attacks of foreign people and make the multitudes of their people dwell in peace, harmony and prosperity.*[3]

The special accomplishment of Lipit-Ishtar's poet lay in his selection, ordering, and expression of the Prologue's goals. The need for implementation of those political purposes and the manner in which that need was to be realized were concerns deeply rooted in Mesopotamian tradition.

Justice

In Mesopotamia, law was thought to be an aspect of the cosmic order, a gift to the gods from the forces of the universe. When the gods revealed the laws to the human ruler, he became a temporary trustee, responsible to the gods for implementation of the cosmic design. There was no single word for law in the Mesopotamian lexicon:

> *In Akkadian, which merely reflects . . . the antecedent Sumerian, "law" is epitomized by the non-technical phrase* kittum u mesharum, *literally, "truth and right." The two nouns are mutually complementary. In the Epilogue to his celebrated Code . . . Hammurabi states explicitly that the sun god Shamash, patron of justice, bestowed on him the various forms of* kittum . . . *whereas the authority of the legislator was limited to* mesharum. . . . *Shamash himself was not the source of* kittum *but only its guardian, for that boon, being eternal and universal could not originate with the gods, let alone mortals. . . . The independent function of the ruler, whether divine or human, is confined to* mesharum, *that is, just and equitable implementation.*[4]
>
> *In other words, the whole phrase* kittum u mesharum *stands for something like impersonal and immutable order tempered with equity and fairness.*[5]

Akkadian cylinder seal depicting Shamash, Sun-god and god of Justice, rising, pruning-saw in hand, between the mountains. To the left stands Ishtar, goddess of Love and War, and Ninurta, the warrior; to the right, Enki, Water-god and god of Wisdom, ascends the mountain.

An inscription marking the dedication of the Shamash temple by Yahdun-Lim, king of Mari, in the eighteenth century B.C. also indicates that Shamash was not the source of *kittum* but only the one assigned to protect "what is right." The inscription reads: "To Shamash, king of the heavens and the earth, the magistrate of gods and men, whose allotted portion is *mesharum* and to whom *kinatum* [pl. of *kittum*] have been granted as a gift."[6] *Mesharum,* literally, denotes "anything that is straight, such as a straight street, and which is applied metaphorically to what is right, being thus commonly used for 'justice, just law' (Bab. mî/ē̌šārum), or the like."[7] The quality of straightness inherent in the Akkadian *mesharum* has never been far removed from the Western definition of justice.

The moral imperative that lay within *kittum u mesharum,* the command that law adhere to the dictates of an everlasting and unchanging truth, was not far from Colonial and, indeed, contemporary understanding. The early preeminence of the American Constitution was based upon an assumption that it embodied certain eternal and immutable principles of right and justice that were entitled of their own intrinsic excellence to prevail.[8] Most Americans of the eighteenth century took the existence of "Laws of Nature and of Nature's God" for granted. In 1760, James Otis, Boston lawyer and idol of the young John Adams, argued that the Colonial's natural and inalienable rights were founded upon eternal truths when he challenged writs of assistance authorized by the British Parliament because they violated natural equity and the "fundamental principles of law." Otis's explanation of natural law theory was probably representative of Colonial understanding:

> *The supreme power in a state is* jus dicere *only;*—jus dare, *strictly speaking, belongs to God. Parliaments are in all cases to declare what is for the good of the whole; but it is not the declaration of parliament that makes it so: There must be in every instance, a higher authority, viz. God. Should an act of Parliament be against any of His natural laws, which are immutably true, their declaration would be contrary to eternal truth, equity and justice and consequently void.*[9]

This Colonial creed derived from the concept of Israelite religion that all law is "an expression of the will of God, his absolute command."[10]

The roots of Mesopotamian moral and natural law, on the other hand, were nourished in a "primordial realm" that contained "infinite forces other than and transcending the gods,"[11] but the *kinatum* of Sumer and Akkad also postulated an eternal, unchanging, and universal absolute, intimately associated with justice. Moreover, the decisions of Mesopotamian courts indicate that, granted a share of the divine capacity of reason, their jurists applied their conception of immutable truth in a manner that would merit acceptance in any enlightened age.

In the great Third Dynasty of Ur, an official of the *erén* people (mostly agricultural workers and military support units) instituted an action alleging that in allocating fields inherited from his father, Awîlumšalim had deprived three *erén* people of their subsistence. The court decided the fields should be remeasured and ruled that if Awîlumšalim had allocated too little, he was to make up the deficiency. Further, the judges said, "If Awîlumšalim, after the death of his father, has taken the best part of the producing fields for himself, he has committed a transgression" (NG #215). In this case, clearly, it was not positive law, but the mandate of natural justice that prompted the Sumerian judges to label Awîlumšalim a malfeasor and to order a reallocation of the fields if the facts established he had unjustly enriched himself by retaining the best lands.

The same justification underlies today's law of quasi-contracts, or "Restitution," in the United States. When a person holds title to property acquired under circumstances indicating that he will be unjustly enriched if allowed to retain it, the law will hold him a constructive trustee for the benefit of the person whose right he has usurped. The transgressor's sole obligation as trustee is to convey the property to the person wronged. The rule emerged from the common law, where Lord Mansfield, writing in the same year as James Otis, seized upon the same "natural justice and equity" rationale to award a plaintiff six pounds held "iniquitously" from him by the defendant: "The gist of this kind of action is that the defendant, upon the circumstances of the case, is obliged by the ties of natural justice and equity to refund the money."[12]

In Mesopotamia, the king's failure to implement the cosmic design would presumably have entailed dire consequences, for "it was an axiom of royal prudence that, if a king paid no heed to justice, his subjects would rebel and his kingship be laid waste, his destiny reversed and misfortune follow close upon him."[13] Mesopotamian rulers, therefore, from earliest times, never ceased to claim they had done "the straight thing" and established justice in their realms. Sargon (lit. "the king is just") of Akkad, who reigned after the middle of the third millennium, always proclaimed himself "the king of justice, one that speaks justice."[14]

The prologue to the Laws of Ur-Nammu reads: "Then did Ur-Nammu . . . verily establish equity in the Land." Here, Finkelstein translates the Sumerian *ni-si-sá* (Bab. *misarum*) as "equity"; Yildiz in "Animadversiones" translates the same word as "justice": *ni-si-sá kalam-ma hu-mu-ni-gar*, "Justice I established in the land." How the Sumerian *ni-si-sá* came to mean justice is uncertain. The word, literally, as Dr. Kramer explained by letter, suggests a comparison of horns: "As for *si-sá*

= *mesarum* (or *misarum*). . . the first member *si* usually means horn . . . and *sá* usually means to compare, to be like, etc."

Hammurabi, Babylon's great sovereign, identified himself as King of Justice. In the prologue to his Code, he maintained that he received his mandate to establish justice from the gods: "At that time Anum and Enlil named me, Hammurabi, the devout and god fearing prince, to cause justice to prevail in the land." In the epilogue to his laws, where the efficient king revealed that he had set up laws of justice and caused the land to take the right way and to have good government, he registered his intention:

> *I wrote my precious words on my stela,*
> *and, in the presence of the statue of me, king of justice,*
> *I set it up in order to administer the law of the land,*
> *to prescribe the ordinances of the land,*
> *to give justice to the oppressed . . .*
> *By the order of Shamash, the great judge of heaven and earth,*
> *may my justice prevail in the land . . .*
> *I, Hammurabi, am the king of justice,*
> *to whom Shamash committed law* (ANET, 178).

Royal bards, not surprisingly, paid lavish tribute to their masters and constantly emphasized their commitment to the dispensation of justice. Royal hymns dedicated to Shulgi repeatedly named him the "righteous shepherd," "righteous man," "righteous lord"; his firm and just decisions prevented the strong from oppressing the weak.

Composed a century after Shulgi lived, an eloquent eulogy to Lipit-Ishtar consisting of sixty-three adulatory lines addressed him as the "King of Justice, Wisdom and Learning." In the following excerpt, "Truth and justice" of line 26 is a translation of the Sumerian *nì-zi nì-gi-na*, a phrase similar to the Akkadian *kittum u mesharum*.

> 25. *Lipit-eštar, you are Enlil's son;*
> 26. *Truth and justice you make manifest;*
> 27. *Lord, your goodness covers even the horizon.*
> 28. *King Lipit-eštar, counsellor of great judgment,*
> 29. *(Whose) word never falters, wise one (whose) decision provides justice for the people;*
> 30. *Great mind, knowing all things deeply,*
> 31. *In order to lay down the law for all foreign countries,*
> 32. *You perceive falsehood and truth even from the words hidden in the heart.*
> 33. *Lipit-eštar, you rage against the enemies,*

34. *From evil and oppression you know how to save people,*
35. *From sin and destruction you know how to free them.*
36. *The mighty do not perpetrate robbery,*
37. *And the strong do not make the weaker into hirelings—*
38. *Thus you established justice in Sumer and Akkad,*
39. *And made pleasant (the life of) everybody in the Land.*[15]

These grandiloquent lines embellish what is essentially a political tract. Once again they set forth the purposes of the Prologue, for the king's counsel and wise decisions provide justice for the people; he protects them from enemies, saves them from moral and physical oppression, and brings happiness to the land. The same lines also convey other important ethical and political ideas that were to become traditional in later Akkadian, Greek, and Hebrew writings.

It is axiomatic that power exercised without sanction will provoke resentment and encourage resistance. Here, the Sumerian eulogist calls the king of Isin the son of Enlil, clothing him in a divine mantle that verifies the legitimacy of his power and validates his right to rule. By making truth and justice apparent, Lipit-Ishtar obeys the divine command and duplicates the eternal cosmic order on earth. He is celebrated for his goodness, as Colonial America exulted in the infinite goodness of the Puritan God. He is the "counsellor of great judgment" as Isaiah's Messiah was thereafter to be the "Wonderful Counsellor." His great mind possesses the only form of knowledge that Plato later claimed "deserves the name of wisdom," the ability to distinguish truth from falsehood, good from evil (*Rep.*, 429).[16]

At the beginning of their reigns, Mesopotamian kings traditionally gave positive evidence of their commitment to the implementation of justice by proclaiming a *mesharum.* Such a proclamation was an "Act of Mercy," a royal edict intended to remit certain specific kinds of obligations, primarily financial in nature, for a limited period. When equity required that the law be adjusted to restore the *kittu* ("correct" or "normal") status, it was the "official duty of the king to 'make (Akk.: *šakânu*, Sum.: *gar*) *mîšaru* (Sum.: *níg.si.sá.*),' i.e., to readjust the law to the necessities of an ever changing world" (ANET, 269 n. 1).[17]

It was not always easy to foresee all consequences of the king's Edict of Mercy. Ammisaduqa's *mesharum* (1646 B.C.), the best preserved of the genre, had a chilling effect upon the steward Gimillum of Sippar, who had deposited a quantity of his master's grain with a warehouseman and authorized the warehouseman "to lend it further," which was done (the interest rates were attractive). When the king's moratorium took effect and it appeared the borrower's obligation to repay might thereby be discharged and the grain lost, a concerned Gimillum removed an equal amount of grain from the warehouse by force, prompting an action for its recovery by the warehouseman.[18] The parties reached a friendly settlement of this lawsuit and the case teaches us little else, but the court's ready acceptance of the warehouseman as plaintiff is interesting; succeeding civilizations, in Rome, Continental Europe, England, and America, have debated to what extent, if at all, a bailee should be allowed to recover commodities taken wrongfully from his possession. California concurred with the Babylonian view when it defined the warehouseman's right in 1922.[19]

Justice is, alas, a will-o-the-wisp, an unattainable or, at best, an evanescent goal. In his last days, when Hammurabi, the great King of Justice, the quintessential judge and father, fell ill, his son, Samsuiluna, assumed the throne and, honoring his obligation to the gods, immediately remitted the arrears of the tenant farmers, broke the debt tablets of soldier, fisherman, and *muskenum*, and once again "established justice in the land."

In a community enlightened by the notion of a truth that transcended the power of the gods, its rulers enjoined by those gods to implement that truth by just administration, the promulgation of just laws became an obligation of the highest order. The first written Law Code, that of Ur-Nammu, expressly proscribed the violent offenses, viz., batteries, mayhem, murder, robbery, false imprisonment, and rape, which no society may countenance if order and justice are to prevail. From the intentional trespasses that were the primary concern of Ur-Nammu, through the Laws of Eshnunna and those of Lipit-Ishtar, Mesopotamian lawmakers increasingly focused their attention upon the management of family relationships, regulation of the economy, and responsibility for damages caused by nonintentional injuries. By the time of Hammurabi, disputes in major fields of modern law—contracts, torts, testamentary dispositions, real and personal property, and commercial law—had been adjudicated. These judgments helped crystallize legal principles and concepts, some of which appeared, subsequently, in legal compilations, or codes.

A *ditilla* (the record of a completed legal proceeding), for instance, marks the entry of a judgment in 2032 B.C., during the reign of Šu-Sin, King of Ur, against the owner of a house who had failed to keep it in good repair and thereby caused injury to his neighbor (NG #143). There is no provision for such a liability in the Laws of Ur-Nammu, which are roughly contemporary, nor in the Laws of Eshnunna, which followed closely. The principle is stated in unmistakable terms for the first time in the eleventh provision of the Law Code of Lipit-Ishtar, a century later. Again, in an action brought during the reign of Amar-Suen, a later King of Ur (1984-1978 B.C.), a defendant accused of the theft of sheep attempted to establish his innocence by claiming over against his seller and proving that he had bought the sheep from him (NG #127). This technique, seeking to prove the corrupt link in a chain of title, duplicated in a "vouching to warranty" procedure employed in Medieval England, first became part of the written law in Hammurabi's Code, Sects. 9-13.[20]

That Mesopotamian law validated attitudes, customs, and institutions which contemporary standards regard as unjust is hardly debatable. Slavery and a class society were accepted and punishments were likely to be harsh. Direct participation by the citizenry in the political process was not possible (although Sumerian mythology suggests that in the very first days it might have been otherwise). These early laws, however, were not arbitrarily imposed by rulers motivated solely by self-interest. Within the limits of the existing culture, the laws sought truly, and in many cases with remarkable sensitivity, to adjust conflicting interests in a reasonable manner and to prescribe standards of humane behavior for the community. As will be shown, the first laws of Sumer encompassed most of the "moral" commandments of the Decalogue, those of the second table that deal with purely human relationships.

In the final analysis, decisions reached by those administering the law will determine the extent to which a legal code will be given effect and a course of conduct judged lawful or unlawful. In that early era when the city-states of Mesopotamia were still largely independent and the administration of justice was the responsibility of the *ensi* (ultimately the *lu-gal,* "big man," or "king"), he participated in the decision-making process, assisted by others of his class who served as nonprofessional judges. As larger political entities gradually absorbed early Sumerian cities, conflicts sometimes arose between the local judiciary, seeking to preserve the traditional and its own prerogatives, and the consolidating power, bent upon a uniformity of interpretation and a strengthening of the federal, or royal, authority. Latent animosity surfaced on one reported occasion in Sumer when the bold *ensi* Urlama overruled the "word of the royal judge" (NG #113). Later, Hammurabi also experienced difficulty with an entrenched judiciary when he attempted to put his laws into effect. He therefore removed local judges who were unable or unwilling to implement his measures and replaced them with "royal" judges sympathetic to his reforms.

James Madison anticipated that dual state-federal jurisdictions in America were likely to generate similar frictions and wrote to George Washington shortly before the Constitutional Convention urging that national supremacy be extended to judiciary departments:

> *If those who are to expound and apply the laws are connected by their interests and their oaths with the particular States, wholly, and not with the Union, the participation of the Union in the making of the laws may be possibly rendered unavailing. It seems at least necessary that the oath of the Judges should include a fidelity to the general as well as the local Constitution.*[21]

From the very beginning, the reports of Sumerian litigation demonstrate a high regard for fair and orderly process. When a plaintiff challenged a personal or property interest before the court, he gave the defendant notice of the proceeding and an opportunity to appear and defend his right. One Sumerian plaintiff in the twentieth century B.C. utilized a summons that resembles contemporary forms to compel the appearance of the defendant: "If you do not appear at the trial concerning the garden within seven days (and) if you do not bring the tablet stating that you bought the garden from Dudum, you may not stay in the garden" (NG #109). A second summons from the same period warned, "If in the morning you do not appear [*in court?*] a final judgment will be passed" (NG #122). This document is noteworthy for its apparent reference to the possibility of a default judgment, a remedy not fully available in English jurisprudence until the eighteenth century A.D.

Colleges of judges, usually numbering three or four, conducted trials during the neo-Sumerian period, although the size of the court varied from a single judge to the community elders sitting in a judicial capacity. During the trial the parties adduced documentary evidence and called witnesses, including experts, to testify. Reporters who could write as fast as a man can talk recorded the proceedings and at times included verbatim testimony. The court interrogated the witnesses and, when necessary, informed itself by visiting and inspecting the location about which the dispute had arisen. The most elementary conception of justice requires that any such hearing be held before an impartial judge, and the activities of neo-Sumerian judicial officials were closely scrutinized. One tablet described the exposure of a corrupt *mashkim*, a court functionary who served variously as bailiff, notary, and judge. The *mashkim* had been assigned to investigate the alleged conversion of a flock of sheep; two witnesses testified at his trial that he had received a number of sheep from the accused as a bribe. He was removed and fined a sum three times the amount of the bribe (NG #138).

Decisions reached by Sumerian courts became a matter of permanent record. Officials charged with responsibility for their care tagged the reports and filed them in archives according to subject matter, year, and presiding judge. Many reports described the penalties imposed upon irresponsible plaintiffs who instituted frivolous actions; some suffered the indignity of having their "front hair" cut off.

A plaintiff who obtains a judgment in his favor gains little if he has no means to realize upon it. In the earliest times, Sumerian judgments were privately executed, and if a plaintiff was not a man of great prestige or lacked a powerful patron capable of enforcing a decision, the judges would not deign to hear his case. Those learned men would obviously have agreed with England's Chief Justice Lord Coke, who thundered in a language they could not have known, *Lex neminem cogit ad vana seu inutilia peragenda,* "The law compels no one to do vain or useless things." Kings of the third millennium, therefore, undertook to protect the rights of men of little substance by providing that if they swore their contracts pursuant to the king's oath and the contracts were subsequently breached, the crown itself would ensure that the court's orders and decisions were carried out—a precedent of great significance in establishing justice in the land.

In the Near East, civilian officials and later, in large measure, priests or judges appointed by the High Temple gradually assumed the trial function. By the time of the Hammurabi dynasty, trial procedures had been established by long usage. In fifteen reports from Babylon, when issues remained unresolved, the court imposed an oath upon one of the parties to the litigation: thirteen times upon the defendant and twice upon the plaintiff. The expensive oath had a formidable effect, for in all cases, the party opposed to the one charged with swearing was dismissed, withdrew, or agreed to a settlement.

The availability and use of expert testimony during the Babylonian hegemony attests to an increasingly sophisticated trial process. In a case involving a dispute over the measurement of a plot of ground purchased from the plaintiff, an expert witness brought the "Houseplan" from the land registry of the Uras temple and the plot was remeasured (AR #275). In a second case, the secretary of the registry office who recorded a conveyance was called to testify before the judicial commission (AR #286). On another occasion, a priestess testified as to how much weight a baby placed under the care of a wet-nurse should have gained and what fees were appropriate for the nurse's services (AR #241). One remarkable tablet describes the judges of Babylon examining two promissory notes in the presence of the *akil tamkarim,* the scribe of the merchants, called as an expert to assist in their evaluation (AR U 1070 348). This was similar to the tack taken in the eighteenth century A.D. by England's great Lord Mansfield, who had the vision and uncommon sense to dine with London merchants and become familiar with their problems and practices. The illumination and understanding those interviews afforded Mansfield subsequently enabled him to incorporate much of the law of merchant into English common law.

The phrase "to establish justice," therefore, for a Mesopotamian ruler was no idle boast. By means of his *mesharum,* the promulgation of just, positive laws, and the regular administration of justice under the control and guidance of a supervised judiciary, he tried to honor his mandate to do "the straight thing" and be adjudged *šar mīšarim*, a just king.

A final note: Casual and irregular tribunals also made a significant contribution to the administration of justice in the ancient Near East. Informal methods of resolving disputes without burdening an existing judicial system later found favor in Plato's *Laws* and have been urged as essential by prominent jurists of the present age. In an address at a meeting of the American Bar Association, then Chief Justice Warren E. Burger, decrying the proliferation of lawsuits in the federal system, urged the bar to try other ways of settling differences. He suggested arbitration and mediation:

> *There is, of course, nothing new about the concept of arbitration to settle controversies. The concept of mediation and arbitration preceded by many centuries the creation of formal and organized judicial systems and codes of law. Ancient societies, more than 25 centuries ago, developed informal mechanisms, very much like mediation and arbitration, to resolve disputes.*[22]

Mesopotamia frequently used "informal mechanisms" to resolve disputes as early as the first half of the second millennium B.C. There, citizen assemblies, usually chaired by the mayor, decided cases at the "city wall," not only in the principal cities of Babylon, Sippar, Dilbat, and Nippur, but also in smaller localities. In one report, the "arbitration people" at Sippar's temple of Shamash resolved a dispute about nonpayment of a debt (AR #270); in a second, an "arbitration court" at Dilbat, a committee consisting of family acquaintances heard a complaint over a conveyance of real property and decided the issue (AR #279); a third, another Sippar report, discloses the occupations of members of a group who appear to have been "arbitration people" before whom a matter was heard and a friendly settlement reached: three herdsmen, a soldier, and the scribe of the merchants (AR #310).

Security

The second and third objectives of the Prologue, "to wipe out complaints from the mouth," and "to return enmity and violence into their house," may be read as intended to achieve internal order and to provide a defense against foreign aggression, but the distinction is not made entirely clear. Other sources, however, confirm that those objectives looked to both the internal and external security of the state.

In the mythology of Mesopotamia, *En-Líl* (lit. "Lord Storm") was master of all free space between sky and earth. As force, he compelled obedience and executed the verdicts of the gods; as divine sheriff, he kept the peace internally and led the gods in war. So closely were those responsibilities identified with the Storm God that they became known as the "Enlil functions."[23]

In the earthly state of Mesopotamia, the tutelary deity of each city owned the land that man worked for the god's well-being. Chief amongst the god's human representatives on earth was the *ensi,* manager of the god's estate, upon whom the Enlil functions devolved, making him responsible for the maintenance of law and order within the city and for its defense against the onslaughts of neighboring tribes. The following lines from the prologue to his Code tell how Hammurabi inherited the Enlil functions through Marduk, who had replaced Enlil in the Babylonian pantheon:

> *When lofty Anum, king of the Anunnaki,*
> *(and) Enlil, lord of heaven and earth*
> *the determiner of the destinies of the land,*
> *determined for Marduk, the first born of Enki,*
> *the Enlil functions over all mankind . . .*
> *at that time Anum and Enlil named me*
> *to promote the welfare of the people,*
> *me, Hammurabi (ANET, 164).*

In the United States, the federal government has assumed the Enlil functions over the states. A provision that has survived from the first drafts of the Constitution reads: "Art. IV, Sect. 4: The United States . . . shall protect each of them *(the States)* against Invasion; and . . . against domestic Violence." Art. I, Sect. 8 (15), also empowers Congress "To provide for calling forth the Militia to execute the Laws of the Union, suppress Insurrections and repel Invasions."

Mesopotamian kings always acknowledged their obligation to establish and maintain the peace, constantly proclaiming themselves defenders of the land, guarantors of tranquility. Ur-Nammu wrote that he had "abolished malediction, violence and strife" and made "outcry for justice disappear." The metaphors of the Shulgi hymns portrayed the king as the *ig-gal*, the "great door" of the city: "You are the 'great wall' (*bàd-gal*) of the homeland / You are a net, spread over heaven and earth, you are a band encompassing Sumer."[24]

Lipit-Ishtar's "Hymn of Praise" said the king "raged against the enemies" and silenced "the loud strife of foreign countries." Hammurabi's Code described him as the "protector of the land and terror of the enemy," who subdued "the settlements along the Euphrates," saved "his people from distress," established "in security their portion in the midst of Babylon," and silenced the "growlers." He made "the four quarters of the world subservient," rooted out "the enemy above and below," brought an end to war, and made "the people rest in friendly habitations" (ANET, 163ff).

In actual practice, faced with the constant threat of attack and the fearful consequences of defeat, wise Mesopotamian rulers took pains to provide a strong defense against external aggression. Generally, military levies were drawn from male members of the community, citizen soldiers, organized and trained in the arts of war. Assyria appears to have been the first nation to forego a yearly conscription in favor of a standing army, although Sargon of Akkad in the twenty-fourth century B.C. boasted that a force of fifty-four hundred men ate daily before him.

Eannatum's limestone Stele of the Vultures, named for the birds of prey shown gorging on the corpses of fallen warriors, conveys some idea of how the redoubtable Sumerian faced his enemies in battle. There, an armed Lagashite contingent of the early third millennium endures; assembled in a tight phalanx, heads encased in heavy leather and copper helmets, they are protected by full-length shields held by the first rank. Led by a ruler clothed in a fleece robe and bearing a short sword, their long, expertly fashioned spears held at the ready, the unit gives every evidence of being a resolute and disciplined force. An auxiliary troop appears wearing helmets but no body armor, carrying long lances, and following a leader mounted on a light two-wheeled chariot, indicating that the evolving military science of the time was sufficiently advanced to utilize specialized bodies, armed and armored, to perform specific functions.[25]

City leaders responsible for maintaining internal order delegated responsibilities to appointed officials and frequently employed the services of the ubiquitous *mashkim* to assist them in discharging the policing function. They invested the *mashkim* with a broad authority to investigate breaches of the civil peace and resolve complaints. In a case reported in 2038 B.C., the *ensi* dispatched the *mashkim* Urmami to investigate an alleged robbery. After hearing the facts, Urmami concluded there was no substance to the charge (NG #121). The *mashkim* who accepted a bribe has been encountered before.

In addition to the preservation of public order, the prevention and investigation of crime, the policeman's duties included the apprehension of wrongdoers. In two neo-Sumerian reports, the interesting *Ukus,* or "constable," attended to his routine chores. In the first, he seized two men accused of the theft of a donkey in order to bring them before the judges (NG #202); in the second, the royal *Ukus* took custody of twenty-two sheep and ten goats found grazing unattended (NG #120a).

The various titles of the "constables" suggest an organization of lawmen-soldiers. The *Uku-us-gal* was the "great" *Ukus*; the *Uku-us-galgal* was presumably his superior or senior. In a case often cited to demonstrate the participation of the king himself in the administration of the law, *Ukus lugal*, the king's constable, Asad-Sarrum, was in attendance when Hammurabi delegated to the judges at Nippur the hearing of a matter that had been brought directly before him (AR #292).

Duties of the Sumerian *Ukus* were not always so prosaic. Serving on the staffs of various high officials of the crown, temple, or individual cities, he fought where and when necessary and traveled the length and breadth of the land, as courier, envoy, or as a member of a military escort accompanying commercial caravans. The Akkadian *rē/dûm,* literally a "runner," "follower," or "driver," but also a soldier-policeman, eventually inherited the duties of the *Ukus*. One tablet recorded a *rē/dûm*'s cry for reinforcements, without which he claimed his troop of one thousand men would be unable to hold a fort.[26]

Welfare

Succeeding to the *ensi*'s responsibility to manage the city-god's estates prudently, rulers of Mesopotamia tried to acquit that obligation and "make good the flesh of their people" by developing the country's natural resources, including the potential latent in the fertile soil of the area.

Rainfall was scarce in their lands; intermittent winter storms delivered barely eight inches of rain annually. For eight months of the year, during which temperatures might exceed one hundred and thirty degrees, there was none. In the spring, the snow melt from the northern Taurus and eastern Zagros mountain ranges flooded the country's two principal rivers. Held in check through half their courses by the hard limestone of the north, the Tigris and Euphrates ravaged the alluvial plain of the south when not confined by an elaborate system of dykes, dams, sluices, and managed diversions. Diligent maintenance of the river banks became ever more essential as the water-borne silt settled, gradually raising the beds of the rivers, until eventually they flowed higher than the land about them. From these main sources, water was directed into reservoirs, channels, ditches, and was raised, when necessary, by water-lifting devices until even the smallest holdings received a portion of the flow. Constant effort was required to keep the waterways clean, and local governors drafted corvées of adult males to care for the vital arteries upon which the well-being of the entire civilization was dependent. It is small wonder that Hammurabi, in enacting his 53rd law, saw fit to impose a positive duty upon his citizen land-occupiers to maintain their portions of the common irrigation system.[27]

Before salinization became a serious problem, the soil of Mesopotamia yielded rich harvests of barley, wheat, dates, melons, and vegetables. Temple lands, administered on behalf of their divine owners, constituted the economic core of early communities. Those lands were divided into three parts; the first was cultivated by the community as a whole, the second, allotted to persons for special services rendered to the crown or temple, and the third, leased to individuals or groups who paid one-third to one-sixth of the produce as a rental. A land allotment (*ilkum*) was highly prized. Hammurabi received many letters from tenants who charged they had been wrongfully evicted from their fiefs, and one chief *rē/dûm* complained his name had been deleted from the register by a comrade who had then substituted his own in its place.[28] With the output of communal land and revenues received from rentals, contributions, and assessments, the income of palace and temple came to exceed immediate needs. Accumulated reserves that filled the magazines inside the city walls were available for loan, barter, or trade, provided capital to fund business ventures, and were distributed to the people in time of emergency.

Mesopotamia lacked many of the raw materials it needed to prosper. Without good native wood, stone, gold, silver, or copper, it was compelled to exchange its agricultural surpluses for essential items. Later, because manufactured goods were more easily transported than bulky agricultural products, its people concentrated their energies and skills on the production of articles of high quality. They became accomplished metalworkers, manufactured tools and weapons, fashioned items of jewelry adorned with precious stones, wove textiles and carpets, all of which their indomitable merchants traded from central Anatolia to the east coast of Africa.

Because trade was critical to the prosperity of the state, the crown did its utmost to stimulate commercial activity; it attempted to discourage fraud and ensure fair dealing in the marketplace by adopting a standardized system of weights and measures, a topic to which Ur-Nammu devoted a share of the prologue to his Laws:

What is one sila, I standardized
I made a ban-measure of copper
(and) I standardized it as 10 sila;
I made the current royal ban-measure of copper
(and) I standardized it as 5 sila
The stone weight of 1 shekel
I standardized it as 1/60 mina
made a bronze-measure of one sila
and standardized (it?) (as?) one mina.[29]

Before the American Revolution, Colonists utilized weights and measures that came largely from an uncertain English system. As Ur-Nammu had before them, American leaders recognized the necessity for achieving uniformity by fixing more precise standards. When drafting the United States Constitution, they deemed the measure of sufficient importance to merit inclusion as a specific power of Congress: "Art. I. Sect. 8 (5): The Congress shall have Power to . . . fix the Standard of Weights and Measures."

In Mesopotamia, the crown established criteria for assessing the quality of silver, attempting to make the metal a more certain medium of exchange. It assured the safety of foreign merchants trading within its borders (when to its advantage) and expected its merchants to be protected by the rulers of foreign states. In the epic *The King of Battle,* Sargon of Akkad is seen leading an expedition into Anatolia to support the cause of Mesopotamian tradesmen.[30]

Mesopotamian rulers were well aware of the incentive provided by the hope of private gain. Their toleration of private enterprise and the aggregation of individual wealth throughout the economic system became a factor of major importance to the well-being of the city. The merchant who began as an agent of the temple found opportunities to trade for his own account; other skilled workers utilized their special abilities to realize private commissions. "The shepherd could dispose of any increase in his flock beyond the statutory figure; the fisherman could dispose of his catch after delivering to the temple his monthly quota."[31]

It goes without saying that the fisherman had to deliver to temple or crown whatever was due. In the eleventh month of the year 2032 B.C., the enterprising Sumerian Adaga failed to turn over four *kur,* ninety *sila* (about 30 bu.) of fresh fish which had been entrusted to him for delivery to the palace. He was charged, convicted, and assessed a fine of sixty *kur.* On that same day, which must have been the most trying day of his life, at least until then, he was also convicted of having harbored a bowman who had been absent four years without leave from a troop of the king's archers. The court fined Adaga an additional "rental" of forty shekels of silver for the services of the bowman (NG #189). For misappropriating the fish, Adaga became the first carrier-bailee of record to be convicted of embezzlement, as defined in Cal. Penal Code 505:

> *Every carrier or other person having under his control personal property for the purpose of transportation for hire, who fraudulently appropriates it to any purpose inconsistent with the safekeeping of such property and its transportation according to his trust, is guilty of embezzlement.*

The prologue to Hammurabi's Code is more than generous in describing the efforts of the king to provide for the people's welfare. He "made affluence and plenty abound," "furnished in abundance all sorts of things for Nippur-Duranki," "made Ur prosper," "supplied water in abundance to the people of Uruk," "extended the cultivated land belonging to Dilbat," and "stored up grain for mighty Urash." He established law and justice in the language of the land, thereby promoting the welfare of the people. The epilogue reports that Hammurabi "was not neglectful of the black-headed people Enlil had entrusted to him," that he "promoted the welfare of the land," and that he "carried the peoples of the land of Sumer and Akkad in his bosom"; they "prospered under his protection."

Mesopotamian poets often attributed the nation's prosperity to the king's benevolent and just administration. One of the Shulgi hymns, however, describes a special amenity that elicited comment later from such diverse notables as Plato and James Madison:

> 29. *I determined the danna-s [*road stations?*] built there (lodging-) houses,*
> 30. *Planted gardens by their side, established resting-places,*
> 31. *Installed in those places experienced (men);*
> 32. *(He) who comes from 'above,' he who comes from 'below,'*
> 33. *May refresh themselves in their cool shade;*
> 34. *The wayfarer, who passes the night on the road*
> 35. *May seek haven there, like in a well built city.*[32]

Thus, by attempting to control nature's forces, by developing the land's natural resources, by encouraging trade and commerce, and by direct grants of rations and land, rulers of the ancient land between the Tigris and Euphrates strove to make their nations prosper and the flesh of their people good. But the high civilization achieved there would have been impossible, or its impetus slowed, without a system of laws designed to augment and defend it. With adoption of the earliest laws, assuring the individual's right to his life, property, and liberty, and the painstaking regard Mesopotamian judges displayed for the protection of those rights, the welfare of the people was nurtured and enhanced.

Numerous studies have examined the close correspondences between Biblical and Babylonian law, but historians have scanted the effect of Babylonian law on Western jurisprudence and political thought. We are told that Hammurabi's Code was not meant to be implemented in day-to-day practice, that it was forgotten a week after his death, and that it was merely a religious testament directed to his gods.[33]

Dr. Joan Oates concludes her splendid history of Babylon with a chapter entitled "The Legacy of Babylon," in which she describes with impressive authority the educational, literary, religious, scientific, mathematical, astronomical, astrological, technological, and agricultural contributions of the Babylonians.[34] Except for incidental references to Hammurabi's Code, however, Dr. Oates makes no attempt to address the Babylonian legal and political legacy. This is a grievous omission, for that legacy, derived from Sumer, with its understanding of law as an expression of an eternal, immutable, and universal order, encompassing the remarkable corpus of positive law and the paradigm of righteous government proclaimed by Hammurabi, may constitute Babylon's greatest gift to later generations.

---

[1] John Milton, *Pro Populo Anglicano Defensio* (1651).

[2] Wolkstein and Kramer, *Inanna*, 137ff. See also Alexander Heidel, *The Babylonian Genesis* (Chicago: Univ. of Chicago Press, 1951), 15.

[3] Jacob Klein, *Three Šulgi Hymns—Sumerian Royal Hymns Glorifying King Šulgi of Ur* (Ramat-Gan: Bar Ilan University Press, 1981), 32. The Shulgi hymns are entitled: Shulgi (D), "The Avenger of Sumer"; Shulgi (X), "The Favorite of the Gods"; and Shulgi (A), "The King of the Road." Klein advises that these are amongst 125 compositions of which 55 are assigned to Isin; of these, 25 to Ishme-Dagan (father of Lipit-Ishtar), a "great admirer and imitator of Šulgi," and 6 to Lipit-Ishtar himself (24 n. 17).

[4] Speiser, "Cuneiform Law and the History of Civilization," 536.

[5] Speiser, "Early Law and Civilization," 863-67.

[6] G. Dossin, "L'inscription de fondation Iahdun-Lim, roi de Mari," *Syria,* 32 (1955), lines 4-6.

[7] G. R. Driver and John C. Miles, T*he Babylonian Laws,* vol. I (Oxford: Oxford Univ. Press, 1952), 21.

[8] Corwin, *'Higher Law' Background,* 152, citing definition incorporating this view in Holland, *Elements of Jurisprudence* (12th ed.).

[9] James Otis, *The Rights of the British Colonies Asserted and Proved* (Boston: Edes and Gill, 1764), 47.

[10] Yehezkel Kaufmann, *The Religion of Israel,* trans. Moshe Greenberg (New York: Schocken Books, 1972), 327.

[11] Ibid., 21ff.

[12] Moses v. Macferlan, 2 Burr. 1005 (K.B. 1760).

[13] H. C. Rawlinson, *Cuneiform Inscriptions of Western Asia,* cited in Driver and Miles, B*abylonian Laws,* I:5. See also the late Assyrian (or Babylonian) tablet DT 1, where divine retribution follows the king's failure to heed justice (W.G. Lambert, *Babylonian Wisdom Literature* [Oxford: Clarendon Press, 1960], 112; hereafter cited in the text as BWL).

[14] Driver and Miles, *Babylonian Laws,* I:5.

[15] H.J.L. Vanstiphout, "Lipit-Eshtar's Praise in the Edubba," *JCS,* 30/1 (Jan. 1978): 33. The number of school copies discovered and the relatively simple grammatical construction leads Vanstiphout to conclude that the poem "was composed in and primarily for the *Edubba,* to be used there as a beginner's text."

[16] Plato, *The Republic,* trans. Paul Shorey (Cambridge: Harvard Univ. Press, Loeb Classical Library, 1978); unless otherwise indicated, all subsequent citations in the text are from this edition.

[17] Some of the new American states adopted similar measures during the economic depression that followed the Revolution when their legislatures passed "Stay Laws," moratoria on the collection of debts and mortgage foreclosures.

[18] M. Schorr, *Altbabylonische Rechtsurkunden* (Leipzig: J.C. Hinrichs'sche Buchhandlung, 1913), #273, hereafter cited in the text as AR.

[19] See Appendix, Exhibit C, "The Earliest Laws of Conversion" (205).

[20] Ibid., 213-14.

[21] *The Founding Fathers—James Madison,* ed. Merrill D. Peterson (New York: Harper & Row, 1974), 107.

[22] Chief Justice Warren E. Burger, "Isn't There a Better Way?" *American Bar Association Journal,* (March 1982): 274.

[23] Thorkild Jacobsen, "Mesopotamia: The Cosmos as a State," in H. and H.A. Frankfort, *Before Philosophy* (Harmondsworth: Penguin Books, 1954), 207.

[24] Klein, *Three Šulgi Hymns,* Shulgi (X), ll.121-22, 143. "Sulgi is characterized as the great protector of Sumer against its enemies. . . . It [*bàd-gal*] frequently occurs in parallelism with *si-gar* 'lock,' which in the present is replaced by *ig-gal,* 'great door'. . . . The king as a large net, spread out menacingly, ready to capture all criminals and foes, is likewise a well attested motive" (ibid., ll.160-61).

[25] Sir Leonard Woolley, *The Beginnings of Civilization* (New York: New American Library, 1936), 187.

[26] Driver and Miles, *Babylonian Laws*, I:114.

[27] See Appendix, Exhibit B, "The Negligent Sumerian—Misfeasant and Nonfeasant" (195).

[28] Driver and Miles, *Babylonian Laws,* I:150.

[29] Yildiz, "Animadversiones," 87.

[30] Henri Frankfort, *The Birth of Civilization in the Near East* (Bloomington: Indiana Univ. Press, 1959), 76.

[31] Ibid., 66.

[32] Klein, *Three Šulgi Hymns,* Shulgi (A), 11. 191-93.

[33] See Appendix, Exhibit E, "The Mesopotamian Law 'Codes': In Real Life, Meant To Be Ignored?"

[34] Joan Oates, *Babylon* (London: Thames and Hudson, 1979), 163.

IV

AN OVERVIEW OF BABYLON'S LEGAL AND POLITICAL HERITAGE

The Code of Hammurabi

The original stele upon which the laws of Hammurabi were inscribed was discovered by French archaeologists in 1902 and is now in the Louvre Museum. The stele is a black, cone-shaped diorite block about eight feet high. At its top, the Sun-god Shamash is shown entrusting the laws to the Babylonian king.

The prologue and epilogue to Hammurabi's laws lack the precise focus of the Prologue, but both sections contain an extravagant imagery describing the same virtues of an ideal ruler and the same transcendent goals of a perfect state. Many qualities of the just king appear there that later became associated with the gods, good kings, and magistrates of Greece, Western Europe, and America. An early *speculum principis* ("mirror of a prince") was the mirror Hammurabi held to himself, displaying his resplendent image for the instruction of the future lords of Babylon. But then, Babylonians believed that "Man is the shadow of a god and a slave is a shadow of a man, but the king is the mirror ['reflecting copper'] of a god."[1]

Hammurabi's scribes engraved his Code in the middle of the eighteenth century B.C. A collection of almost three hundred laws, it illuminated the world's dominant civilization for a thousand years. Its provisions were widely distributed; royal copyists reproduced the laws for the instruction of judicial officials and bureaucrats staffing the administrative centers of Hammurabi's realm. His educators prepared copies to be used as exercise tablets in the training of Babylonian students. The entire Near East admired and attempted to imitate Hammurabi's laws and highly efficient administration. So effective were the practices, customs, and institutions which evolved from the legal and philosophical ideas endorsed by Hammurabi that Babylonian influences spread to neighboring nations and brought a common, homogeneous culture to much of

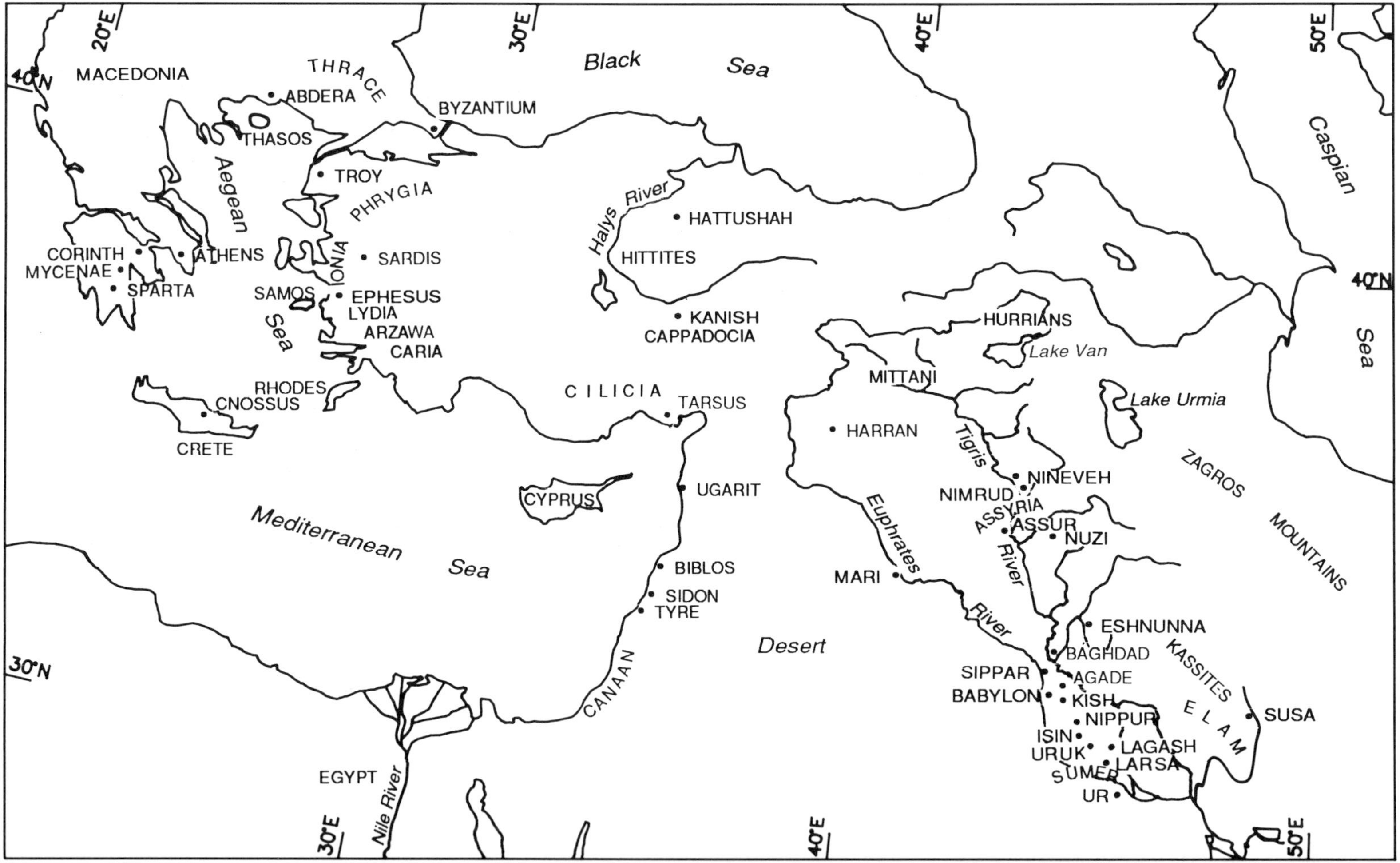

20°E
30°E
40°E
50°E
40°N
30°N
MACEDONIA
THRACE
ABDERA
THASOS
BYZANTIUM
Black
Sea
Caspian
Sea
Aegean
Sea
TROY
PHRYGIA
IONIA
SARDIS
CORINTH
MYCENAE
ATHENS
SPARTA
SAMOS
EPHESUS
LYDIA
ARZAWA
CARIA
RHODES
CNOSSUS
CRETE
Halys River
HATTUSHAH
HITTITES
KANISH
CAPPADOCIA
CILICIA
TARSUS
HURRIANS
Lake Van
Lake Urmia
MITTANI
HARRAN
Tigris
River
NINEVEH
NIMRUD
ASSYRIA
ASSUR
NUZI
ZAGROS
MOUNTAINS
CYPRUS
UGARIT
Mediterranean
BIBLOS
SIDON
TYRE
Euphrates
River
MARI
Desert
CANAAN
ESHNUNNA
BAGHDAD
KASSITES
SIPPAR
AGADE
BABYLON
KISH
ELAM
SUSA
NIPPUR
ISIN
URUK
LAGASH
LARSA
SUMER
UR
EGYPT
Nile River

western Asia. Despite their underlying differences, Elamite, Hurrian, Syrian, and Palestinian states "were drawn into the orbit of a single civilization, notably in such essentials as the concept and practice of law."[2] The correspondences between Hammurabi's laws and later Assyrian, Hittite, and Hebrew enactments have given rise to an entire literature.

Six hundred years after its adoption, as Aegeans entered their dark and illiterate period, Hammurabi's Code was still so highly regarded that the Elamite Shutruk-Nahhunte carried off the ponderous stele upon which the laws were inscribed and installed it at Susa, the capital of ancient Iran. There he had Hammurabi's name chiseled from the stone, apparently in preparation for the insertion of his own, a plagiarism never completed.

In light of its broad distribution and pervasive effect upon the commerce and social organization of the Asian West, there can be little doubt that Greeks of the mid-first millennium were also familiar with the provisions of Hammurabi's Code, the goals of the Prologue, and the Mesopotamian concept of a perfect prince. Incidental trading contacts had exposed Greek merchants to sophisticated forms, laws, and procedures developed in Mesopotamia long before the earliest Aegean trading colonies were established on the shores of Asia Minor. Greek scholars for centuries sought out the wisdom and, specifically, the data accumulated in the East. Greek writers before Plato accepted as best Hammurabi's political goals, expressed earlier in the Prologue and evident later in the *Republic*.

Scribes of Assyrian kings still copied the provisions of Hammurabi's Code during Solon's lifetime (640-560). Scholars have used reproductions from Assurbanipal's collection at Nineveh to restore damaged portions of the original stele. The last great Assyrian monarch, Assurbanipal, boasted that he could read "the cunning tablets of Sumer [and] the dark Akkadian." He established his famous library by sending emissaries to copy and translate into Akkadian the tablets stored in ancient archives, "notably those attached to temples at Babylon, Kûta and Nippur."[3]

Persian lawmakers of the late sixth century B.C., in preparing an ordinance for which Xenophon and Plato expressed their admiration, consulted Hammurabi's compilation and cast their law in the same conditional style. The prologue-corpus-epilogue convention used by Hammurabi in recording his laws appears also in Plato's dialogue the *Laws*. Many of its provisions correspond closely in form and content to the enactments of the Babylonian ruler.

Greek maritime contracts of the fifth century B.C. resembled those used earlier by Sumerian and Babylonian traders. Hammurabi addressed nine sections of his laws to the subject. Chapters of a third-century B.C. Rhodian Sea-Law, which still obtained in the Mediterranean when Viking raiders sailed there, compare to Hammurabi's instructions.

In Hammurabi's lifetime, the highly developed mercantile practices of Mesopotamia, based upon his laws and utilizing the Akkadian cuneiform language, produced much of the legal accoutrement of a modern commercial society. Business transactions memorialized by written agreements had long been the rule; the provisions of some had been reduced to standard form. Express warranties accompanied contracts of sale; surety bonds supported contractual undertakings; sureties in turn secured themselves by taking pledges of personal property.[4] Sumerian traders had worked out the debt, deposit, and carrying contracts necessary to confirm and finance the purchase, storage, and transportation of commodities centuries before. Merchants utilized documents that resemble contemporary negotiable instruments; some Babylonian promissory notes were bearer in form. Delivery orders addressed to grain warehousemen, which functioned as drafts, date from the beginning of the second millennium.[5] Negotiable warehouse receipts facilitated the transfer of commodity surpluses.

Businessmen formed trading associations, partnerships, and joint ventures and allocated company capital for specific business purposes. Tablets record many actions for accountings upon dissolution of business enterprises. ("I have gone shares in business; loss is unending" [Babylonian proverb, BWL, 278].) An advanced system of accounting made this extensive mercantile activity possible. Mesopotamian bailees issued periodic recapitulations of deposits, withdrawals, and resulting balances that correspond in form to modern bank statements.

The Usages of Trade

It was barter, not Homer, that made the Greeks literate.[6]

The beginnings of Aegean-Asian trading contacts are obscure. There is credible evidence that Aegean merchants established trading colonies at Ugarit, on the Levantine coast, as early as 1400 B.C., although other reporters, equally believable, argue that proof of a Greek presence there at the time is unpersuasive. In any case, during the following two centuries, shipments of vases, perfumes, and cosmetics from Mycenaean Greece arrived at all ports on the Asiatic shore.

As the thirteenth century closed, events not completely understood destroyed Bronze Age civilization in the eastern Mediterranean.

Whether due to climatic changes or other natural or man-made disasters, entire populations moved. Egyptian texts recorded that northern countries "quivered in their bodies." Their peoples came from "islands in the midst of the sea" to attack Egyptian armies (ANET, 263). Sea peoples destroyed Canaanite cities, overran central Anatolia and the capital of the Hittites. Widespread disruption reduced life in the region to a primitive level that lasted almost four hundred years.

During those dark centuries, the art of writing disappeared in Greece. It was not until the beginning of the eighth century B.C. that the Greeks, drawing also upon Syrian and early Canaanite letters, acquired a consonantal alphabet from the Phoenicians, the Greek *phoinika grammata*. Soon Greek traders were challenging their Phoenician teachers for the markets of the Aegean. The very inception of Greece's reemergence as a Mediterranean power was coincident with its exposure to the forms, skills, and practices essential to trade, i.e., the basic bookkeeping, written contracts, receipts, releases, and commercial instruments it came upon in the East. Particularly important were documents originating in the cities of Canaan, where Babylonian scribal schools had been maintained, the Akkadian language used in legal documentation, and the laws of Babylon known for centuries.

Greek public and private law, based upon immemorial custom, was first reduced to writing in the discrete codes of individual city-states during the seventh century; no Greek common law may be spoken of before the fifth, if then. A uniform commercial law, however, developed earlier in the port cities; it was shaped in part by international treaty and implemented by metics, resident aliens, who understood and conducted much of the banking, industrial, and commercial activities that reached a high degree of maturity in Periclean Athens. Maritime contracts prepared there in the fifth century B.C. utilized legal concepts that were well known in Hammurabi's Babylon.

Because of the poverty of Attica's soil, Athens, at the peak of its power, imported large quantities of grain to feed its expanding population. It paid for those purchases with capital acquired, to a great extent, from the profits of its trading enterprises. Each Athenian trading venture was a separate and distinct transaction. In a typical "double voyage" (a single voyage might be either out from Athens or in from a foreign port), a merchant who wished to undertake a maritime trading expedition borrowed the necessary funds from a local lender to purchase a cargo, engaged the services of a shipowner to transport it, and frequently accompanied the shipment to its destination. There, with the profit from the cargo's sale, he acquired another for the return voyage, and upon arrival at his home port, delivered the cargo to his lender to be held until sold and his debt repaid.

The parties memorialized their understanding in a standard form of contract that has become known as "respondentia."[7] These agreements set out the amount of the loan to be advanced for acquisition of the cargo, specified its nature and the rate of interest to be charged. The merchant affirmed that no prior lien existed on the merchandise and agreed not to use it to secure any other debt. His obligation was terminated if the vessel was lost, and it was reduced to the extent he was forced to jettison the cargo or make payments to enemies or pirates.

Although no respondentia contracts from the Babylonian period have been recovered, Hammurabi devoted no fewer than nine laws, viz., 99-107, to the rights and duties of the *tamkārum,* the Babylonian trader, and his *samallum.* (The *samallum*'s precise relation to the *tamkārum* is obscure. He was at once "agent," "debtor," "partner," the carrier of a bag or purse containing weighing stones.) Hammurabi's preoccupation with the activities of *tamkārum* and *samallum* testifies that similar contracts must have been common and of great economic importance at the time.

Babylonian practice and the procedures adopted in Greek maritime contracts had much in common; the latter are in writing, an imperative of Babylonian law. They are executed in the usual Babylonian manner; i.e., they are acknowledged and sealed in the presence of witnesses. The particulars of the loans set out in the Greek contracts are similar to numerous Babylonian promissory notes that have been recovered. Deposit of the cargo with the lender upon return of the ship to its home port, pending payment by the merchant of his debt, constituted a contract of pledge, an ancient Mesopotamian security device.

Force majeure defenses utilized in the respondentia agreements are similar to those enumerated by Hammurabi. CH #103 also provided that if an enemy caused the *samallum* "to jettison" whatever he was carrying, he went free if he so affirmed. In at least one Babylonian case decided by the judges of the Shamash temple, the defendant lessee argued with apparent success that the ship he leased had been lost to enemy action (AR #302), a defense that also exculpated the Greek merchant. A similar rationale in earlier Sumerian litigation might have accounted for the shipowner's denial that he had leased the ship at all when it was returned to him after it had been wrecked without fault on the lessee's part (NG #62).[8]

The Rhodian Sea-Law ("RSL")

Several important mercantile provisions authorized by Hammurabi facilitated trading practices in the Near East well into the first millennium. A code of maritime law that regulated trade in the eastern Mediterranean fourteen centuries after Hammurabi's death demonstrates that laws he promulgated and practices he inaugurated were still useful to the water-borne traffic of the later period.

From the heights of the mountain range stretching across the island of Rhodes, the southwestern shore of Asia Minor is clearly visible. In the third century B.C., this small island threw off a Macedonian rule and established itself as the hub of international commerce and banking in the eastern Mediterranean. Blessed with magnificent natural harbors and boasting the best port facilities available, it became the transshipment depot for the products of Europe, Egypt, and the East. Its powerful navy swept pirates from the seas and made the island a safe haven for merchant vessels of all nations.

Prosperous and secure, Rhodes produced a maritime law that was widely respected and accepted.[9] So efficacious were the Rhodian regulations that more than a thousand years later Byzantine rulers used them as a basis of their maritime codes. Italian republics in turn adopted the Byzantine enactments, which had an effect upon Mediterranean law and commerce for hundreds of years.

Recurring issues that arise from the storage and transportation of goods dealt with in RSL may be matched, in style and substance, against sections of Hammurabi's collection.

I. The boatman's liability for negligence

RSL Part III, Chap. 10:

If the captain and the crew are negligent, and there is an injury or wreck, let the captain and crew be responsible to the merchant for making the damage good.

CH #237:

When a seignior hired a boatman and a boat and loaded it with grain, wool, oil, dates, or any kind of freight, if that boatman was so careless that he has sunk the boat and lost what was in it as well, the boatman shall make good the boat which he sank and whatever he lost that was in it.

II. Formalities of deposit

The first two sentences of RSL Part III, Chap. 12:

If a man makes a deposit in a ship or in a house, let him make it with a man known to him and worthy of confidence before three witnesses. If the amount is large, let him accompany the deposit with a writing.

CH #122:

If a seignior wishes to give silver, gold, or any sort of thing to a(nother) seignior for safekeeping, he shall show to witnesses the full amount that he wishes to give, arrange the contracts, and then commit (it) to safekeeping.

The Greek of RSL Part III, Chap. 12 reads, *ean tis parathētai en ploiō ē en oikō,* i.e., "If a man makes a deposit in a ship or in a house." Ashburner advises that RSL Chap. 12 was originally confined to deposits made in a house (see CH #125, below) and that the extension to deposits made in a ship was added by a compiler of the Sea-Law.

The Greek verb *parathētai* derives from the root *the,* as does the noun *parakatathēken,* "deposits." Lawsuits relating to *tēn parakatathēken,* property entrusted by one man to another, became common in fifth- and fourth-century Greece. Isocrates, in fact, argued that the "deposit theme," which had become a hackneyed exercise in the schools of rhetoric, was too trivial for serious oratory.[10]

III. Bailee's liability for failure to return deposit. Theft as a defense.

The second and third sentences of RSL Part III, Chap. 12:

If a man who agreed to take charge of the deposit says that it is lost, he must show where the wall was broken through or how the theft took place and take an oath that there was no fraud on his part. If he does not show it, let him restore the goods safe as he received them.

CH #125:

If a seignior deposited property of his for safekeeping and at the place where he made the deposit his property has disappeared along with the property of the owner of the house, either through breaking in or through scaling (the wall), the owner of the house, who was so careless that he let whatever was given to him for safekeeping get lost, shall make (it) good and make restitution to the owner of the goods, while the owner of the house shall make a thorough search for his lost property and take (it) from its thief.

Under the Sea-Law, if the bailee met his burden of proof by offering evidence of a theft and by swearing that he had committed no fraud, he escaped liability. The bailee of CH #125, on the other hand, is presumed negligent if a theft occurs, and he is held liable, but only for the value of the property lost, the theft of his own property indicating he is innocent of a wrongful conversion. Hammurabi's legislators appear to have had no difficulty in deciding that the bailee, upon reimbursing the depositor, should succeed to his right against the thief, presumably for the same considerations of equity and good conscience that underlie current subrogation doctrine.[11]

Greeks Look To The East

The commercial regulations and mercantile practices of Mesopotamia may have constituted the first exposure to Eastern customs and procedures experienced by Greek writers and scholars who traveled there. Many financed their voyages by trading. Solon as a youth had "applied himself to merchandise," as did Pythagoras, whose father was a merchant. Other Greek traveling traders were Thales, Hippocrates the mathematician, Herodotus, and Plato, who "defrayed the charges of his travels by selling oil in Egypt."[12] Those illustrious tradesmen undoubtedly learned much on their voyages of the customs and laws that had evolved from Hammurabi's masterwork and its Sumerian antecedents.[13]

The principal incentive of Greek intellectuals who visited the East, however, was not the rewards judicious bargaining might bring. According to ancient sources and their own testimony, they were eager to see the awe-inspiring citadels, extant and crumbled, of the East, and to learn of the rules of behavior, laws, and principles of political organization that had brought order and security to the East's innumerable peoples.

Sometime after Homer and before giving the Spartans their constitution, Lycurgus studied the laws and forms of government he found on Crete; then he sailed to Ionia to compare the "manners and rules of life" of the luxury-loving Ionians with the more sober laws of the land he was leaving. There, says Plutarch, he transcribed and digested into order the "lessons of state and rules of morality" that Homer had expounded for use in his own country, and Lycurgus was the first to make them "really known" to the Greeks. Greek readers of Lycurgus undoubtedly recognized the good king and his government from the *Odyssey,* where Homer had described them in terms Hammurabi would have approved:

> *. . . as of some king, who as a blameless man and god-fearing, and ruling as lord over many powerful people, upholds the way of good government, and the black earth yields him barley and wheat, his trees are heavy with fruit, his sheepfold continues to bear young, the sea gives him fish because of his good leadership and his people prosper under him (XIX, 107-114).*[14]

That the gods would bless the subjects of a powerful, just, and pious king with a full measure of the earth's bounty was a predicate as old as Mesopotamia.

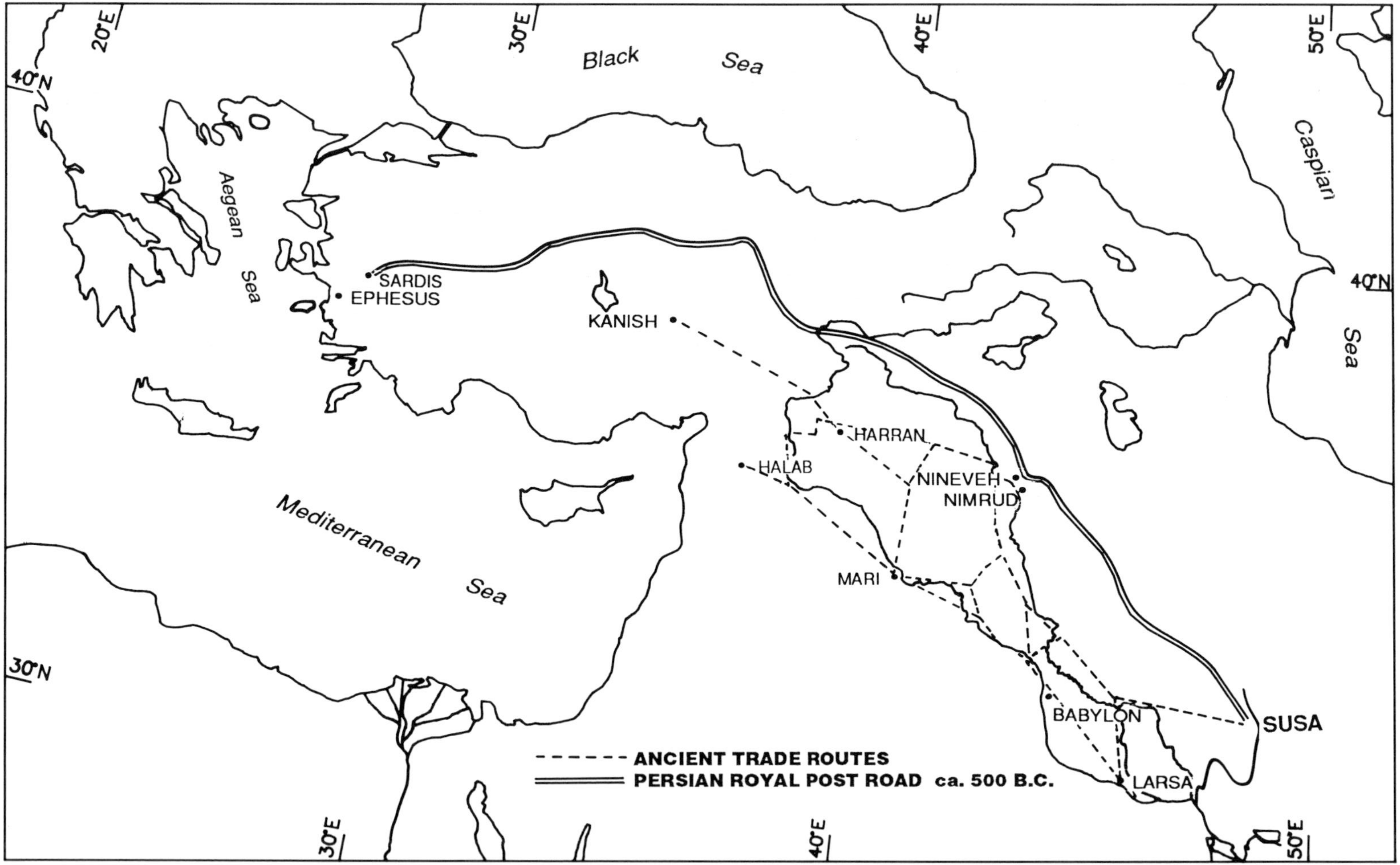

20°E
30°E
40°E
50°E
40°N
30°N
Black Sea
Caspian Sea
Aegean Sea
Mediterranean Sea
SARDIS
EPHESUS
KANISH
HARRAN
HALAB
NINEVEH
NIMRUD
MARI
BABYLON
LARSA
SUSA
ANCIENT TRADE ROUTES
PERSIAN ROYAL POST ROAD ca. 500 B.C.

By the first half of the sixth century B.C., the industrial power of the ancient world was concentrated in the Lydian Empire, which dominated all of Asia Minor west of the Halys River. Sardis, the Lydian capital, amassed riches and reputation by expediting the movement of goods and ideas to and from Mesopotamia and the Greek coastal cities of Asia Minor. Through Lydian territories, caravans passed, bearing the products of Mesopotamia to Ionian seaports and thence to south and west. "Here ran the route along which Persian armies marched to impose Oriental culture on Greece, along which diplomatists, scientists and merchants travelled to transmit more peacefully and successfully Babylonian ideas to the young Ionian states."[15]

Descendants of early Greek-Ionian settlers who met and married into families of Hittite ancestry adopted the Lydian system of weights and measures, learned to work metals and mint coins. They adapted the art, architecture, crafts, music, science, and literature of the Orient to produce a brilliant civilization. Ionian cities, with immediate access to Eastern influence, became the intellectual and political centers of the Greek world. Great teachers, philosophers, scientists, and lawgivers from Ionia and the Greek mainland journeyed to the East, intent upon acquiring knowledge.

The Ionian experience was unique. None of the numerous early Greek settlements, trading ports, and cities around the Black Sea, in Egypt, along the northern rim of the Mediterranean, Italy, and Sicily produced anything comparable to the intellectual achievements of those who studied Oriental culture. The following notables from the West who lived before Plato were clearly enlightened by their exposure to the wisdom and learning of the East.

Solon (640-560 B.C.)

Of all the Greeks to visit Sardis, the Lydian capital, trading center, terminus of the Royal Road to Susa, and wealthiest city in the world, the most distinguished, said Herodotus, was Solon the Athenian. Upon the ruin of his father's estate, Solon traveled extensively on trading missions, leading one writer to conclude: "The probability that he gained from travels the knowledge of constitutions and of foreign commerce exhibited in his laws is very great."[16]

When Solon embarked upon his Ionian voyages, his homeland was struggling to emerge from a semibarbaric dark age. The petty and disorganized towns of mainland Greece had experienced social turmoil, political disruption, and a sharp decline in population. Homes were no more than mud and rubble hovels; there was little wealth; the arts were primitive. Even Greek heroes lived a rudimentary existence. The "palace" in Ithaca to which Odysseus returned was a large, probably windowless, farmhouse where his old tic-ridden dog, Argos, lay asleep on a dung heap in the front yard. It is entirely possible that the *Odyssey* described a Greek scene closer to Solon's lifetime than an imagined thirteenth- or twelfth-century Mycenaean world.[17]

For most of Solon's adult life, a resurgent Babylonia dominated the Near East. Its armies helped destroy an Assyrian supremacy, conquered Jerusalem, Syria, and, in the northwest, extended Babylonian rule to the borders of Lydia. In Babylon itself, Hammurabi's Code was still a respected authority in the seventh and sixth centuries; an Assyrian king consulted Hammurabi's laws while Solon was alive; a Persian ruler copied them half a century after Solon's death. A recently published cuneiform text describes a Babylonian king, thought to be Solon's contemporary, Nebuchadnezzar II, concerned about the rich man's exploitation of the poor, as Mesopotamian rulers always were, working night and day to draw up laws for his city. His labors were extensive; "Not only is a code of laws ascribed to him . . . but also regulations for his city, Babylon, and his own royal office."[18] Earlier, kings of the Hammurabi dynasty had also differentiated *dinat,* laws, from *simdat* or *simdatum,* ordinances framed to deal with such specialized measures as interest rates and wage and price regulations. Later, the Athenians, too, distinguished their laws (*nomoi*), permanent, general, more authoritative enactments, from decrees (*psēphismata*), temporary, particularized measures.

For a Greek politician of the sixth century B.C., determined to relieve the tensions that gripped his native city by providing it with a constitution founded in wisdom and justice, Eastern civilization offered much to be evaluated and emulated when appropriate. Many of Solon's accomplishments have parallels in venerable Oriental usages. When he was chosen arbitrator and archon by the people and notables of Athens in 594, for instance, Solon limited the power of the ruling class to interpret the unwritten law to its own advantage by drafting a code of written laws for his city, just as Sumerian kings had done for theirs from the close of the third millennium. And, as Ur-Nammu upon his accession had installed a system of weights and measures to facilitate commerce, so, Aristotle advises, Solon "raised the standard of measures and weights" in Athens when he rose to power.[19]

Aristotle also says that in Athens, before Solon, the poor were *hectemoroi,* sixth-part tenants, for that was the rent they reputedly paid for farming the rich man's land. In the ancient Near East, part of the temple land, the *uru-lal,* was also let out to tenants at a minimal rental amounting to one-sixth of the yield. Enslavement of debtor and family upon default was characteristic of Mesopotamian and Greek practice before Solon, who ameliorated the plight of Athenian debtors by prohibiting loans secured on the person.

One provision of Solon's legislation parallels Mesopotamian law older than that of Hammurabi, for he distinguished daytime thefts from those committed at night, as had the thirteenth law of ancient Eshnunna ("A man . . . caught in the house at night shall die, he shall not get away alive"); he also advocated death for the nocturnal thief. Solon's laws, according to Demosthenes, whose attribution may have been merely conventional, were presented in the old conditional Eastern mode "If a man"—a form used often by Demosthenes in his orations as well. Demosthenes claimed Solon had introduced a law that "if a man stole anything in the daytime of greater than fifty drachms, he might be taken off to the Eleven, and if he stole anything by night, it should be lawful to kill or wound him in pursuit."[20]

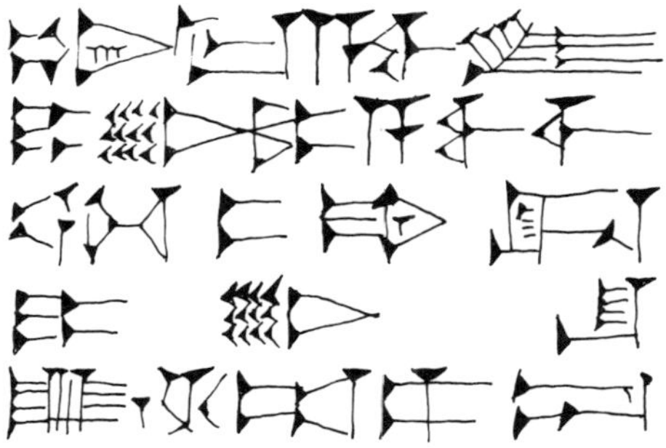

BABYLONIAN—
CH #196:
Šumma awīlum īn mār awīlum uḫtappid insu uḫappalū.
(If a man destroys the eye of another man, they will destroy his eye.)

According to Roman tradition, in the fifth century B.C., the Plebeians, impatient with the administration of an unwritten and uncertain law by Patrician magistrates, demanded that written laws be drawn up. In 451 B.C., ten men, the *decemviri,* sent to Greece to study the laws of Solon, compiled a code of ten tablets, to which two were subsequently added, the result providing the basis of Roman law for centuries. The opening passage of the XII tables reads, "If a man is killed while committing theft at night, that killing is lawful."

Solon's famous proclamation, nicknamed the *Seisachtheia* (the "Shaking off of Burdens"), sought to adjust imbalances of economic power disrupting the tranquility of his city. His measure invites comparison with the *mesharum* acts of Mesopotamian kings. Both edicts were proclaimed upon the ruler's coming into power; the *Seisachtheia* was Solon's first official act; the *mesharum* of Eastern rulers was traditionally accomplished in the first full year of the king's accession, although recent research has shown they might occur later as well. By canceling indebtedness, both attempted to alleviate the severe economic distress endured by a particular subordinated class. The Greek *Seisachtheia*, directed at abuses perpetrated by large landowners, was probably broader in effect: Aristotle considered it a complete remission of all debts, public and private. The *mesharum* acts were at first more limited, targeting specific obligations exacted by an oppressive bureaucracy. Both were issued as proclamations. It appears the *Seisachtheia* was not inscribed on the *axones*, the revolving pillars bearing the Greek laws; the *mesharum* acts were not, per se, part of the Mesopotamian law codes. Both decrees were intended to have an immediate, one-time effect: the nullification of debts that had burdened an impoverished class to the point of confiscation.

In presenting an account of his archonship, Solon claimed that he "set free" debtors who had been reduced to an ignoble slavery and that he removed the "mortgage stones," or boundary markers, stuck everywhere in the black earth of an enslaved Greece. Thus, Solon's *Seisachtheia* established justice by releasing debtors and real property from the grasp of the overreaching creditor, thereby realizing the purport of many Babylonian enactments. In the ancient literature, date formulae and inscriptions frequently applied the Akkadian phrase *andurārum sakanum* to the king's *mesharum* acts, *andurārum* being the equivalent of the Sumerian *amargi*, "freedom." *Andurārum,* however, first signified the "'release' or 'return' of persons held in bondage for debt or real estate so held," and seems to have been a more precise term than *mesharum*, "justice," with which it later became interchangeable.[21]

Solon has left an eloquent testament in which he prophesied that Athens would never be ruined by Zeus or the immortal gods, but that the wantonness and love of money of the townspeople and their false-hearted leaders would bring destruction to their great city.

They are rich because they yield to the temptation of dishonest courses. . . . They spare neither the treasures of the gods nor the property of the state, and steal like brigands from one another. They pay no heed to the unshaken rock of holy Justice. . . . Our beloved city is rapidly wasted and consumed in those secret conspiracies which are the delight of dishonest men . . . the poor and needy in great numbers are loaded with shameful bonds and sold into slavery in foreign lands. . . . Thus public calamity cometh to the house of every individual.[22]

The troubles within Athens that Solon deplored—conspiracies, injustices, and lawlessness, oppression of the weak and the poor by the strong, corruption of officials, greed and dishonesty of the townspeople, looting of private places, and impious desecration of the sacred—were also evident in the Babylon devastated in 689 B.C. by the Assyrian monarch, Sennacherib, and his Ionian mercenaries. The inscription of his son, Esarhaddon, explained why Marduk, angry at the sins of its citizens, turned his back on his city and allowed it to be reduced to ruins:

> *They [*the citizens of Babylon*] oppressed the weak and gave him into the power of the strong. Inside the city there was tyranny, the receiving of bribes; every day without fail they plundered each other's goods; the son cursed his father in the street, the slave (abjured) his master, (the slave girl) did not listen to her mistress . . . they put an end to offerings and entered into conspiracies . . . they laid hands on the property of Esagil, the temple of the gods, and sold silver, gold and precious stones to the land of Elam. . . . Marduk, the Enlil of the gods, was angry and devised evil to overwhelm the land and destroy the peoples (BWL, 5).*[23]

Esarhaddon's inscription is stated in the past tense; Solon's is a prediction of what will happen and is typical of the "prophecies of social disorder," the "If a king heeds (or heeds not) justice" genre, a form with a long history in the omen literature of Mesopotamia. Significantly, in neither the Greek nor Assyrian declaration is the people's distress caused by a divine retribution visited upon an unjust king. Rather, individual excesses of the "citizens of Babylon" and the "townsfolk" of Athens have brought, or are likely to bring, their cities to grief. The Babylonian inscription implies a degree of individual and civic responsibility not often associated with its supposedly lock-stepping citizenry. In both societies, fortune and misfortune result from social and not natural or supernatural causes.

Pythagoras (570-500 B.C.)

The island of Samos, where Pythagoras was born, lay a few kilometers off the shore of western Asia. As a youth, Pythagoras heard the great Ionian philosophers: Thales of Miletus, originator of Greek astronomical and mathematical sciences, shared a Mesopotamian belief that the earth floated on water, and predicted the sun's eclipse using centuries-old Babylonian calculations;[24] Anaximander, his pupil, introduced Pythagoras to the concept of the infinite and produced Greece's first horoscopes in imitation of ancient Babylonian configurations;[25] most influential of all was Pherekydes of Syros, a student of the secret books of the Phoenicians, from whom Pythagoras may have taken the doctrines of reincarnation and psychic immortality.[26]

Pythagoras is supposed to have spent thirty years visiting the known world of his time, including the territories of the Near East. Historians may have exaggerated the extent of his journeys of instruction, but

Pythagoras could not fail to have been impressed by the ancient Colossus to the east, which for most of the sixth century was dominated by the Chaldeans, the "wise men" of Babylonia. In Pythagoras's youth, Babylonian armies under Neriglasser penetrated into western Cilicia, on a direct line within three hundred miles of his birthplace.

At the urging of Thales, who had grown too old to teach, the story runs, Pythagoras proceeded to Egypt to continue his investigations. He became the disciple of Egyptian priests and the first Greek to learn to decipher the Egyptian hieroglyphic. When the Persian king Cambyses overran that country in 525 B.C., he deported Pythagoras as a captive to Babylon. There Zaratas, an important Magos of the Zoroastrian religion, cleansed Pythagoras with magical herbs and initiated him into the choir of the divinely inspired. In Babylon, Iamblichus says, Pythagoras "learnt about a very mystical worship of the gods. He also reached the acme of perfection in arithmetic and music and other mathematical sciences taught by the Babylonians, remaining there another twelve years."[27] Babylonian mathematics, based upon a Sumerian sexagesimal notational system, was in fact a fully developed discipline one thousand years before Pythagoras visited the city. The right-angle theory attributed to him had been in use there for thirteen hundred years.

Despite the testimony of Iamblichus, the length of Pythagoras's stay in Babylon is uncertain. Why or how he left is unknown. In 518, however, he is reported to have met with Leon, the tyrant of Phlius. In a conversation with that ruler recorded by Heraclide Ponticus, a pupil of Plato, Pythagoras compared the life of man to a fair celebrated by athletic competitions and attended by the whole of the Greek world (i.e., the Olympic Games). Some people there

> *seek the glory and nobility of victory in the athletic exertion of their bodies; some go to buy and sell in the hope of gain and profit; but there is a certain class of person, the noblest, who seek neither applause nor gain, but come only to watch and view intently what and how things happen . . . a chosen few who study the universe, considering themselves of no importance. These people call themselves lovers of wisdom, in other words, philosophers.*[28]

Here, if we may believe the report, Pythagoras identified the three classes of men who would appear later in the society of Plato's *Republic*: Lovers of Wisdom, Lovers of Honor, and Lovers of Gain. Their identification "perhaps implies a correlative doctrine of the Three Parts of the soul; Reason, Spirit and Appetite. The debt of the *Republic* to Pythagorean doctrine on these points is both obvious and profound; the whole framework of the *Republic* . . . may be said to be Pythagorean."[29]

Philosophers have devoted volumes to the confluence of Pythagorean and Platonic thought. Some early writers claimed that Plato had plagiarized Pythagoras; others maintained he was simply another Pythagorean, his ninth successor, and regarded their teachings as one and the same. Cicero, recording a Roman view in the first century B.C., said that Plato visited Egypt and studied with disciples of Pythagoras in Italy and Sicily. There he acquired the notes of the disciples and devoted himself entirely to the "ponderous learning" of Pythagoras "in so many fields of knowledge."[30]

Protagoras (500-430 B.C.)

Socrates deemed Protagoras of Abdera, foremost Sophist of the fifth century, to be the wisest of all living men. Plato said the simple word-of-mouth message "Protagoras is come" attracted an enthusiastic audience of Athenian philosophers and students. To Protagoras, skeptical of the gods, man was the measure of all things; virtue was teachable. Men could learn to become better citizens by studying the art of politics that he taught.

Upon what meat did this our Thracian feed? How came he from a northern land, whose inhabitants were still shooting arrows at flashes of lightning, to command large fees for explaining the art of government to eager Athenian aristocrats? The city of Abdera was founded in the middle of the sixth century by Ionians who fled from their settlement at Teos, on the Asian coast, when it was besieged by Cyrus's generals. Their respite from Persian domination was short-lived, for in 513, when Darius took his hasty and inglorious leave of Scythia, he left his general Megabazus behind with a large force to subdue Thrace, a mission that distinguished Persian managed to accomplish. Abdera became a Persian stronghold, where Thasian ships were anchored upon their surrender, where Xerxes was entertained after the battle of Salamis. The Persian presence continued in Abdera until 475. Protagoras, born in 500 B.C., and therefore a Persian subject, grew up under a Persian administration based upon Darius's laws, which had been adapted from Hammurabi's.

In his dialogue named for the Thracian sage, Plato turned to the legends of the past to describe how the state first came into existence and to reveal how its three necessary functions were first implemented. In the beginning, Protagoras tells Socrates, gods existed, but mortal men did not. When it came time for mortals to be created, he explains, the gods fashioned them out of earth and fire, a sequence also described in an earlier legend: "In the beginning, according to Sumerian and Babylonian speculation, only the gods existed. Man was a later creation" (BWL, 4).

And when it was man's time, the Sumerian god Enki also modeled him from the clay that lay above the underground waters.

In Protagoras's telling, the gods charged the slow-witted Epimetheus and his clever brother Prometheus to equip man with whatever faculties were necessary for his survival. Unfortunately, Epimetheus, being less than wise, began the distribution and exhausted all the qualities he had to bestow with the creation of the animal species. When Prometheus, the benefactor of man, saw it was time for man to go forth into the light of day but that he was still naked and defenseless, he stole the technical skill of using fire from the workshop of Hephaestus and Athene and gave it to the human race. Thus man acquired the means of sustaining life and began to worship the gods; he invented speech, constructed houses, made clothes and furniture, and drew sustenance from the earth.[31]

While they lived apart from one another, however, men were incapable of defending themselves against wild beasts. They had acquired food and the means of life, but not the art of government, which included their mutual defense. The need for self-preservation eventually led them to gather in cities, but once there and still lacking the art of government, they behaved unjustly toward one another and began to disperse, to their certain destruction.

Thereupon, Zeus, fearing that the entire race of men would be exterminated, sent Hermes to them, swift as the wind on his winged sandals, "bearing reverence and justice to the ordering principles of cities and the bonds of friendship and conciliation." Hermes, the child of Zeus, was thereby appointed intermediary between man and the divine and was charged with the duty to establish justice in the land, for Zeus's explicit command was to "make a law by my order, that he who has no part in reverence and justice shall be put to death, for he is a plague of the State."[32] Greek mythology, in this instance, parallels the Mesopotamian precisely; in Akkadian prophecy literature, Anu, the god of Heaven, also dispatched Enlil, the divine sheriff and Lord of the Wind, "to establish justice" (*mi-sa-ra sa-ka-na*) on earth.[33]

It thus became the responsibility of Zeus's son and herald to bring the art of polity to the Greeks, to teach them that by discontinuing their cattle raids and other outrages against one another, they will establish justice, ensure domestic tranquility, and enhance the ability of the community to defend itself. The patron god of commerce was to persuade the Greeks that by putting aside piracy and brigandage and by entering into peaceful trading relationships with their neighbors, especially those capable of defending themselves, they will promote their own welfare.

Herodotus (485-425 B.C.)

"There are many kings of Babylon who helped fortify the city and adorn its temples, and I will tell their stories in my History of Assyria."[34] Unfortunately, Herodotus never kept his promise to tell these stories, for he could have saved much speculation as to what he and his contemporaries knew about the kings of Babylon. Obviously the "Father of History" believed he had acquired a sufficient fund of knowledge concerning "Assyrian" (i.e., Babylonian) history to undertake a work his *Histories* attest would have been comprehensive in scope and rich in detail.[35]

Born in the town of Halicarnassus, on the southwest coast of Asia Minor, Herodotus as a young man had journeyed to Egypt, the north African coast, Italy, mainland Greece, the Black Sea, and parts of southern Russia. Some authorities claim Herodotus actually traveled the Royal Road from Sardis to Susa, where the stele bearing Hammurabi's Laws was maintained. It appears that he visited Babylon; the year might have been 450. Living there at the time were the sons of Babylonian priests and scribes who, seven decades before, had consulted Hammurabi's Laws in order to frame the laws of the Persian Darius. Herodotus says that he spoke to the "Chaldeans," presumably priests, in the temple at Babylon. They told him of a solid golden statue of a man some fifteen feet high, which had been present in the temple at the time of Cyrus, but was later carried away by Xerxes. Immediately after his conversation with the Chaldeans, Herodotus made his promise to write a history of Assyria, suggesting that the priests of Babylon were to be the source for part, at least, of what he would relate.

According to this peerless historian of Ionia, five days after Darius and his companions had slain the two Magi who had usurped the throne of Persia, they met to discuss the form of government that should be installed. Their views—Otanes favored a democracy, Megabyzus an oligarchy, and Darius a monarchy—set out, for the first time, the relative strengths and weaknesses of the stages in the constitutional cycle studied later by Greek philosophers and the Founding Fathers of the United States.[36] It cannot be completely without significance that the first historian, a Greek of western Asia, chose to place the arguments on forms of government in the mouths of Persian nobles. If the tenor of the conspirators' arguments is totally Greek, Darius's espousal of monarchy—that the rule of one best man will most surely provide justice and security and maintain the country's freedom—is totally of the ancient East, although Darius is noticeably silent with respect to the ruler's obligation to make good the flesh of his subjects.

Darius argues: "One ruler: it is impossible to improve on that—provided he is the best. His judgement will be in keeping with his character." The best ruler, then, will render the best judgments, and those judgments will be best that are wisest and most just. Monarchy will enable the ruler to maintain order more effectively and better provide for the security of the state: "His [*the monarch's*] control of the people will be beyond reproach; his measures against enemies and traitors will be kept secret more easily than under other forms of government." Darius asks, "Where did we get our freedom from and who gave it to us? Is it the result of democracy or of oligarchy or of monarchy? We were set free by one man" (III:240). Thus, the "freedom" of the Persians was a beneficence of Cyrus, who liberated them from Median rule, as Ur-Nammu and Lipit-Ishtar had long before procured the freedom of Sumerian cities.

Finally, after telling the story of a deceit perpetrated by his groom that enabled Darius to be chosen king over his co-conspirators, Herodotus recalls a Persian saying that made "Cyrus a father . . . in the kindness of his heart always occupied with plans for their [*his subjects'*] well-being," an indication that the Persian people believed a just ruler would extend himself on their behalf (III:238-43).[37]

In 447 B.C., Herodotus reportedly left Ionia and emigrated to Athens. There, and in adjoining towns, he conducted public readings of his *Histories,* much of which had already been written. In Athens, Herodotus enjoyed the friendship of the playwright Sophocles, a prominent political figure, general, and ambassador to Ionic cities, as well, who dedicated several elegaic poems to his well-informed friend from the East. It is fascinating to imagine those two learned and historic personages comparing Antigone's "immutable and unwritten laws of Heaven" (443 B.C.) with the unchanging order of the Mesopotamian *kinatum,* as well as discussing the essential functions of good government that appeared shortly thereafter in Plato's *Republic.*

Democritus (470?-380? B.C.)

If the wanderings throughout the East of most Greek scholars are obscured by imprecise and often conflicting reports, there can be little doubt that Democritus of Abdera, Protagoras's countryman, spent much time there studying the ancient lore of Babylon and Persia. His written works, *A Phrygian Treatise,* demonstrating his familiarity with the interior of Asia Minor, the *Chaldean Treatise, On the Sacred Writings of Those in Babylon,* and his numerous tracts on mathematics, astronomy, zoology, physiology, embryology, and the Persian religion testify to the scope of his Eastern research and the wide range of this Thracian scientist's interests.[38]

Democritus proposed that all phenomena, including the human soul, were composed of eternal and indivisible atoms that could be neither created nor destroyed; they moved and combined only in accordance with their own intrinsic natures. Atoms of the soul, arranged side by side with those of the body, pervaded the entire structure and were the finest of all, exercising discrete functions in different organs of the body; in the head resided reason, in the heart, anger, and in the liver, desire.

In *Timaeus,* Plato reaffirmed the threefold division of the soul earlier assumed in the *Republic.* He told there how the lesser gods encased the immortal principle of the soul in the skull of mortal man; they set the mortal parts of the soul in the heart, the seat of courage, passion, and ambition. In the liver, they secured like a wild beast his appetite for food, drink, and other natural needs. To Plato, the liver was the seat of the irrational and imaginative element in the soul of man; it housed a special god-given sense of the hidden things from which all poetic and prophetic inspiration emanated.[39]

Perhaps something of the mystique Greek philosophers associated with that unprepossessing organ came from a Near Eastern tradition. Numerous clay and bronze models of the liver and related texts recovered there attest to the importance of hepatoscopy in the ancient divination process. Earliest Semitic folklore had long since singled out the liver as the seat of man's emotions.[40] Much later, Ezekiel (21:21) advised that before putting Jerusalem to the sword, Nebuchadnezzar consulted his diviners: "For the king of Babylon stands at the parting of the way, at the head of two ways, to use divination; he shakes the arrows, he consults the teraphim, he looks at the liver."

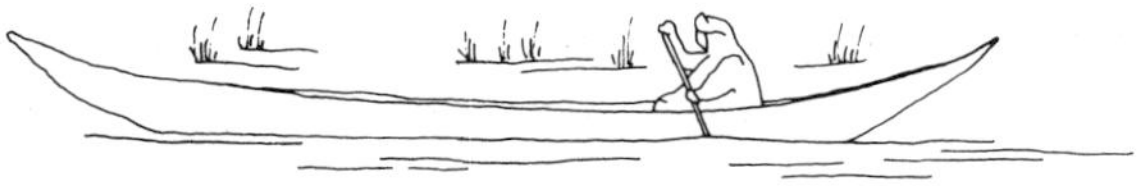

It is regrettable that we shall never know what the Greeks took from Babylon, nor shall we ever fully appreciate the intellectual product of that Old City. Its high-water table has frustrated the efforts of archaeologists to penetrate deeper than neo-Babylonian levels. Some indication of the possible extent of Western indebtedness to the East may nevertheless be gleaned from the numerous parallels that lie on the surface between the two civilizations, waiting like fragments of a shattered clay tablet to be joined. Surely when the thousands of cuneiform documents already recovered but not yet translated and some part of the hundreds of thousands estimated to lie still buried become available, a less disjointed story will emerge.

For twelve hundred years after Hammurabi had gone to his fate, Assyrian, Hittite, and Persian nations, which at one time or another were masters of all or much of the Anatolian land mass, took Babylonian laws for their own. Late in the second millennium and early in the first, Greek colonies studded the Anatolian littoral. These early settlers married into Hittite families and adopted Hittite customs. Hittite leaders married Assyrian and Babylonian royalty; copious evidence of their correspondence survives. Hittite scribes wrote a Babylonian script and studied the Sumerian language. The bulk of Eastern culture—its laws, art, music, sciences, and religion—meandered down the Ionian coast and became accessible to Greek newcomers. A specific and grisly appropriation of Oriental thought occurs in Greek mythology where Kronos is said to have castrated his father Uranus, the god of Heaven, as the cup-bearer Kumarbi had dragged Anu from the sky and bitten off his male parts in an earlier Hittite-Hurrian story.

In the sixth century, Cyrus the Persian conquered the nations of Asia Minor, the fledgling Greek cities of Ionia, and Babylon itself. As "King of Babylon, Sumer and Akkad," Cyrus set Mesopotamian scribes to work administering his holdings. At the end of that century, Darius's legislators, assisted by Babylonian scholars, used Hammurabi's Code as precedent for their own laws. Plato called Darius a great king and statesman because those laws had enabled the Persian state to endure.

In Canaanite cities, the principal documents essential to trade, originally prepared in the Akkadian language, based upon Babylonian laws, and studied in Babylonian scribal schools, enabled Greek merchants to buy, sell, finance, store, and transport their wares. Legal provisions important to commerce that had begun in Sumer appear as modified by Hammurabi in the laws of a third-century B.C. Rhodian banking community located a short distance off the southwestern shore of Asia Minor.

Greek intellectuals and statesmen in the second quarter of the first millennium sought the technical data accumulated by the observations of Babylonian priests. They studied the myths, philosophy, laws, and political organization of Eastern cities and brought home an inestimable corpus of information. Solon's *Seisachtheia* resembled Mesopotamia's *mesharum* acts. He railed against a corrupt Athens that ignored the "rock of holy Justice," fomented civil strife, and reduced the people to a degrading bondage. Esarhaddon had described an equally sinful Babylon several generations before and attributed Marduk's rage and retribution to the personal transgressions of Babylonian citizens. Pythagoras learned mathematics in Babylon and introduced Greeks to the three classes of men who were to function in Plato's *Republic*. Protagoras told how people first provided for their physical needs and security and how Zeus sent justice with Hermes to be an ordering principle of cities. The Sumerian Sky-god Anu had dispatched Enlil on a comparable mission millennia before. Herodotus described how Darius convinced his colleagues that monarchy was the best form of government because it ensured the best judgments and enabled the leader to maintain order and defend the state. Darius's subjects looked to him for their well-being as a successor to "Father" Cyrus. Herodotus discussed these ideas with political dignitaries and dramatists in Athens shortly before Plato's birth.

A few generations ago, reputable historians taught that ancient Greece had no models, that everything, and particularly all political theory, began there. Since then, archeological finds and the interpretation of volumes of Eastern literature have shown how fallacious was their "lightning stroke" explanation for the origin of Greek civilization. Well before Plato, the strange, long-haired gentlemen of Babylon described by Herodotus, clad in their full-length tunics, turbaned and perfumed all over, each carrying his seal and specially carved walking stick, had developed a sophisticated body of law and understood very well what an ideal state and its ruler should try to accomplish. Greeks of the mid-first millennium B.C. took liberally from the Babylonian legal and political heritage of their exotic neighbors.

---

[1] R.F. Harper, "Letter to Esarhaddon," *ABL* 652 rev. 9-13.

[2] Speiser, "Early Law and Civilization," 871.

[3] G.R. Driver, *Semitic Writing,* The Schweich Lectures of the British Academy (London: Oxford Univ. Press, 1944), 73, 76.

[4] See Appendix, Exhibit F, "Some Early Mesopotamian Contracts of Suretyship."

[5] See Appendix, Exhibit G, "The Clay Commodity and Money 'Paper' of the Ancient Near East" (242ff).

[6] Speiser, "Cuneiform Law," 541.

[7] See Walter Ashburner, *The Rhodian Sea-Law* (Oxford: Clarendon Press, 1909) for its principal provisions.

[8] Oliver Wendell Holmes Jr., in *The Common Law,* undertakes to prove that "the exemption from liability for acts of God or the public enemy is characteristically English" (199).

[9] The laws are set out in Ashburner, *The Rhodian Sea-Law.*

[10] Isocrates, *Panegyricus,* trans. George Norlin (Cambridge: Harvard Univ. Press, Loeb Classical Library, 1980), 188, 240 n.a. See Leviticus 6:2-5, and Appendix, Exhibit I, "The Babylonian Bailee's Obligation to Redeliver."

[11] See Appendix, Exhibit C, for the bailee's right to recover property taken from his custody without authorization (205).

[12] *Plutarch's Lives,* "Solon," trans. John Dryden (New York: Modern Library, reprint of Clough's ed., 1864), 98.

[13] For an example of the sophistication of Near Eastern commercial documents of the sixth century B.C., see Appendix, Exhibit H, "An Ancient Disclaimer."

[14] See also *Hesiod and Theognis,* trans. Dorothea Wender, ed. Betty Radice (New York: Penguin Books, 1984), 225-38.

[15] V. Gordon Childe, *The Dawn of European Civilization* (St. Albans: Paladin, 1973), 71. Childe adds: "The development of industry and commerce in Greece and subsequently in Temperate Europe was as much dependent on Oriental capital as the industrialization of India and Japan was on British and American capital last century" (ibid. 396).

[16] Kathleen Freeman, *The Work and Life of Solon* (London: H. Milford, 1926), 158. Linforth advises: "But it seems altogether probable that he *[Solon]* should have been often in Ionia and for somewhat prolonged periods. This assumption is almost necessary in order to explain his ability to use the Ionic language and the elegaic verses of Ionia as his natural medium of expression . . . he must have been charmed by the brilliant society which he found in Asia. It was here that he learned the pleasures of Aphrodite, Dionysus, and the Muses, whose attractions he frankly acknowledged" (Ivan M. Linforth, *Solon-the Athenian* [Berkeley: Univ. of California Press, 1919], 37).

[17] In Solon's day, western Anatolia, which he admitted was a revelation to him, had been exposed to Mesopotamian influences for many centuries. Six levels below Homer's city, Troy's first settlements have produced numerous artifacts resembling earlier Mesopotamian fashion; mud brick walls constructed in the traditional Sumerian herringbone pattern, stone gate-sockets, face urns, and many items of jewelry, soldered beads, and filigree work utilizing motif and technique employed in ancient Sumer (Childe, *The Dawn of European Civilization,* 73).

[18] W.G. Lambert, "Nebuchadnezzar, King of Justice," *IRAQ*, 27 (1965): 3. Lambert says that if the identification is correct, Nebuchadnezzar must be considered a "second Hammurabi."

[19] *The Athenian Constitution,* trans. H. Rackham (Cambridge: Harvard Univ. Press, Loeb Classical Library, 1971), X.1. The Babylonian *manah* was adopted by the Greeks as a standard of weight for their *mna.*

[20] Demosthenes, *Private Orations,* ed. J.H. Vance (Cambridge: Harvard Univ. Press, Loeb Classical Library, 1936), vol. III, Adv. Timocrates, 736; also, vol.II, Adv. Macartatus, 61: "And if any man shall commit any outrage against them *[the widow and orphan]"*; vol. I, Adv. Lacritus, 279: "And if anyone shall lend money contrary to this enactment"; vol. VI, Adv. Neaera, 391: "If anyone shall give a woman in marriage."

[21] J.J. Finkelstein, "Ammisaduqa's Edict and the Babylonian 'Law Codes,'" *JCS,* 15 (1961): 104 n.19. There, J. Lewy reads *andurārum sakanum* as "to establish a (general) release" and *mesarum sakanum,* "to establish (social) justice" (*Eretz-Israel*, 5[1961]: 28).

[22] Linforth, *Solon,* Frag. XII, 141.

[23] *BWL,* 5 n. 3 cites R. Borger, *Asarhaddon,* 13-15, and advises that the translation is a combination of pieces from different inscriptions.

[24] A. Jardé notes that "Thales does not seem to have progressed much beyond his Oriental masters" (*Formation of the Greek People* [New York: Cooper Square Pub., 1970], 96).

[25] Cuneiform documentation today assures the Babylonian origin of the Greek zodiac and other significant features of the Greek system. See "Elements of the Babylonian Contribution to Hellenistic Astrology," *JAOS,* 108 (Jan. 3, 1988).

[26] Peter Gorman, *Pythagoras—A Life* (London: Routledge and Kegan Paul, 1979), 36.

[27] Iamblichus, *Life of Pythagoras,* trans. T. Taylor (London: 1818), cited in Gorman, *Pythagoras,* 63.

[28] Cicero, *Tusc.*, V 3,8. In *Diogenes Laertius*, "Pythagoras ," trans. R.D. Hicks (Cambridge: Harvard Univ. Press, Loeb Classical Library, 1979), vol. II, VIII, ll.6-8, Sosicrates is cited as the immediate source of this quote.

[29] Sir Ernest Barker, *Greek Political Theory* (London: Methuen, 1979), 56.

[30] Cicero, *De Re Publica, De Legibus*, trans. Clinton W. Keyes (Cambridge: Harvard Univ. Press, Loeb Classical Library, 1977), *Rep.*, I. x. 19. All subsequent citations are from this edition. Professor Georges Dumézil of the College de France has pointed out that all Indo-European-speaking societies tended to organize themselves in a tripartite social organization, a community of those who prayed and ruled, those who fought, and those who worked. A corresponding set of gods and heroes represented each rank in myth and epic. Dumézil notes that Plato phrased his conception of the ideal commonwealth and the Just Man in terms of these same functions. The earliest datable evidence to support Dumézil's theories, however, occurs in a fourteenth-century B.C. treaty between the conquering Hittites and the vanquished Mittani, whose king calls upon the gods Mitra-Varunna (sovereign), Indra (warrior), and the Asvins (herder-cultivator) to witness his oath. See C.Scott Littleton, *The New Comparative Mythology*, 3rd ed. (Berkeley: Univ. of California Press, 1982).

Babylonian priests of Pythagoras's day, their kings always Judge, Warrior, and Father, had succeeded to a recorded tradition of tripartite social organization far older than the Indo-European. Littleton, in his assessment of Dumézil's theories, grants the possible derivation of proto I-E social organization from Mesopotamian prototypes, and Richard N. Frye, Professor of Iranian at Harvard University, comments: "Iranian ideals of social organization must have changed when the Iranians came into close contact with the Mesopotamian culture area where settled people had developed certain norms of society over the centuries. Under such circumstances, the persistence of any Indo-European ideology about social classes into Achaemenid times is rather unlikely" (*The Heritage of Persia* [New York: The World Publishing Company, 1963], 52).

[31] In Protagoras's version, Prometheus steals fire from Hephaestus, and not from heaven, as Hesiod reports (*Works*, 50). Prometheus appears to have been an old Greek deity, the son of a Titan, who later was superseded by Hephaestus, an Oriental deity from Lycia in Anatolia. As a skilled metallurgist, Hephaestus became an important god in the industrialized Athens of the sixth century. Southern Anatolia was overrun in the middle of that century by Babylonian armies, who may have carried artifacts first fashioned by the unsurpassed metalworkers of Sumer. See Childe, *The Dawn of European Civilization*, for the numerous artifacts and items of jewelry incorporating Sumerian elements found further north at Troy.

[32] *The Works of Plato*, "Protagoras," trans. Benjamin Jowett, ed. Irwin Edman (New York: Modern Library, 1956), 209-10.

[33] A.K. Grayson and W.G. Lambert, "Akkadian Prophecies," *JCS*, 17 (1964): 7-30.

[34] Herodotus, *The Histories*, trans. Aubrey de Selincourt (New York: Penguin Books 1977), I:115. The following citations in the text are from this edition.

[35] Herodotus does name Nineveh capital of Assyria and tells of a vast treasure stored there by Sardanapalus (Assurbanipal), which was stolen by thieves who tunneled into a storeroom (ibid. II:190).

[36] For indications that democratic organizations were known in prehistoric Mesopotamia, see Thorkild Jacobsen, "Primitive Democracy in Ancient Mesopotamia," *JNES*, 2 (July 1943): 159.

[37] In Herodotus's lifetime, the original stele upon which the Code of Hammurabi had been inscribed was maintained at Susa, the winter palace of Persian kings. Herodotus fully appreciated the importance of Susa as the administrative and political hub of the Persian Empire; the *Histories* is filled with anecdotes of happenings there, of the assassination of the Magian usurpers, of the reception accorded prisoners of war (generally merciful), political refugees, and detainees. Some authorities say that Herodotus actually traveled the Royal Road from Sardis to Susa, which he describes. True or not, other Greeks had visited Susa and returned. Two young Spartans went there and offered their lives in atonement for the murder of two of Darius's messengers. They were pardoned and allowed to return home. One Callias and a "number of other Athenians" were at Susa on "quite different business" when representatives from Argos arrived to interview Artaxerxes. Histiaeus of Miletus, a politically suspect guest of Darius, who was entertained at Susa, was permitted to return to the Ionian islands.

It is possible, therefore, that the Laws of Hammurabi came to be known in fifth-century Greece by reason of the contacts of its citizens with the original stele held at Susa, but this seems unlikely. Access to the stele might have been restricted and translation difficult. Moreover, the importance and even the location of Susa was not common knowledge throughout Greece. When Aristagoras of Miletus attempted to persuade the Spartan king, Cleomenes, to invade Persia, describing the riches available for the taking at Susa, Cleomenes was at first enthusiastic. When, however, Aristagoras advised that it would mean a three-month march, Cleomenes, shocked at the thought of taking a Spartan army that far into Persia, warned Aristagoras in a manner that has become a Western cliché: "Milesian," he said, "you must leave Sparta before sunset."

[38] A.T. Olmstead, *History of the Persian Empire* (Chicago: Univ. of Chicago Press, 1978), 331ff.

[39] Kaufmann, *Religion of Israel,* 52.

[40] See A. Leo Oppenheim, *Ancient Mesopotamia—Portrait of a Dead Civilization* (Chicago: Univ. of Chicago Press, 1977), 213-15.

V

PLATO

Babylon and the *Laws*

Darius's Ordinance of Good Regulations

In 539 B.C. the Persian great king Cyrus took Babylon and appropriated its rulers' traditional titles as "King of Babylon, King of Sumer and Akkad, King of the world quarters." Nine years later, he was killed in battle somewhere east of the Caspian Sea, leaving an empire that extended from the Indus in the east to the Aegean and the borders of Egypt in the west. Cyrus's vast holdings were administered by a bureaucracy made up of Mesopotamian and Syrian scribes, who undoubtedly had mastered and passed on an understanding of Babylonian law and legal procedures to those subject nations.

Cyrus's son Cambyses succeeded in annexing Egypt to his inherited empire, and when Cambyses died in 522, Darius I, with the aid of six nobles who rallied to his cause, assumed the throne. After several years of arduous campaigning Darius succeeded in restoring order to his kingdom.

Faced with the necessity of reorganizing the extensive territories subject to his rule, Darius ordered that a new and suitable set of laws be prepared for his approval. Historians agree he based his subsequent "Ordinance of Good Regulations" on the Code of Hammurabi. A.T. Olmstead concludes that in view of all the detailed parallels between Akkadian texts of parts of Darius's inscription and the beginning and ending of Hammurabi's work,

> *there can no longer be any reasonable doubt that Darius and his legal advisers had before them an actual copy of Hammurabi's lawbook. Quite possibly he used the original stele, preserved in the temple of Inshushinak at Susa; orperhaps the tablets in late Babylonian writing . . . were copied for translation and adaptation.*[1]

A.R. Burn concurs: "He [*Darius*] established the rule of law, adopting as his own the great body of Babylonian case-law codified long before by

Hammurabi and applied by the Assyrians."[2] When Darius wished to turn his Persian dictation into Akkadian, Olmstead notes, he looked to Babylonian temples and their priesthoods for the scribes who labored on his new code.

Two years after his accession, Darius presented his Ordinance to the city of Babylon and claimed, on the Behistun inscription, that he had installed his laws throughout the whole of his empire:

> *By the will of Ahuramazda I made stelae of other sorts, which was not done before, on baked tablets and prepared leather. My name and seal I ordered affixed to them. Writing and order were read before me. Then I had these stelae carried into all distant lands to my subjects.*[3]

Darius, therefore, intended that his Ordinance should guide all peoples subject to his governance, including the inhabitants of Greek cities living under Persian rule. Within a decade of his ascent to the throne, Darius had entered Scythia, subdued Thrace; his western domain included all the important nations of the eastern Mediterranean except the tiny and unorganized city-states of western Greece.

Darius's law, which has since been completely lost, nevertheless was known to Athenians by the end of the fifth century. At that time, Xenophon lived under the Persian king's code and observed the administration of the Persian provincial system when he served Cyrus the Younger as a civilian advisor. In his treatise on estate management, Xenophon described advantages of Darius's law that made it preferable to the Greek, stressing the necessity for the "perfect bailiff" to be honest and not

> *touch his master's property. . . . I guide the servants into the path of justice with the aid of maxims drawn from the laws of Draco and Solon. . . . By applying some of these clauses and other enactments found in the Persian king's code, I try to make my servants upright in the matters that pass through their hands.*[4]

It is perhaps significant that Sections 253-56 of Hammurabi's Code also dealt with thefts and misappropriations committed by the seignior hired by the owner of a field. The seignior was a contract employee, or "bailiff," to whom the field was entrusted for cultivating; his punishments ranged from fines to mutilation.

Plato, too, admired the Persian king and spoke of his laws with respect. In his Seventh Epistle, he wrote that in Darius's career "we see an ideal example of the character which the statesman and the good king should display; for the laws which he framed have been the preservation of the kingdom of Persia even up to now."[5]

An Iranian lawbook of the second century B.C., the *Videvat* or *Antidemonic Law*, also reflected Darius's laws in its use of the ancient "If a man" form to introduce each of its provisions. A *tukum bi* ("If a man") formulation, originating and employed without exception in the Sumerian Laws of Ur-Nammu, was later favored in a similar *summa awilum* construction by Hammurabi and in the *tak-ku LU-as* protasis of Hittite laws.

Preambles, Prologues, and Preludes

The tripartite prologue-legal corpus-epilogue conformation utilized by Hammurabi and Lipit-Ishtar in promulgating their laws may have been characteristic of all early Mesopotamian compilations, although the Laws of Ur-Nammu, as presently known, bear only a fragmented prologue and the Laws of Eshnunna possess neither introductory nor concluding sections.

Sir Ernest Barker has identified a similar tripartite structure in Plato's *Laws*. Books I-IV of that dialogue, which deal with the place of song, dance, and wine in education, the development of states, and the principles of politics, are, he suggests, "in the nature of a preface." The four books following, Books V-VIII, are occupied with the construction of a constitution. Books IX-XI, the main section, contain civil and criminal codes, the corpus, or essence of the work. Book XII, suggesting an afterthought and postscript, he contends, may properly be "termed an epilogue."[6]

Plato, who was engaged for a period in drafting preambles to the laws of Dionysius, the tyrant of Sicily, insisted that explanatory preludes to laws were indispensable for their proper and complete presentation. In order to render his hearer as receptive as possible, the legislator was to provide a prefatory address that would persuade people to listen to the law with open and receptive minds. "Prelude" was the right term for this persuasive part preceding the unblended law; "the lawgiver must never omit to furnish preludes as prefaces to the laws as a whole and to each individual statute." By stressing the moral principles from which the laws proceeded and by making the reasons for their promulgation known, the prefaces would persuade citizens the laws flowed naturally from their own beliefs and should therefore be willingly accepted, rather than obeyed solely from fear of fines and punishments (722D-723C).[7]

In addition to the similarity in overall form of Plato's *Laws* and the Law Codes of Hammurabi and Lipit-Ishtar, the preludes to Plato's laws are like the prologues to Mesopotamian law codes in their poetic and religious orientation. The prologue to the Laws of Hammurabi has been called, in fact, "a religious introduction in the form of an encomium written in the language of poetry," and the Prologue itself was first identified as part of a hymn to Lipit-Ishtar.[8] The difference in style and content between the personal, imaginative, and emotionally charged verses of the Mesopotamian prologues and epilogues and the steady, precise, juristic prose of the laws themselves is obvious even on a casual reading.

When constructing preludes, the lawgiver must, to some extent, rely upon the language of poetry. According to Plato, the poet, "seated on the Muses' tripod . . . not in his senses," produces contrary utterances without knowing which is true, but is able, thereby, to provide two statements about a single subject, an option denied the lawgiver (719C). As the Italian priest Marcilio Ficino later explained:

> *Plato was right in his view that poetry springs not from technique, but from a kind of frenzy . . . those who are in a frenzy utter many wonderful things which a little later, when their frenzy has abated, they themselves do not really understand, as if they had not spoken them, but God had sounded through them, as through trumpets.*[9]

The prelude to Book X of the *Laws*, is a lengthy "religious" exposition, in which Plato proves the nature of the soul, that gods do exist, that they are concerned for mankind and cannot be persuaded to flout justice. It serves as an introduction to the law of heresy, the failure to worship gods specified by the state. The Athenian provides another moral introduction when he preaches that it is God, not man, who is the measure of all things, and that those men who become as near as they can to the temperate God and follow his goddess Justice are most dear to him, while those who are intemperate and unjust are unlike and at enmity (716C). After God, the wise man will worship the daemons, heroes, ancestral deities, and next, living parents. Gradually, by means of his religious prelude, Plato leads the reader to a ready acceptance of his duties toward children, relations, friends, and fellow citizens.

Eastern Influences

Several passages in Plato's *Laws* suggest its author had Eastern historical precedent in mind when, at the beginning of Book III, he speculates as to the probable origin of governments. The Athenian speaks of the "vast and immeasurable" space of time during which "thousands upon thousands" of states came into existence, demonstrating that Greeks of Plato's age knew that the truly ancient civilizations of Egypt and Phrygia had existed an "infinitely long period of time" before their own. Elements of the great *cataclysmos*, or Deluge, to which Plato refers, associated with

Deucalion in Greek mythology, may be derived from a Sumerian original of the early third millennium, repeated thereafter in numerous tales of Gilgamesh throughout the territories and languages of Asia Minor. When survivors of the Flood, simple, brave, temperate, and righteous, but not yet wise shepherds, moved down from the hills into a broad and noble plain and rediscovered the art of metalworking (a Lycian specialty), they founded, not Athens, Corinth, or Thebes, but the city of Ilium (Troy).

Kudurru. Boundary stone from Sippar (ca. 1100 B.C.), inscribed with symbols of various deities. Kudurru texts frequently called upon the gods to destroy anyone who attempted to remove the stone or change its inscription.

Many customs, laws, and procedures adopted in the *Laws* had older counterparts in the East. Greek, Hittite, Babylonian, and Sumerian laws contained similar provisions dealing with runaway slaves. The older laws allowed anyone to take a runaway and earn a reward from the owner. Ur-Nammu (LU #14) specified two shekels of silver, as did Hammurabi (CH #17); the Hittite stipulated that the owner give silver or shoes to the captor, depending upon where the capture is made (HL #22-24). Plato limited the right to stop the runaway to relatives and friends and made no provision for a reward.

The very first of Plato's agricultural laws, sanctioned by Zeus, god of boundaries, provided that no one was to move a boundary stone:

"Sooner let a man try to move the largest rock which is not a boundary-mark than a small stone which forms a boundary, sanctioned by Heaven, between friendly and hostile ground" (843A). Plato's "small stone" is clearly not one of the "huge, black and rugged stones" that served as boundary markers in Homer's *Iliad* (XXI, 405). His reference to a little stone marking a boundary and protected by an oath to the gods calls to mind the *kudurru* stones utilized in the Near East from the Kassite to the Achaemenid era to mark royal grants of land. These oval-shaped markers, frequently less than two feet in height, owed their authority, not to bulk, but to the inscribed symbols of divinities that proclaimed their sacrosanct natures. Like the Kassite grants, mortgages in Greece before Plato were deemed grants or conveyances, voidable upon repayment of the debt, as in American common law.

The "criminal" laws of Book IX, 864-882, dealt with the violent offenses—homicides, woundings, and assaults—that the Sumerian Ur-Nammu had proscribed in the first written law code. Plato's single, comprehensive rule that would bar all falsehood, fraud, and "adulteration," in word and deed, in the marketplace (916E) encapsulated Hammurabi's particularized measures to deal with the dishonest merchant or trader, the fraudulent wine-seller (CH #106-8).

Plato's designation of fifteen "Guardians of the Laws" to act as fathers to orphaned boys and girls echoed the age-old concern of Mesopotamian rulers for the widow and the orphan. Both Greek and Babylonian set out procedures for disinheriting a son; the latter required a court appearance (CH #168-9), while the *Laws* provided the father need merely assemble his kinsfolk to expel the son from the family (929B).

The *Laws*' utilization of neighbors, as arbitrators, to resolve differences before resorting to the courts continued a custom developed in Babylon more than a thousand years before. Also repeating earlier Mesopotamian practice was the *Laws*' provision for credit-worthy sureties ("If anyone gives a security") and its insistence that their contracts be "in express terms, setting forth the whole transaction in a written record," and executed before at least three witnesses (954A).

The frequent specification of both sexes in the phrase "If a male or a female slave" (*Laws* 936D, and elsewhere) affords another parallel, for the usage is found in many of Hammurabi's provisions. So, CH #118: "When a male slave or a female slave" et passim. It appears throughout the Hittite Laws as well: HL #8: "If anyone blinds a male or a female slave and knocks out his/her teeth, he shall give 19 shekels of silver and pledge his estate as security" (ANET, 188).

Piety, the obsessive virtue of Mesopotamia, dropped from the

Greek canon in the *Republic*, is restored in the *Laws* and becomes again the "noblest and truest" rule, "superlatively fitting" for the good man: "to engage in sacrifice and communion with the gods continually, by prayers and offerings and devotions of every kind, is a thing most noble and good and helpful towards the happy life" (716D).

Finally, in his tirade against innkeepers, Plato described the conveniences a weary traveler should be able to expect at inns established in remote areas: "welcome resting places . . . calm tranquility to those driven by the violence of storms . . . refreshment in stifling heat." These amenities compare to the accommodations planned by the Sumerian Shulgi, the "King of the Road," who planted gardens and established "resting places" where wayfarers might "seek haven like in a well-built city" and there "refresh themselves in their cool shade."[10]

Specific Parallels to Hammurabi's Code

The concurrence of the following provisions from the *Laws* with others promulgated by Hammurabi and his predecessors is so explicit in manner of presentation and substantive purpose and effect, there can be no doubt the Greek laws ultimately derived from the Mesopotamian. Like Sumerian, Akkadian, Middle Assyrian, Hittite, and Persian draftsmen before him, Plato made liberal use of the conditional "And if a man," "And if anyone" (*Ean tis*) form in drafting his laws.[11] The phrase appears throughout Books VIII-XII, and was used later by Demosthenes, compilers of the Rhodian Sea-Law, and many others.

Trespass

Laws (VIII, 843D):

If a man lets his cattle graze on someone else's land, these officials must inspect the damage, . . . and assess the penalty.[12]

CH #57:

If a shepherd . . . has pastured sheep on the field without the consent of the owner . . . the shepherd . . . shall give in addition twenty kur of grain per eighteen iku to the owner of the field.

Negligence

Laws (VIII, 844C):

And if, when rain comes, any dweller . . . on higher ground damages the man below by letting out the floods carelessly, . . . and if convicted [of refusing to pay the magistrate's order] *he shall pay to the injured party double the damage.*

CH #53:

If a seignior was too lazy to make [the dike of] *his field strong. . . and a break has opened up in his dike, and he has accordingly let the water ravage the farmland, the seignior in whose dike the break was opened shall make good the grain that he let get destroyed.*

CH #55:

If a seignior, upon opening his canal for irrigation, became so lazy that he has let the water ravage a field adjoining his, he shall measure out grain on the basis of those adjoining his.

A poorly preserved tablet of the Neo-Babylonian period contains fifteen laws. The third reads:

[The seignior, who *opened*] *his well for irrigation purposes, but did not make [*his *dike] strong and hence caused a flood and inundated [a field] adjoining his, shall give [grain to the owner of the field on the basis of] those adjoining (*ANET, *197).*

Theft from Temples

Laws (IX, 854E):

If any citizen is ever convicted of such an act [robbing a temple] . . . . *For him the penalty is death.*

CH #6:

If a seignior stole the property of church or state, that seignior shall be put to death.

Receiving Stolen Goods

Laws (XII, 955B):

If anyone knowingly receive any stolen article, he shall be liable to the same penalty as the thief.

CH #6:

. . . also the one who received the stolen goods from his hand shall be put to death.

Involuntary Homicide

Laws (IX, 865B-D):

And if one man kills another of his own act, but involuntarily . . . If he kill a slave he shall secure the master against damage and loss . . . if it be a slave of his own that he has killed he shall be set free after the legal purification . . . and if anyone kill a free man involuntarily, he shall undergo the same purification as the man that has killed a slave.

CH #206:

If a seignior has struck a(nother) seignior in a brawl and has inflicted injury on him, that seignior shall swear, "I did not strike him deliberately.'' CH #207: *If he has died because of his blow . . . and if it was a member of the aristocracy, he shall pay* $^1/_2$ *mina of silver.* CH #208: *If it was a member of the commonalty, he shall pay* $^1/_3$ *mina of silver.*[13]

Justifiable Homicide—Burglary

Laws (IX, 874B-C):

If a man catch and slay a thief who is entering his house by night to steal goods, he shall be guiltless.

LE #13:

A man who is caught in the house of a muskenum . . . at night, shall die, he shall not get away alive.

"Vouching to Warranty" Procedure

(An Anglo-Saxon procedure for testing the chain of title, ascertaining the thief, and recovering stolen goods. The typical Babylonian case involved stolen cattle.)[14]

Laws (XI, 915D):

If anyone claims as his own the beast of any other man, or any other of his chattels, the man who holds it shall refer the matter to the person, who, as being its substantial and lawful owner, sold it or gave it, or made it over to him in some other valid way.

CH #9:

When a seignior . . . whose property was lost, has found his lost property in the possession of a(nother).

(In this, and the next four laws, CH #10-13, Hammurabi describes in detail the procedure for impleading the seller and determining whose rights are to prevail.)

Claim Against Purchased Slave—Buyer's Right

Laws (XI, 916C):

If a man wittingly sells a murderer [a slave], *if the buyer is aware of the fact, he shall have no claim to restitution for the purchase of such a one; but if the buyer be ignorant, he shall have right of restitution as soon as the fact is perceived.*

CH #279:

If a seignior purchased a . . . slave and he has then received a claim (against him), his seignior shall be responsible for the claim.

The sixth Neo-Babylonian law: *In the case of a seignior, who sold a female slave and there was a claim outstanding against (her) and she was taken away—the seller shall give money to the purchaser in accordance with the terms of the deed in the full amount* (ANET, 196).

Breach of Warranty—Buyer's Right

Laws (XI, 916A-B):

If a man sell a slave who is suffering from . . . the "sacred disease" [epilepsy] . . . *if any professional person sell any such slave to a lay person, the buyer shall claim restitution . . . within twelve months.*

CH #278:

If a seignior purchased a . . . slave, and when his month was not yet complete, epilepsy attacked him, he shall return (him) to his seller and the purchaser shall get back the money which he paid out.

This express warranty appears first in Babylonian contracts after Hammurabi's Laws, and later, in Assyrian and Graeco-Egyptian contracts. No ancient Egyptian code of laws has been found.

Adverse Possession

(Generally, the acquisition of rights by one who has maintained an actual, open, and notorious possession of real property under claim of title adverse to that of the true owner. Plato extends the concept to chattels.)

Laws (XII, 954C-D):

. . . in respect of anything else a man has acquired, if the possessor be seen to be using it in the city, market and temple, and if no one lays claim to it—then if some man asserts that he has been looking for it all this time, while it is plain that its possessor has made no concealment of it, and if this goes on for a year . . . at the expiration of the year no one shall be allowed to lay claim to its possession.

CH #30:

If either a private soldier of a commissary gave up his field, orchard and house on account of the feudal obligations and has then absented himself, (and) after his (departure) another took over his field, orchard and house and has looked after the feudal obligations for three years—if he has returned and demands his field, orchard and house, they shall not be given to him; the one who has taken over and looked after his feudal obligations shall himself become the feudatory.

Although the Babylonian law was enacted to ensure that feudal obligations were respected, both sections are consistent in allowing a stranger who acts openly as owner to acquire property rights that the state will honor after a period of time.

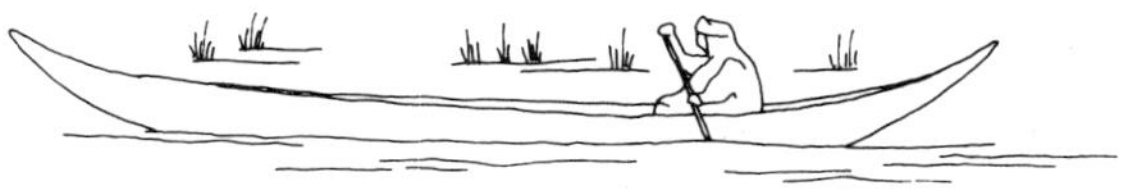

Plato organized his *Laws* according to a three-sectioned pattern—preamble, text, epilogue—employed earlier by Hammurabi and Lipit-Ishtar. His dialogue makes regular use of the "If a man" protasis, a convention favored by all Eastern lawmakers. The numerous specific and significant substantive parallels between Plato's *Laws* and those of Mesopotamian collections and the corresponding practices that grew out of them are too close and too abundant to have occurred independently. The conclusion is inescapable that Mesopotamia had a major effect upon the formulation of Plato's *Laws*.

In his masterful treatise on Greek political theory published in 1918, before much of the ancient materials discussed herein were known, Sir Ernest Barker pointed out that if we attempt to trace the origins of Plato's laws, we must remember that his Academy must have been "in some measure a school of law." The detailed provisions of the last four books of the *Laws,* Barker concludes, "presuppose a technical and systematic study of Greek jurisprudence."[15] If so, is it likely that Plato, whose penchant for acquiring wisdom wherever available is generally accepted, would have ignored two millennia of Eastern experience? His *Laws* indicates he did not.

Ancient Greek law, as Barker acknowledged, has largely perished and the jurisprudential genius he claims for Greece, especially in its formative stages, can only be presumed. Fortunately, explicit evidences of an earlier Mesopotamian legal and political genius, ever more abundant and compelling, survive, tantalizing us with intimations of their effect upon the ideas and institutions of subsequent civilizations.

Babylon and the *Republic*

. . . our city . . . rightly founded . . . will be wise, brave, sober and just.
—The *Republic*

The *Republic* and its Virtues

In the sixth century, Peisistratus, the tyrant of Athens, grew old in office, said Aristotle, for he always worked for peace and safeguarded tranquility. No taint of the opprobrium today associated with the term "tyrant" may justifiably be linked with the name of Peisistratus; that enlightened ruler advanced money to support the industries of the poor and encourage farming; he organized local justices and traveled the country circuit in person, settling disputes and administering everything according to the laws.[16] Early in the fourth century Isocrates advised a young Cyprian prince that a wise king must provide just, expedient, and consistent laws, preserve the state's security, and cause his subjects to believe his plans for their welfare are better than their own.[17]

In Plato's *Republic*, "Government, defence, sustenance—the three necessary functions of the State—are all made into professions and assigned to professional classes."[18] As can be seen, the *Republic*'s professionals, in performing their specialized functions, fulfill the objectives of both Preamble and Prologue (see table below).

Each of the *Republic*'s three classes accomplishes its assigned function through the exercise of its specific virtue. In brief, Plato's rulers, the guardians or philosopher-kings whose cardinal virtue is wisdom, ensure by their decisions that justice, the virtue of specialization, will obtain in the city. The second class of society, the carefully trained "auxiliary" guardians, courageous "watch dogs," enforce the decrees of the rulers, maintain order within the state, and defend it against aggression from without. The third class, the obedient and temperate general population, expends its specialized capabilities to produce the goods necessary to sustain life. (This marks a major difference between the Platonic commonwealth and the state planned by Lipit-Ishtar and other kings of the East. Plato's worker-bees toil for the good of the city-state; Mesopotamian gods mandated that Sumerian and Akkadian rulers provide for the well-being of their people.)

Finally, in the *Republic*, "the governors and the governed will share the same conviction on the question who ought to rule." This principle of freedom, "government with consent of the governed—is thus recognized."[19]

Preamble	***Republic***	**Prologue**
In order to:		
"establish justice"	*Justice a "universal requirement"—the "object of the whole inquiry'"—its realization accomplished by the wise decisions of the rulers*	*"establish justice in the land"*
"ensure domestic tranquility"	*Function of the auxiliary guardians—"to hold down rebellion against the laws from within"*	*"wipe out complaints from the mouth"*
"provide for the common defense"	*Second function of the auxiliary guardians—"to repel aggression from without"*	*"return enmity and violence into their house"*
"promote the general welfare"	*Function of the third class—to satisfy the needs of the people for food, clothing, and shelter*	*"of the Sumerians and Akkadians, to make good their bodies"*
"secure the blessings of liberty"	*"Freedom" achieved by government ruling with consent of the governed*	*"I . . . procured . . . the freedom of . . . the sons and daughters of Sumer and Akkad"*

Plato's ideal city, then, comprises the Rulers, who bear deliberative and legislative responsibilities; the Auxiliaries, who execute their decrees and defend the city against internal and external threat; and the general population, charged with providing its material needs. And the ideal city, "if it has been rightly founded, is good in the full sense of the word . . . . Clearly then it will be wise, brave, sober and just" (427E).

Helen F. North, in providing a brief history of the Greek cardinal virtues, points out that before Plato they were a

> *shifting group, unstable in number and content . . . they first appear in literature in the time of Pindar and Aeschylus, both of whom recognize piety [eusebeia] as a member of the group. What Plato did in* Republic IV *was to exclude piety and establish the other four as the excellences proper to the soul and the state, when each is in its ideal condition.*[20]

North refers, of course, to Greek literature, but Greek poets of the sixth century B.C. were not the first to identify or write of the admirable qualities the *Republic* later consecrated. Xenophon understood those excellences were neither new nor native to Greece. He taught that wisdom, courage, sobriety, and justice were enduring qualities of leadership that an older Persian educational process had impressed upon the hearts and minds of its students.

Xenophon's *Cyropedia*, studied by the freshman class when James Madison attended the College of New Jersey, tells how the virtues of obedience, temperance, piety, courage, and, above all, a conception of justice as a moral quality shaped the characters of Persian princes two centuries before he wrote. Taught early that the art of governorship included an obligation to supply everything necessary and in abundance for those they governed, Persian rulers, according to Xenophon's account, achieved all goals of Preamble and Prologue by means of the training they received at four stages of their lives.

As boys, they learned justice, obedience to their superiors, temperance in eating and drinking. Their instructors trained them to shoot the bow and throw the javelin, taught them not to lie. As young men they guarded the cities, apprehended criminals, sharpened their courage on hunting expeditions under the direct scrutiny of the king. Fully grown, they put aside the weapons of their youth, armed themselves with sword, corselet, and shield for close combat on military expeditions. As elders, the best men, having made their way through all things good and excellent, dispensed public and private justice, appointed magistrates, passed life and death sentences. Xenophon's tale of the education of Cyrus is an imaginative but historically unreliable work. Nevertheless, however fanciful Xenophon's account, it seems unlikely he would have placed virtues so dear to Greeks in the minds and souls of Persian aristocrats had he not believed those ideals had come from the East.

The *Alcibiades I*, a dialogue attributed to Plato, identifies the cardinal virtues in the Persian education process as well. In that dialogue,

Socrates questions the fitness of the Athenian general and politician to rule, pointing out that Alcibiades' preceptor was Zopyrus of Thrace, the oldest and most worthless of Pericles' domestics. Specialists, on the other hand, trained the Persian king, men in the prime of their lives, who excelled in wisdom, justice, temperance, and fortitude. The tutor renowned for his wisdom instructed the Persian ruler in the teachings of Zoroaster, worship of the gods, and the art of kingly government. The man who excelled in justice taught him to profess the truth in words and honor it in deed. The temperate man trained him to control his appetites and be truly a king rather than, by indulging his passions, to become their slave. The last preceptor, leading all in fortitude, made him steadfast and unafraid, since the man who fears is nothing but a slave.

To the author of *Alcibiades I,* the education of Persian nobility was so superior to that of a well-born Athenian that Alcibiades' ascribed deficiencies were measured against the advantages of the Persian system. The Persian discipline was superior to the Greek because it trained those destined to govern in the ancient virtues that would make them fit to rule.

The Virtues in the East

The catalogue of royal virtues canonized by Greek poets and philosophers was, however, an integral part of a cultural heritage far older than the Persian. Before the beginning of history, as the waters of the great Flood receded and kingship descended from heaven into the land of Mesopotamia, thoughtful men had already reached agreement as to what should be the nature of the man who was to lead them and what such a ruler might be expected to accomplish. The first political theorists who struggled to perfect their summary of the Prologue's objectives also sought, with those same phrases, to circumscribe the ruler's authority and limit his power. Priest-tutors, who expected to live under the administration of a mature king charged with a divine command to establish justice and provide for the welfare of his people, always instructed the young princes of Sumer and Akkad to be just, courageous, temperate, pious, and submissive to the law, to value the counsel of older men, to love the truth, and honor the gods. Those young princes grew up and as kings put into effect the laws that enabled Darius to become the "statesman and good king" so admired by Plato in his Seventh Epistle. Clearly, the Greek cardinal virtues—wisdom, justice, courage, temperance, and the old piety—had been honored in the East from the earliest days.

Wisdom

The mythology and epic literature of Mesopotamia frequently associated the epithet *Atrahasis,* meaning "Exceedingly Wise," with its gods and heroes. Utnapishtim, survivor of the Flood, the Babylonian Noah, was also known as *Atrahasis*. The same title identified Etana, mythical king of Kish, depicted on a Babylonian cylinder seal rising to heaven on the

Enki, Water-god and god of Wisdom, established the world order.

back of an eagle while an astonished goatherd exclaims to a potter and baker busy amongst their jars and loaves. From heaven Etana brought kingship back to a people who had theretofore lacked "counseling," a qualification that provides an insight into the nature of early kingship. "The term mitluku 'counseling, consultation' refers here to the function of the maliku, a cognate of the Hebrew word for 'king.' It is a significant commentary on the nature of kingship in Mesopotamian civilization" (ANET, 114 n. 9).

In another Sumerian story, the mortal Adapa, denied immortality by a trick of the gods, is granted wisdom instead, and becomes the wisest of all men. "Wide understanding he had perfected for him to disclose the designs of the land. To him he had given wisdom. . . . The sage . . . the capable, the most wise among the Anunnaki is he. . . . He steers the ship" (ANET, 101), thus introducing the metaphor later favored by Plato and many other writers.

Sumerian hymnists always maintained the gods had bestowed wisdom upon their leaders. Enki, the Lord of Wisdom, the god who knew the food and water of life, awarded Lipit-Ishtar the gift of broad wisdom. Nisaba herself, patroness of the scribal art, looked to the education of Lipit-Ishtar. Radiant with joy, the lady of all knowledge guided the hand of the young prince as he learned to write with a golden stylus upon the clay tablets, to use the measuring rod, the surveyor's line, and the cubit ruler "that gives wisdom."[21] In eulogizing Lipit-Ishtar as the "King of Justice, Wisdom and Learning," his scribe stressed it was the king's good counsel and wisdom that brought justice to the people. The king was the "great mind, knowing all things deeply," the "wise one [whose] decision provides justice," the "counsellor of great judgment."[22]

The god Enki also blessed Shulgi with wisdom; his wisdom perfected, his words true, the rich endowment of Shulgi's understanding amazed Sumerian poets. Hammurabi, god amongst kings, plumbed the depths of wisdom. Granted insight by Enki, he sheltered the people in his wisdom in order that justice be dealt the widow and the orphan. Later, in cursing the future king who might presume to abolish his laws and distort his words, Hammurabi prayed that Enki would deprive that man of understanding and constantly lead him astray.

Greek writers accepted the Sumerian equation of good counsel and wisdom. Zeus also knew "imperishable counsels," his "counsels and perceptions" were beyond all others.[23] Athena, greatest of the Greek goddesses, extracted from the head of Zeus after he had swallowed Metis ("Counsel"), was wisest in counsel. A warrior goddess and defender of cities, in peace she became the protectoress of agriculture, industry, and art. Plato's city, too, was wise in every deed, for it was well counseled "and surely . . . good counsel is a form of wisdom . . . for it is by knowledge that men counsel well" (*Rep*. 428B-E).

Another Babylonian word for wisdom, *nemequ* (adj. *enqu*), usually refers to skill in cult and magic lore, rites of exorcism (BWL, 196). Tablets of the Kassite period (ca. 1500-1100 B.C.), however, have used the term in a broader sense. One such, the *Counsels of Wisdom*, extends the meaning of wisdom to include the deference a wise (*enqu*) man will accord his neighbor, specifically urging that he maintain justice (*mi-sa-ra*) even to his enemies. The same tablet urges him to requite evil with kindness, give food and drink and grant whatever is asked, thus moving wisdom's reach beyond the magistrate's justice and raising it to the level of the holy man's all-embracing charity.

In the *Republic,* the wisdom of the philosophic guardian also contains an element of affection in that he loves the state, whose interests he supposes to be his own, and through the proper practice of the art of government, its subjects (412D-E). Even as Plato composed his *Republic,* Isocrates was advising the young Nicocles that a wise king "must take pleasure in the objects for which it is his duty to care," be a *philanthropon kai philopolin*—a lover of mankind and a lover of his country. [24]

Justice

The finger of Utu, the Sumerian god of Justice, had already touched the heart of man, when, in the twenty-fourth century B.C., Urukagina of Lagash put an end to extortions and other bureaucratic abuses that flouted principles he knew were entitled of their own intrinsic excellence to prevail.[25] Seventeen centuries before Plato posed the central question of the *Republic,* Sumerian philosophers had concluded that the concept of justice involved measurement, a determination that two objects or phenomena were, or were not, equal. Exemplification of justice as a comparison of equals began with the Sumerian *si-sá,* "to compare horns," from which the noun *nig-si-sá,* meaning "justice," derived.

Later, the notion of justice as an equivalence, balance, or equilibrium became a useful figure, expressed often and in many ingenious and imaginative ways. Solon stood between peasant and landowner and tried to establish equality before the law. Pericles claimed that *isonomia* (*isos,* "equal," *nomos,* "law") was characteristic of Athenian justice. To Pythagoras, justice was the product of equal numbers. Plato theorized that disease in the body and injustice in the body politic occurred when the equal balance of their constituent elements was disturbed by an excess of due measure in any one. He agreed with Hammurabi that it was unjust to treat nonequals equally. Aristotle's justice involved the maintenance or restoration of a balance, or proportion (*analogia*), between persons.

Iconography of the European Middle Ages usually depicted justice by a set of balanced scales, but also by the ostrich, because its feathers are of equal length. In the Arabic, "The root 'dl . . . once in the Qur'an is used [*for justice*] depending on the following preposition for moving toward or away from something, thus indicating its intermediate position. The even balancing of camel loads ('dl) is another indication of the equity meaning of the word."[26] To Erasmus, the Papal headdress, which originated as an Oriental cap, was the "two-horned mitre," its peaks signifying the equal perfection of his knowledge of the Old and New Testaments.

The Akkadian *mî/êšarum,* as already noted, meant anything that was "straight," such as a straight road, and came to be used in the sense of that which was right, just (*šar mīšarim*—"just king"), or as a noun for justice. Many later languages describe justice in terms of straightness. In Latin, *rectus* (past participle of *rego,* "to direct") meant ruled or straight and, therefore, that which was right, correct—the English and French rectitude. From the German verb *richten,* "to straighten," the adjective *richtig* described that which was correct, right, just; *Recht* became right, law, justice. The French *rendre droit,* "to straighten," produced *Droit,* "straight," "equitable," "just." *Tortus,* on the other hand, was a "twisting," or "winding." Thus, in Co. Litt. 158b, a tort is "so called because it is wrested, or crooked, being contrary to that which is right and straight."

The English "right" and "wrong" carry the same connotations of straight and crooked.

In early Greek, *dikē* was "the way it is," the "natural order of things." Derived from *deiknumi*, "to point in a direction," *dikē* sometimes denoted a legal decision—a *dikē* was always straight if just, crooked if unjust. Later encompassing the *dikai*, or "decisions of arbitrators," it imported, in a larger sense, justice.[27] *Dikaiosynē*, "justice," "righteousness," a derivative of *dikē*, also conveys a sense of going straight and doing right when used in the *Republic*, and the city's professionals, proceeding straight ahead, perform the tasks their capacities best suit them for, without interfering with the functions being discharged by their neighbors.

Greek poetry made liberal use of the straight-crooked antithesis. In the *Iliad*, Zeus was angered when in violent assembly mortals passed decrees that were "crooked" and drove "righteousness from among them" (16:387). At the legal trial depicted on Achilles' shield, two talents of gold were awarded the judge who "spoke the straightest opinion" (18:508), and Aineias warned, "The tongue of man is a twisty thing" (20:248).

Hesiod repeated the Mesopotamian image of justice as a straight road. "Do not try to practice violence . . . that other road is the better which leads towards just dealings. For Justice wins over violence";[28] and elsewhere: "lightly the crooked man he [*Father Zeus*] straightens" (7); "straight decisions, which are from Zeus, . . . are the fairest" (36); "there is an outcry when Justice is dragged perforce, when bribe-eating men pull her about, and judge their cases with crooked decisions" (220-1); "Beware, you barons. . . . Straighten your decisions, you eaters of bribes. Banish from your minds the twisting of justice" (263-4).

Gnomic poets of Greece who favored the distich form, as had their Sumerian predecessors, are well represented: "Rule one: no honor, prize or cash reward can justify a base or crooked act," said Theognis,[29] and with a patrician equanimity: "It's better, Kurnos, to be poor and good than rich and crooked, if you have to choose" (145-6); "I'll walk a straight true path and not incline to either side; my thinking must be sure" (945-6).

In a passage that could, with some modification, rest comfortably in the epilogue of Hammurabi's Code, Solon, the more even-handed lawgiver, wrote:

These deeds I made prevail,
Adjusting might and right to fit together,
And did accomplish even as I had promised.
And rules of law alike for base and noble,
Fitting straight justice unto each man's case,
I drafted.[30]

Halfway through the seventh century, Kypselos, the Corinthian tyrant, redistributed the land of his city to create many smaller holdings when urged by the Delphic oracle to "put Corinth straight." Pythagoras's list of antinomies carries "straight" as the male, odd number, as opposed to the female, even-numbered "crooked" and "evil."

References to straight and crooked as morally antithetical appear throughout the Old Testament as well: "All the words of my mouth are righteous; there is nothing twisted or crooked in them. They are all straight to him who understands" (Prov. 8:8); "a wicked man goes about with crooked speech" (Prov. 21:18); "I will cause them to walk . . . in a straight path" (Jer. 31:9).

A book written by a twelfth-century author, *Laws of Edward the Confessor,* relates that King William, in the fourth year after the Conquest, summoned English nobles to give testimony as to the customary laws of their country. Twelve men, chosen from each of the counties of the whole land, swore to make known the provisions of their laws and customs "so far as they were able, in a straight path, turning neither to the right nor the left, passing over nothing, adding nothing, changing nothing by walking crookedly."[31]

Modern writers have used the straightness-justice figure, which permeates colloquial expression, to explain aesthetic and spiritual judgments. The critic Walter Kerr, with rare felicity, wrote:

> *One man will insist, as a friend of mine insisted to me, that the clue to all order lies in proportion alone. Pointing to a high, straight, naked stairway in Italy, my friend announced himself willing to settle for the unflinching justice of its functional rise. No ornamentation; no curve to no purpose; no dawdling; no piece out of place. That "justice" which gives every element its proper due, is, in this view, the key to our deep intellectual satisfaction. In one of his plays, Graham Greene has suggested that God is "just" in the way that a straight line is said to be just . . . For my friend, the beautiful, the profoundly pleasing began and ended in the assertion of an incorruptible rectitude."*[32]

An old Irish clergyman, clearly no Calvinist (John Calvin had preached that when we follow God's authority, we never wander from the "straight path"), explained to his flock, "What we have to do, dear brethren, is stay on the straight and narrow path between right and wrong."

Courage

No virtue is more deserving of respect than the willingness to face danger to life and limb without shrinking when the community at large is threatened. However amusing the Greek poets who left their shields—and companions—on the battlefield, mankind owes its very survival to the few ready to sacrifice themselves when necessary for the safety of the greater number. Barely tolerated in peace, fully celebrated in war, their courage is the greatest and noblest virtue, surpassing wisdom, justice, and, above all, prudence.

Courage is an obvious qualification for police and military leaders of all ages and societies. It was the virtue that distinguished the Akkadian *rēdum* and the Sumerian *Ukus,* precursors of the *Republic*'s auxiliary guardians, Plato's fleet hounds. In 400 B.C., Cyrus the Younger shouted, "*orō ton andra,*" "I see the man," and charged to his death against the bodyguard of his brother at the battle of Cunaxa, thus displaying the boldness and martial ardor that Eastern rulers always claimed. Darius boasted of being a good horseman and a good bowman, both mounted and afoot. The great Cyrus fought his bear on foot.

Long before the Achaemenids lived, however, Mesopotamian rulers had made similar claims. Some relished being depicted as ferocious as animals in the wild. Hammurabi was the "fierce wild bull," the terror of the enemy. Lipit-Ishtar, the "great bison," raged against his enemies. Shulgi reminded his contemporaries of "a lion, with wide open mouth." Gilgamesh of the stormy heart was "strong as a wild ox," the onslaught of his weapons had no equal. Enkidu, his antagonist and eventual companion, as a youth had run with the animals of the forest. When the nobles of Uruk, voicing their displeasure at Gilgamesh's arrogant behavior, called out the excellent qualities they had expected to find in the character of their ruler, the virtue courage led all the rest.

The *Republic* holds the courage of a citizen to be his "unfailing conservation of right and lawful belief about things to be and not to be feared" (430B), a definition Socrates promises to discuss more fully at another time. In *Laches,* Nicias argues that the lion, bull, stag, and monkey may not be considered courageous because they lack knowledge of what is to be dreaded or dared, key elements in Plato's incomplete definition of courage. When qualifying Socrates as valiant, however, Laches refers simply to his "manliness" in battle (Gr. *andreiotes,* from *aner,* "man" a term of respect, Cyrus's word above; Lat. *vir, virtus*). In the *Laws,* Plato suggests an appropriate penalty for the cowardly "shield flingers" would be, if it were within human power, to transform them into women (944E). Obviously that brilliant man had never seen a female bear defend her cubs against a male twice her size.

Temperance

Some Greeks scorned the Persian for his subservience, but in an ideal state, appetite willingly yields to reason's lead, and obedience by its numerous worker-producers is an essential virtue in a city to be ruled by a few philosophers. The Greek *sōphrosynē,* the first word of Plato's epitaph, (Lit. *sōos,* "safe," "sound," + *phrēn*, "mind"), interpreted as self-control, temperance, or prudence, was originally the virtue of the men of brass in his *Republic. Sōphrosynē* was used there in the sense of obedience: "Are not the main points of self-control these—to be obedient to their rulers and themselves to be rulers over the bodily appetites?" (389D-E). Eventually, *sōphrosynē* becomes temperance, sobriety and is equated, at times, with wisdom and justice.[33]

In describing the character of the younger Cyrus, whom he served on the ill-fated expedition to Cunaxa, Xenophon employs *sōphrosynē* in the *Anabasis* as meaning a deference to, and the exercise of, lawful authority:

> *For all the sons of the Persian nobility are educated at the gates* [i.e., the palace] *of the king and there one may learn much* sōphrosynē, *but not see or hear anything shameful. The boys see and hear of those honored by the king and also of those in disfavor so that even as children they learn not only to govern but to be governed. There Cyrus seemed . . . to be the most respectful of his peers and to obey his elders far more readily than those even of inferior rank.*[34]

Xenophon here touches upon an aspect of Eastern thought not often emphasized; one that moves the obedience of the king's subjects from an abject capitulation close to a concord based upon rational choice as to who is best suited to rule, the *sōphrosynē* of 432A of the *Republic.* Submission to organized government had long been the measure of civilized man in Mesopotamia:

> *. . . one can say that obedience to the proper authorities was considered by the people of Mesopotamia as a main characteristic of civilized living on the same level as worship of the gods. In the descriptions of the strange ways of the unsedentary sections of the population, this attitude is mentioned together with certain eating habits and burial customs as culture traits which separate the civilized from the uncivilized.*[35]

In the West, *sōphrosynē* tamed the Homeric hero, forcing him to moderate his arrogant individuality and accept the restraints of society as it developed an urban organization. In Mesopotamia, the prototypical untamed hero was the overbearing Gilgamesh, thinker of immortal thoughts and architect of ramparted Uruk, who recognized no one's rights but his own and did with the wives and children of his contemporaries as he would. Responding to the pleas of his distraught nobles, the gods attempted to teach Gilgamesh *sōphrosynē* by creating Enkidu, his equal in strength, to serve as a counterbalance. Gilgamesh's horror as he observed the decomposition of the remains of the befriended Enkidu, and realized the gods had denied him immortality, ultimately shattered his hybris and compelled him to face the inevitability of his own death.

English writers of the early 1600's insisted that the powers of kings, queens, and princes were ordained of God, that it was God's will for society to be arranged in hierarchies, that social inequality was necessary and natural, and that each rank enjoyed distinct prerogatives, the highest's being the right to rule. God expected each person to remain in his allotted place, and obedience to authority was the honorable course. Typically, Bishop Lancelot Andrews proclaimed that "obedience to government ought to be dearer to us than our goods, yea, than our lives."[36]

Early English immigrants brought this conviction with them to America and formed their own patterns of hierarchical social organization. They established and staunchly defended the prerogatives of ordained leadership. Preachers often cited in support the letters of St. Peter and Paul of Tarsus in Cilicia, a city known for its fusion of Oriental and Occidental thought. Romans 13:1 was a mainstay: "Let every person be subject to the governing authorities. For there is no authority except from God and those that exist have been instituted by God." John Calvin, the dominant Christian voice in North America, explained why it is just to be obedient, as will be seen below.

Piety

Habitual reverence and obedience to God (or the gods); Devotion to religious duties and observances, godliness, devoutness, religiousness.

— (O.E.D.)

In *Euthyphro*, Socrates gets no closer to a satisfactory definition of piety than he had of courage in *Laches*. To Euthyphro's attempt, that piety is "learning how to please the gods in word and deed, by prayers and sacrifices," Socrates retorts that piety then is the "science of asking and giving," a sort of business transaction, from which the benefit accruing to the god is difficult to make out.[37]

As modern catechisms teach that man was created to serve God on this earth, so the ancient Mesopotamian, untroubled by Socrates' doubts, believed he had been placed here to serve and honor the deities. With prayer, supplication, benediction, obeisance, kneeling, ritual murmurs, and prostration, he worshipped his great gods, his lesser gods, and the

Votive bronze statue of Babylonian worshiping. Gold foil covers the face, beard, and hands.

benevolent and protecting spirits who walked beside him. At table he invoked the blessing of his goddess. At chapels, holy places, sacred sites and shrines scented with fragrance, he importuned the gods to raise their heads, show their faces, make their wills known. His lower eyelids distended with tears, he cried, in an earlier language, "Miserere! miserere! miserere! Forgive me my debts, forgive me my offences!" (ANET, 384). With freewill offerings of bread, flour, clear libations, honey sweet beer, and pure wine, fattened animals of all sorts, oxen, sheep, gazelles, and dormice (later a Roman delicacy), he made the gods' hearts glow, caused them to be exultant with succulent meals.

For his priests and priestesses, the secret rites of their specialized functions demanded an explicit competence. No activity, however obliquely related to the divinities, escaped their devout observance. They followed procedures for the daily sacrifice to the city-gods, for pageants, the repair of a temple, the observance of special holy days, the ritual to be followed by the *kalu* priest when covering the temple kettledrum, with meticulous attention paid to endless and presumably significant minutiae. The procedures were written, checked, and rechecked when copied.

Eastern kings assumed the awesome responsibility for housing the deities that came to be associated with all phenomena. They spoke with pride and justification of magnificent edifices built, shrines adorned, and altars prepared. Hammurabi, himself the god-fearing prince, devout, suppliant, boasted that he had designed the temple of Ebabbar, which was like a heavenly dwelling. Other Mesopotamian rulers described how they roofed their new and refurbished temples with cedar beams, sheathed their great cedar doors with bands of bronze, lined their walls with gold and lapis lazuli, placed images of shining bronze in their doorways, brightened the great godheads with red gold and shining stones, placed fierce dragons of gold at the pedestals of the gods, confronted the gods with statues made in their own human likeness, and covered these too with red gold and shining stones.

Legendary heroes performed their religious duties and prayed for help from the deities; lesser gods sought the intercession of the more powerful. Childless Etana, praying for the plant of birth, reminded Shamash that he had sacrificed his fattest sheep, that the earth had drunk the blood of his lambs, that he had honored the gods and revered the spirits, that the oracle priestesses had properly presented his offerings. The gods saved Ziusudra, the Sumerian Noah, from the Deluge because of his steadfast devotion. We are left with the touching spectacle of Ninsin, mother of Gilgamesh, herself a goddess, ascended to the roof of the palace, burning incense at the altar of the Sun-god, and lifting her arms to the heavens as she beseeches Shamash to keep her son from harm on his forest journey. Even as, many years later, the circumspect Lady Penelope climbed to the "upper story" to pray that Pallas Athene would enable Telemachus to avoid the suitors' ambush and return safely from his journey to Pylos.

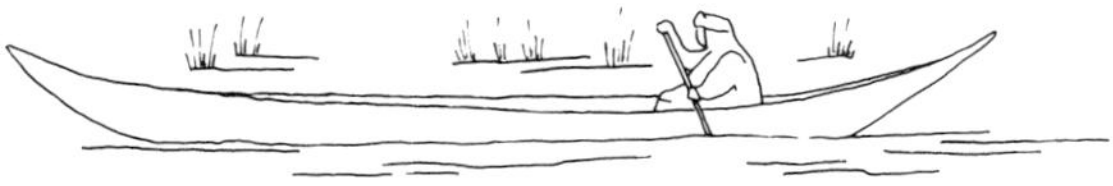

Aristoxenus said that nearly all of Plato's *Republic* was included in the *Controversies* of Protagoras. True or not, Plato's reputation for using materials wherever found is well known. He sought, and bought when necessary, the best information available and enriched it with his genius. The objectives he assigned to the functionaries of his *Republic* were well known to his contemporaries and had a long history in the civilizations of the East, which always recognized the necessity for wise, just, courageous, temperate, and pious leadership.

These, then, were the Eastern virtues: the wisdom of the ideal Mesopotamian ruler was a wide understanding that enabled him to comprehend the "designs of the land" and make their nature known by counseling his people in a kingly manner. His wisdom was the deep and perfect understanding that came from divine inspiration. The wise man and the wise king were expected to display a love and compassion that transcended mere feeling and required them to act, to grant what was asked, to do unto others—the message of the Bible's Golden Rule.

Mesopotamia's concept of justice was bifurcated; it involved comparison, an examination of balances on the one hand, measurement and a quality of straightness on the other. The latter is symbolized by the surveyor's line, the measuring rod, and cubit ruler used by the goddess

Nisaba to teach Lipit-Ishtar. Shamash, the Sun-god, handed similar instruments to Hammurabi as he directed that great king to institute justice in the land. The Mesopotamian definition of justice implied a correspondence between the physical and moral spheres and provided an idiom for discussing the concept of justice that is still in use. As Sir Henry Maine remarked over a hundred years ago in referring to a Roman hypothetical state of nature: "Nature implied symmetrical order, first in the physical world and next in the moral, and the earliest notion of order doubtless involved straight lines, even surfaces and measured distances."[38]

Physical courage, "manliness," the determination to disregard prudence when necessary and confront peril to life and limb in circumstances the less venturesome find valid reasons to avoid, was equally admired and demanded of its rulers in Greek and Mesopotamian civilizations.

If Plato's *sōphrosynē* had no explicit Eastern counterpart, the virtue of piety that compelled devotion to religion and the law was a traditional moderating influence in Mesopotamia. There, religious ritual called for the annual public humiliation of its kings, forcing them to acknowledge they were only trustees of the law, mere participants in a cosmically ordered universe. To the extent the piety of the East defined the limits of royal power, curbed the excess of Eastern kings and prescribed obedience by the populace to the city-god's vicar on earth, that virtue merits comparison with the Greek temperance.

Because the purposes of ideal government and the qualities of an ideal prince, as understood in fifth-century Greece, addressed fundamental human issues of politics and morality, the Greek response of necessity had much in common with the reasoning of earlier Babylonian philosophers and lawmakers. For the same reason, Western students of Greek thought, including statesmen of the new American republic, formulated and decided those ultimate questions in much the same manner.

---

[1] Olmstead, *History of the Persian Empire,* 127.

[2] A. R. Burn, *Persia and the Greeks* (U.S.A.: Minerva Press, 1962), 117. For a previously unpublished Late Babylonian copy of the prologue to Hammurabi's Laws, see D. J. Wiseman, "The Laws of Hammurabi Again," *JSS,* 7, 161.

[3] Olmstead, *History of the Persian Empire,* 128.

[4] Xenophon, *Oeconomicus,* trans. E.C. Marchant, O.J. Todd (Cambridge: Harvard Univ. Press, Loeb Classical Library, 1979), XIV, ll.4-7.

[5] Plato, *Epistle* VII. 332b, cited by L.A. Post, *Thirteen Epistles of Plato* (Oxford: Clarendon Press, 1925), 76. "Even critics who reject the other letters accept the seventh as genuine" (ibid., 56).

[6] Barker, *Greek Political Theory,* 339. Also, Shalom M. Paul, in *Studies in the Book of the Covenant in the Light of Cuneiform and Biblical Law* (Leiden: E.J. Brill, 1970), 27, marks a "striking parallel to the form of Mesopotamian collections in Deuteronomy where the legal corpus (Dt. 12-26:15) is preceded by a lengthy prologue (Dt. 1-11) and followed by an epilogue (Dt. 26:16-31:30), which contains a succession of blessings and curses," as do the epilogues to the Laws of Hammurabi and Lipit-Ishtar. In "true Mesopotamian fashion," the legal corpus of Leviticus also closes with a catalogue of sanctions. Paul's study seeks to demonstrate that the book of the Covenant displays the same prologue-corpus-epilogue sequence.

[7] Plato, *The Laws,* trans. R.G. Bury (Cambridge: Harvard Univ. Press, Loeb Classical Library, 1967), IV:723b. Unless otherwise indicated, all citations of Plato's *Laws* in the text are from this edition.

[8] Driver and Miles, *Babylonian Laws,* I:16,36.

[9] *The Letters of Marsilio Ficino.* Pref. by Paul Oskar Kristeller, 3 vols. (New York: Gingko Press, 1985), I:70.

[10] Klein, *Three Šulgi Hymns,* Shulgi (A) ll.29-35, 191-93.

[11] The Middle Assyrian and Hittite laws may date from the fifteenth century B.C., although a fourteenth- or thirteenth-century dating may be preferable. In recovered form, neither Assyrian nor Hittite Laws contain a prologue or epilogue.

[12] Plato, *The Laws,* trans. Trevor J. Saunders (New York: Penguin Books, 1978), 344.

[13] An inscription of 409/8 B.C. prepared by a Greek commission assigned to republish Dracon's laws on homicide has been recovered. The beginning of the text dealing with involuntary homicide reads: "The First Axon. And if anyone [*Ean tis*] kills anyone without intention" (Raphael Sealey, *A History of the Greek City States, 700-338 B.C.* [Berkeley: Univ. of California Press, 1976], 101). A photograph of the inscription is included on p. 100. Penalties differ in both Greek and Babylonian provisions according to victim's social status.

[14] See Appendix, Exhibit C, "The Earliest Laws of Conversion" (213-14).

[15] Barker, *Greek Political Theory,* 342.

[16] Aristotle, *Athenian Constitution,* XVI, 2-10.

[17] Isocrates, *To Nicocles,* trans. George Norlin (Cambridge: Harvard Univ. Press, Loeb Classical Library, 1980), I:18-24.

[18] Barker, *Greek Political Theory,* 175.

[19] *Republic of Plato.* trans. Francis MacDonald Cornford, (New York: Oxford Univ. Press, 1945), 125 and n. 1.

[20] Helen F. North, *Dictionary of the History of Ideas* (New York: Charles Scribner's Sons, 1974), IV:386b.

[21] Vanstiphout, "Lipit-Eshtar's Praise in the Edubba," 50. "It is remarkable that truth and justice are viewed rather as manifestations of wisdom than as administrative measures" (ibid.).

[22] Ibid., 37.

[23] Hesiod, *Works and Days and Theogony,* trans. Richmond Lattimore (Ann Arbor: Univ. of Michigan Press, 1973), 561, 656.

[24] Isocrates, *To Nicocles,* II:15. "Later . . . some *[Pythagoreans]* went beyond the application of number to the conception of justice and taught a definite theory of politics. The essence of the theory was the divine right of wisdom to rule the state" (Barker, *Greek Political Theory,* 55).

[25] "The law of nature is that which God at the time of creation of the nature of man infused into his heart, for his preservation and direction; and this is Lex Aeterna, the moral law, called also the law of nature. And by this law, written with the finger of God in the heart of man, were the people of God a long time governed before the law was written by Moses, who was the first reporter or writer of law in the world" (Sir Edward Coke, 7 Co. 12a-b). "Good men tremble / Wise men nod / When lawyers speak / Of the fingers of God" (Anon.).

[26] Franz Rosenthal, "Political Justice and the Just Ruler," *Israel Oriental Studies,* 10, 92.

[27] In neo-Sumerian legal documents, the *di-ku* is the one who passes, or "cuts," the judgment, the judge.

[28] Hesiod, *Works and Days,* 214-18. The following quotations in the text are from this Lattimore edition.

[29] *Hesiod and Theognis,* "Elegies," ll.29-30. The following citations in the text are from this Wender edition.

[30] Aristotle, *Athenian Constitution*, XII, 4-5.

[31] Charles Howard McIlwain, *The Growth of Political Thought in the West* (New York: Cooper Square Publishers, Inc., 1968), 193, citing Liebermann, *Gesetze der Anglesachen,* I, 627.

[32] Walter Kerr, *The Decline of Pleasure* (New York: Simon and Schuster, 1965), 167.

[33] On the many uses and meanings of *sōphrosynē,* see North, "Temperance [Sophrosyne] and the Canon of the Cardinal Virtues," in *Dictionary of the History of Ideas,* IV:365.

[34] *Xenophon's* "Anabasis," eds. William W. Goodwin and John Williams White (Boston: Ginn and Company, 1894), I.9.1-6.

[35] Oppenheim, *Ancient Mesopotamia,* 103.

[36] T.H. Breen, *The Character of the Good Ruler* (New Haven: Yale Univ. Press, 1970), 6.

[37] *The Works of Plato,* "Euthyphro," ed. Irwin Edman, 53, 54.

[38] Maine, *Ancient Law,* 49.

VI

THE HERITAGE OF THE *REPUBLIC*

The conviction, expressed in the Republic, *that the highest life is that not of pleasure and power but of philosophical contemplation remained the governing ideal of ancient thought.*—W.G. De Burgh, *The Legacy of the Ancient World*

After Plato's *Republic,* the traditional goals of the modern state were never far from the forefront of Western political theorizing. Whether proclaimed expressly as the objects of an ideal state or implicit in the character of an ideal ruler who alone possessed all the virtues of the *Republic*'s three classes, writers of every age before the United States Constitution was drafted argued for the primacy of a government capable of satisfying the economic, military, and philosophical-political needs of its people. Philosophers and statesmen, poets and churchmen of all lands west of Babylon reasserted the same old and honored themes; that wise, just, brave, pious, and sober princes should know and love the truth, be subject to the law, magnificent and high-minded, properly educated, shepherds of their flocks, and fathers to their peoples.

The good princes, surpassing all in personal appearance, forsaking private advantage in the administration of public affairs, would protect the widow and the orphan, curb the malice and extortions of public officials, qualify themselves to rule by learning to obey, and so serve as true pilots of their ships of state.[1] Such leaders were expected to create and maintain states that were just, tranquil, and bountiful. Although expressed in light of contemporary events and changing religious beliefs, these themes were a restatement, without substantial alteration or addition, of ideas that began in the West with Isocrates, Xenophon, Aristotle, and, most often, Plato.

400 B.C. to 400 A.D.

Aristotle (384-322 B.C.)

The Greek *polis* is believed to have developed, historically, about a height easily defended, an *acropolis,* where natural resources were available to provide the needs of gathering family and village units. Surpluses accumulated from surrounding village farms and pastures were exchanged at the *agora*, or marketplace, where arbiters sat to settle disputes. Eventually, the defensive heights came to house religious and secular authorities, not unlike the conformation of Sumerian cities, where gods and kings resided on or near the *ziggurat* within the refuge of the city wall and were fed by those who tilled the land and tended the flocks and herds outside the enclosure. Judges heard causes and meted out justice at the gates of the walls.

At the beginning of his *Politics*, a work studied in Colonial American colleges, Aristotle explained how human associations progressed from the household through the village, to the final and perfect association, the *polis*. Each phase contributed: the family to satisfaction of daily recurrent needs, the village to satisfaction of defense and simple justice, and the *polis* to satisfaction of all needs—sustenance, defense from external aggression, and the highest spiritual satisfaction, the attainment of a complete system of justice.[2]

Aristotle defined his state as a body of citizens adequate to achieve self-sufficiency. In the seventh book of the *Politics* he listed the elements necessary for a state to be self-sufficient. The first necessity was food, the next arts and crafts. The third was arms, in order to repress disobedience and meet any threat of external aggression. The fourth was a certain supply of property; the fifth an establishment for public worship. The last and "most vitally necessary" was a "method of deciding what is demanded by the public interest and what is just in men's private dealings" (vii 8.7).

The enduring legacy of the *Politics* to Western civilization is said to be its concept of "constitutionalism," the presumption that "the king is, and shall be, below the law."[3] There is dramatic precedent for this Aristotelian insight, however, in the most ancient East, for, in the very first days, did not the fate-decreeing gods of Sumer seize their king, Enlil, and banish him to the netherworld for raping the lovely young goddess Ninlil? (The child born of this attack was the Moon-god Nanna, shown on the stele of Ur-Nammu [p. 21 supra] holding the instruments of justice before the Sumerian king.) On earth, three powerful influences, the state, religion, and the law, had, in fact, circumscribed Mesopotamian kingship from earliest times.[4]

In prehistoric Mesopotamia, sovereignty appears to have resided in general assemblies of free adult males who could grant kingship to an individual in time of war, for a limited period.[5] At the dawn of history, in the Sumerian poem *Gilgamesh and Agga*, Lord Gilgamesh is depicted putting the question to the convened assembly of the elders of Erech: Should he submit to demands from the city of Kish or smite it with weapons? Later he posed the same question to an assembly of the men of the city. And Utnapishtim, the Babylonian Noah, sought the counsel of the people as well as the elders of Shuruppak before building his ark.

In actual practice, Eastern rulers, including fierce Assyrian kings, were not insensitive to the interests of officials and institutions important to their rule. The power of Hittite kings, in particular, was delimited by legislative assemblies—in Akkadian, the *nagbāti* and the *kabtūti*—councils of greater and lesser nobility, who fought with the king and with each other.[6] In the sixteenth century B.C., the Hittite king Telipinus decreed that the king himself was subject to the law, an acknowledgment that may have merely confirmed a traditional power possessed by the *pankus,* or assembly, to constrain the royal authority.[7]

Because Babylonian kings were responsible to their city-god for the management of earthly affairs entrusted to them, interpretation of the god's wishes became an increasingly complex task and source of power for those competent to offer an expert judgment as to how the divine will might best be carried out on earth. The king was therefore dependent upon the counsel of his priests, and they were not always reluctant to demand royal recognition of their prerogatives.

At the New Year's *akitu* festivals celebrated in Babylon, for instance, the *urigallu*-priest permitted the king to enter the innermost sanctuary and approach the god Bel (lit. "Lord"—later Marduk), but only after the priest had stripped him of his royal insignia and humiliated him by slapping his face and pulling his ears. Then, bowing to the ground, the king in a formal declaration swore to the god that he "did [not] sin," that he had not been "neglectful" of the "requirements" of godship, that he did not "rain blows on the cheek of a subordinate," that he "did not humiliate them," that he did not forget the rites of the temple Esagil, and that he had "[watched out]" for the sacred city of Babylon (ANET, 334). Thus the king assured the divinity that he had been a just, temperate, pious, caring, and zealous leader of his people. Later in this annual rite, the high priest, having informed the king that his prayer had been accepted, reinvested him with the authority and trappings of office, gave back his scepter, circle, and sword, and slapped his face again—hard enough to draw tears—for only in this manner was Bel made friendly.

Despite a reputation for despotism at times honestly earned, the kings of the ancient Near East were not free to act on whim; as noted, they were mere agents of the law, reigning under an unqualified divine mandate to establish justice in the land. Those who disregarded the strictures of *kittum*'s eternal truth exercised power without right and were vulnerable to a tradition that justified rebellion against their rule.[8]

A document recovered from Assurbanipal's palace at Nineveh, the "Advice to a Prince" tablet, DT 1, pointedly cautioned the Babylonian king against self-aggrandizement and other abuses of royal power, urging him to heed justice (BWL, 12). He was to accept the advice of his nobles and counselors and reject the counsel of rogues, as post-Platonic literature constantly reminded the just prince to prize good counsel and avoid flatterers. DT 1 also specified the nature of the divine retribution that awaited a Mesopotamian ruler who paid no heed to justice. Such a king might expect his people to be thrown into chaos, his land devastated, his own life cut short. The gods would never cease from pursuing him hostilely; they would send foreign soldiers to slaughter his soldiers, give his wealth and possessions to the enemy.

The DT 1 document marks an important milestone in the history of man's search for political recognition and protection, for it provided that the gods would also invoke these dread sanctions against a monarch who violated basic rights enjoyed by citizens of Nippur, Sippar, and Babylon. Those fortunates were exempted from the obligation to pay taxes or perform forced labor; they were not to be imprisoned or have their silver, fodder, or livestock taken from them; they were to be judged by a dedicated and honest judiciary, and not have their "treaties" declared void by the king. Here, with the principle established that certain privileged citizens, at least, possessed property rights upon which the king could not arbitrarily encroach, lies a forerunner of the great constitutional lever, the power of the purse, which ultimately enabled the peoples of England and Colonial America to set limitations upon the powers of ambitious Western kings.

A fine scholar has traced the "long line of transmission" of the precept that the king shall be below the law from Aristotle to St. Thomas, from St. Thomas to Richard Hooker, from Richard Hooker to John Locke, and from John Locke to Edmund Burke.[9] That line of transmission may be extended to James Madison in the West at one end, and at the other, back through Aristotle's parents, who came from Asia Minor, to their more distant ancestors from the East.

Cicero (106-43 B.C.)

Marcus Tullius Cicero, Roman politician-statesman, lawyer, orator, philosopher, and elegant essayist, freely acknowledged that Rome's indebtedness to Greece was "no little rivulet that flowed . . . into our city, but a mighty river of culture and learning" (*Rep.*, II.xix.34). In his youth, Cicero studied in Athens for three years and was greatly influenced by Greek political theory. His *De Re Publica* owed much to the *Republic* of Plato and Aristotle's *Politics*.[10] Cicero's *De Legibus*, a sequel, contains the laws of his *Republic*.

Colonial America knew the *De Re Publica* only through intermediate works. Except for the "Dream of Scipio" of Book VII, Cicero's manuscript was lost until 1820, when fragments were discovered in the Vatican library. John Adams was, nevertheless, well aware of Cicero's devotion to Plato:

> *Cicero was educated in the Groves of Academus where the name and Memory of Plato were idolized to such a degree, that if he had wholly renounced the Prejudices of his Education, his Reputation would have been lessened, if not injured and ruined. In his Volumes of Discourses on Government, We may presume, that he fully examined Plato's Laws and Republick as well as Aristotle's Writings on Government. But these have been carefully destroyed; not improbably with the general Consent of Philosophers, Politicians and Priests.*[11]

In the preamble to the Constitution of Massachusetts, as we have seen, Adams declared that the end of government was

> *to secure the existence of the body-politic, to protect it, and to furnish the individuals who compose it, with the power of enjoying, in safety and tranquillity, their natural right, and the blessings of life . . . .It is the duty of the people . . . to provide for an equitable mode of making laws . . . that every man may, at all times, find his security in them.*

These are Cicero's views, expressed by him repeatedly. Law was the bond (*vinculum*) of civil society, the state, an association in justice enforced by law (*Rep.*, I.xxxii.49). As "supreme law" was the right reason of supreme Jupiter, so the perfected reason of the wise man was also "law." Inherent in that term, (*lex*—"law," from *legere*, "to choose") is "the idea and principle of choosing what is just and true" (*Leg.*, II.v.12); "Laws were invented for the safety of citizens, the preservation of States, and the tranquillity and happiness of human life" (*Leg.*, II.iv.11).

Of the simple forms of government, Cicero deemed kingship the best, "but only so long as it retains its true character. But it does that only when the safety, equal rights, and tranquillity of the citizens are guarded by the life-long authority, the justice, and the perfect wisdom of a single ruler" (*Rep.*, II.xxiii.43). He cited Numa Pompilius, an early king of Rome, as such an exemplary king: "Thus he implanted in them [*the citizenry*] a love for peace and tranquillity, which enable justice and good faith to flourish most easily, and under whose protection, the cultivation of the land and the enjoyment of its products are most secure" (*Rep.*, II.xiv.26).

St. Augustine (354-430)

Although much of Cicero's *De Re Publica* had been lost to the West in the eighteenth century, American Revolutionaries were familiar with Cicero's political and ethical thought through the works of St. Augustine, a churchman who lacked the language but dearly loved the Greek Plato.

Augustine's voluminous writings made him the leading figure in Catholic philosophy for eight hundred years. His opus, *City of God*, which ultimately ran to twenty-two volumes, began as a refutation of the charge that Christianity was responsible for the fall of Rome to Alaric and the Goths in 410 A.D. The Bishop of Hippo claimed that the corruption and wickedness of Rome itself had brought about its ruin. The strongest bond of security in any community, he maintained, is the harmony or accord which marks a just society. He argued that when justice ceased to exist in Rome, as it had, and when the welfare of its people was forgotten, as it was, there was no common recognition of rights, nor mutual cooperation for the common good, and therefore no commonwealth.[12]

In *The City of God* Augustine turned often to Cicero for precedent. The Roman had called a commonwealth "an assemblage of people in large numbers associated in an agreement with respect to justice and a partnership for the common good" (*Rep.*, I.xxv.39). Augustine cited Cicero when he called a republic the "weal of the people," and the people, "a multitude bound together by a mutual recognition of rights and a mutual cooperation for the common good" (XIX.23.478). (The Preamble to the Massachusetts Constitution is again similar in concept and language: "a social compact, by which the whole people covenants with each citizen, and each citizen with the whole people, that all shall be governed by certain laws for the common good.")

Augustine offered a Christian interpretation of the venerable "true virtues" to men living by faith:

> *. . . what is a life of virtue save one unending war with evil inclinations . . . that arise within ourselves and are our very own . . . temperance—*sophrosyne, *as the Greeks call it—which must bridle our fleshly lusts . . . prudence . . . to distinguish what is good from what is evil . . . what prudence preaches temperance puts into practice . . . there is justice . . . to see that to each is given what belongs to each . . . the great virtue called fortitude—to bear patiently with misfortune (XIX. 4. 438).*

The Middle Ages

The Republic *Lost*

Europe's Middle Ages knew Plato's *Republic* only through intermediate sources, for the dialogue itself was lost to the West for a thousand years after the fall of the Roman Empire:

> *What the Middle Ages knew of Plato came from a Latin translation of a large part of the* Timaeus *made by Chalcidus in the fourth century, and from references in Aristotle, Cicero, St. Augustine and Macrobius, in Apuleius'* De Dogmate Platonis *and in Boethius'* De Consolatione Philosophi. *Something of the* Republic *was contained in Cicero's* De Republica.[13]

The *Republic* nevertheless had an important effect during the millennium of its disappearance:

> *The Four Cardinal virtues of popular doctrine in the Middle Ages, familiar in preaching and allegory, are according to the division and arrangement of Plato . . . .It might be fanciful to derive the three estates*—oratores, bellatores, laboratores—*from the* Republic, *though nowhere in history are the functions of the three Platonic orders of the Sages, the Warriors and the commons more clearly understood than in the medieval theory of the Estates, as it is propounded, for example, in the book of* Piers Plowman. [14]

In this period, too, symbolic representations of the four classical virtues, Latinized as *Justicia, Prudentia, Fortitudo, and Temperantia*, were painted in oils, modeled in mosaics, sewn into tapestries, illuminated in books, Bibles, and breviaries, and carved into the facades of mausoleums; altogether they became so much a part of the iconography of the Middle Ages that by the time of the Renaissance few Europeans, literate or otherwise, could have remained unaware of the political and personal ideals embodied in these all-pervasive figures.

Thomas Aquinas (1226-74)

Thomas Aquinas, the Dominican genius who synthesized Christian faith and Aristotelian reason, outlined his political views in a short treatise *On the Training of Princes*. He taught there that man was by nature a social and political animal and that he entered into social organizations in order to obtain the necessities of life. Peace was essential to the realization of the common good; the possibility of war necessitated guarding against all potential enemies. Aquinas noted that one of the main difficulties threatening the good order and very existence of the state was the "radical," or chronic objector (Hammurabi, too, had his "growlers"), who was to be corrected by laws, precepts, and punishments. He distinguished carefully divine, natural, and man-made positive law, and was willing to depart from his heavenly speculations when necessary to advocate legislation for the mundane activities of everyday life. Like Ur-Nammu and Solon before him, Aquinas understood the necessity for uniform values and equivalents, and recommended that the prince install a system of standard weights and measures. He also urged that roads and highways be kept open to promote internal peace and stimulate commerce. The ruler was always to do his best "to keep firm the bonds of peace and mutual good will within the state and to provide for the essentials of a normal life."[15]

Aegidius Romanus, a pupil of Aquinas, enlarged upon his master's political views in a three-volume work *On the Governance of Princes,* published in 1287. The perfect prince, Aegidius wrote, should be possessed of all the virtues: prudence, justice, courage, and moderation. He should love the common good; desire only the welfare of the state; be powerful enough "to keep off enemies from his realm" and "keep the country well policed." He was to spend his time only on the larger problems of the state, including "the preservation of wealth, commerce, especially in providing food for cities and towns, trade laws, maintenance of internal order, declaration of war and the formulating of laws."[16] Four years later, three Swiss communities drew upon these venerable rules of good government when they formed a League with goals much the same as those of the Prologue and Preamble.

The Forest Cantons of Switzerland

The first "Federal Constitution of Switzerland," the "Perpetual League of the Forest Cantons, 1291," may be compared to the New England Confederation of 1643.[17] Both leagues were defensive in nature: the Swiss cantons formed their "Perpetual League" to resist the encroachments of Hapsburg-Austria; the New England settlers united in a "firm and perpetual league" to keep themselves safe from the threat of Dutch, French, and Indian attack. The Swiss League was more truly a union, however, in that its regulations, "established for the common welfare," were to be given internal effect.

The "Agreement" by the "people of the valley of Uri, the democracy of the Valley of Switz and the community of the mountaineers of lower valley [the canton of Nidwalden]" provided that "public welfare" is enhanced "when agreements are entered into for the proper establishment of quiet and peace." The league was formed "in order that [*the cantons*] may better defend themselves and their own" against "all and every, who may inflict upon any one of them any violence, molestation or injury." Proscription of the crimes of murder, arson, and robbery, forbidding seizure of another's goods without "special permission of his judge," and a provision for arbitration by prudent men to settle disputes amongst the confederates helped establish justice and ensure domestic tranquility.

It is noteworthy that draftsmen of the Swiss Constitution set out many of the Swiss laws in the same casuistic "If a man, If anyone," formulation characteristic of all early law codes of the ancient Near East.[18] The Swiss Constitution also purported to renew "by means of the present [agreement] the ancient oath-confirmed confederation." No one knows the nature of that ancient confederation.

The Republic *in the East*

If the *Republic* was lost to the West during the Middle Ages, the writings of Syrian Christians made that dialogue known in the Arab world at least from the middle of the ninth century, when Arabic Nestorian Hunain ibn Ishaq and his school translated the *Republic* for study by their Muslim readers. A portrait of the philosopher-king in Islam is seen in the description of Alp Arslan, a Seljuk sultan who began his reign in 1058:

> *In appearance he was tall, with mustaches so long that he used to tie up their ends when he wished to shoot; and never did his arrows miss the mark. He used to wear a very high kulah on his head, and men were wont to say that from the top of this kulah to the ends of his mustaches was a distance of two yards. He was a strong and just ruler, generally magnanimous, swift to punish acts of tyranny, especially extortion and exaction, and so charitable to the poor that at the end of the fast of Ramadan he was wont to distribute 15,000 dinars in alms . . . .He was also devoted to the reading of the chronicles of former kings, and of works which threw light on their character, institutes, and methods of administration.*[19]

This righteous king was killed when his arrow missed an onrushing assailant.

As the twelfth century came to an end, Baha' ad-Din, retainer and confidante of the great Saladin, wrote a biography of his master, who had imposed a crushing defeat upon the Frankish armies ("God Damn Them!") of the Third Crusade. He began the first chapter, "Saladin's Character," by setting out the countless manifestations of Saladin's extraordinary piety: his study of, and devotion to, the Qur'an, his assiduous performance of the canonic prayers, his discharge of the fasts of *Ramadan,* his devout preparations for the Pilgrimage.[20]

Saladin was an orthodox Muslim and no philosopher-king, for he hated all philosophers and other enemies of the Law; nevertheless, the subheadings of Chapter I reveal the Platonic—and Christian Godlike—virtues of the Sultan's character: "His Justice," "Examples of His Generosity," "His Courage and Steadfastness," "His Zeal in the Holy War," "His Endurance and Determination to Win Merit in God's Eyes," "Examples of His Humanity and Forgiveness," and finally, "His Unfailing Goodness."[21]

Mohammed II, Sultan of Turkey, poet, linguist, lawmaker, and patron of the arts and Italian artists, conquered Constantinople in 1453 and thereupon drew orthodox Christians into an Ottoman state that had been structured much as Plato had imagined his *Republic*. Guardians, administrative and military (the famed Turkish Janissaries), recruited from the enslaved Christian class, were rigidly trained to serve the state and its ruler. An intellectual elite governed. Candidates for the learned professions, legal, educational, and priestly, schooled at the Court of the Eight Colleges, came only from free Muslim families.[22]

The European Renaissance

Marsilio Ficino (1453-1499)

At the beginning of the fifteenth century, Manuel Chrysoloras, Byzantine Ambassador to Italy and later Professor of Greek literature at the University of Florence, made a translation of Plato's *Republic* available to Western scholars, who had for centuries sought to augment their understanding of Greek civilization and culture. As the gathering power of Mohammed's Ottoman Empire loomed ever more menacingly over the Byzantine capital, Greek intellectuals fled to the West, bringing with them manuscripts that intrigued and challenged Roman, Venetian, and Florentine students of classical literature and philosophy. For the first time, these enthusiasts reviewed ideas and customs that had originated in Mycenaean and Oriental civilizations long before.

The task of editing and translating the new literature fell largely to Greek émigrés and Italian humanists, teachers, and students of Latin rhetoric and grammar, who labored to acquire an equal proficiency in Greek. In 1445, Cosimo de Medici provided financial support for Marsilio Ficino, the son of his physician, to enable him to continue his studies of

Plato and the Greek language. By the end of the century, Ficino had translated the complete works of Plato into Latin, and copies of his edition, published by the new bookmaking process, were available to purchase.

Ficino's influence was enormous. His translations of Plato remained the standard edition into the last century. A priest and voluminous correspondent, his writings rekindled European interest in the doctrines of the "divine" Greek. His vision was all-encompassing. He reminded Church dignitaries and the Pope himself of their pastoral obligations, that part of man's soul was immortal. He elevated Italian painters from their journeyman status and directed Botticelli in the preparation of his "Primavera." He tutored and remained a life-long friend of Lorenzo de Medici, the leading statesman of his time. His Academy, devoted to the study of Plato's compositions, included Michelangelo and the brilliant Pico della Mirandola. His skills as a doctor made him the preferred physician of the Medici, and he believed, as had Babylon-trained Pythagoras, that serious music could cure diseases of body and soul. Most engaging is a contemporary bishop's description of Ficino, an accomplished musician, improvising on his lyre: it was "as if a curly-headed Apollo took up the lyre of Marsilio and fell victim to his own song. Frenzy arises. His eyes catch fire . . . and he discovers music which he never learnt."[23]

By the end of the fifteenth century, Ficino, his colleagues, and successors had reproduced in Latin the entire available body of Greek literary, mathematical, medical, and astronomical learning. Due in large part to their efforts, over the span of the next three hundred years, Plato's philosophical and political ideas were absorbed into the intellectual processes of the West and were consulted as a matter of course by those who sought to devise social organizations suited to accommodate man and state in peace and happiness.

Italian humanists became the teachers and scribes of western Europe. Masters of classical literary forms and techniques, they served as chancellors and secretaries to heads of state, drafted documents, wrote letters, speeches, and orations, composed moral and philosophical treatises that spread their learning and their insistence upon the dignity and value of the individual throughout the capitals and salons of the Western world. In northern Europe, the writings of Erasmus and Thomas More displayed a profound regard for Platonic theory and the traditions of Italian humanism.

Erasmus (1466?-1536)

Pope Julius II had been dead but a year, when, in 1514, a sketch passed through the courts and academies of Europe that depicted him attempting to browbeat Peter into admitting him into Heaven. He is seen depreciating the mere Sanctus Peter bore, compared to his own triple Sanctissimus, and threatening to excommunicate the Apostle and storm the gates of Heaven with a ghostly horde of sixty thousand. Although he was reluctant to acknowledge authorship, the work is attributed to Erasmus. It is outrageous—and very funny—but then it was said that Erasmus could cause more hurt to the Papacy by his jesting than Luther could with his raging.

Born the illegitimate son of a Dutch canon, himself at one time a priest of the Augustinian Order, Desiderius Erasmus was the preeminent Renaissance scholar and writer of Latin in northern Europe. His research disclosed errors in the Latin Bible of Catholicism, and his translation of the New Testament, based upon a reevaluation of Greek sources, shook the authority of both Book and Church.

The following theories espoused by Erasmus represent ideals to which all political writers of the time paid at least nominal homage and which were well known in Colonial America. They provided the criteria by which the actions and characters of the great men—and ladies—of Europe were judged. In the salon of the Duchess of Urbino, at the height of the Renaissance, Italian noblemen enthusiastically reaffirmed the classical virtues the "Perfect Courtier" would encourage in the character and deeds of the good prince, with constant reference to Plato, Aristotle, Xenophon, and Roman authorities.[24] Courtiers of Ur would have readily accepted the immaculate figure that emerges from their discussions, a paragon described at times in the very phrases of the hymnists of Shulgi.

Even Machiavelli, the contemporary Dark Spirit who denied everything, could not discard entirely the positive virtues espoused by Erasmus. Although he valued the state more highly than his own immortal soul, urging his prince to do good as he was able and evil as necessary, good arms, good laws, and the common good were always part of Machiavelli's testament. *Il Principe,* written in 1512 and published twenty years later, was studied in American colonies, whose leaders professed to believe that classical principles of honor and good faith better befitted an American prince than the amoral wisdom of the Florentine Secretary.

Erasmus was popular in eighteenth-century America, where college students and men of substance owned his books. His *Institutio principis Christiani,* published in 1516, was written as an instruction to the young prince Charles, the future Charles V, who shortly thereafter was to inherit the new Spanish colonies in America. In the *Institutio,* Erasmus drew upon his great knowledge of classical literature to describe what sort of man the perfect Christian prince should be and to enlighten Charles as to what such a prince should do to realize the "blessed state." Innovation and originality were not his purpose. Much of his instruction was taken bodily from writers of ancient Greece and Rome and, less frequently, from those of Medieval Europe and the Bible. Throughout the whole of his dissertation, Erasmus acknowledged his sources by citation, quote, or obvious allusion. Because he was as deeply impressed by the works of Plato as Ficino had been, much of Erasmus's writing on law and justice, the obligation of citizen and ruler to honor the law, and the education of youth corresponds closely to the ideas of the Italian priest.[25]

The rule of the state, Erasmus began, should be entrusted to the man "who excels all in the requisite kingly qualities of wisdom, justice, moderation, foresight, and zeal for the public welfare" (140). Wisdom, above all, is essential. "But a prince should excel in every kind of wisdom. That is the theory behind good government . . . his wisdom will be used for the good of the country, not himself" (174, 188).

Erasmus considered the education of the prince of major importance. He should "study the precepts of the Bible and classical writers . . . from the *Politics* of Aristotle and from the *Offices* of Cicero many passages that are worth knowing can be culled out. . . . But Plato is the most venerable source of all such things" (200-201). The prince must be a philosopher: not one trained in the pseudorealities but one who seeks and follows the truth with an open mind. He must be like a father to the state, for "what else is a kingdom but a great family? . . . God is the unquestioned prince of all the world and we call him 'Father.' . . . He must be the shepherd of his people, as 'Homer' in giving a man the honorary title of 'king' calls him the '*pasteur de peuple*,' 'shepherd of the people'" (170).

To ensure internal security in his land, "The prince must seek out the means . . . by which his country is freed from robbery and criminals [and that with the least bloodshed] and by which he may foster and strengthen lasting agreement among his people" (246). For the people's welfare, Erasmus advocated measures that were customary in ancient Mesopotamia. The Christian prince was to "adorn the cities with public buildings, bridges, . . . churches, river walls, and aqueducts. . . . Streams that flow to places of no advantage he should change to other courses; he should let in or shut out the sea as the need of his people demands" (246-47).

Thus Erasmus continues, describing the wondrous virtues and beneficent activities men have always associated with a perfect prince. He draws perhaps his most succinct conclusion from Plato: "The most felicitous condition exists when the prince is obeyed by everyone, the prince himself obeys the laws, and the laws go back to fundamental principles of equity and honesty, with no other aim than the advancement of the commonwealth" (221).

Despite the appealing and convincing presentation of the model ruler's character in *Christian Prince,* readers of Erasmus would have known that his discourse could not be accepted entirely without reservation, for he had already argued that the Platonic, and Stoic, philosopher, ruled only by reason, devoid of all emotion, is a "marble statue," a "monstrous apparition," and utterly incompetent to deal with the affairs of everyday life. His *Moriae Encomium* ("Praise of Folly"—*Moriae* a play on the surname of his friend Thomas More), published in 1509, a book possessed by First Gentlemen of Virginia, proved that the princely virtues of wisdom, courage, industry, and prudence are truly the offspring of Folly alone. "Nothing happens in this world which is not full of folly, performed by fools amongst fools."[26] Only someone from the ordinary run of fools, therefore, is suitable to hold office, lead troops, marry, or host guests. Such a man, unlike the self-satisfied, gloomy, silent, tiresome, and friendless wise man, "Would be pleasant to his wife, and agreeable to his friends, a congenial guest for a meal and good company for a drink, a man in fact, who thinks every human interest is his concern" (107). Man, Erasmus concluded, is the most unfortunate of animals, for he seeks to "step outside" his natural limitations and become something more than human (115).

Here, in recalling that man's fate is inexorable and that life is to be relished, the great humanist relied upon Ecclesiastes 9:2, 7-9.

> *. . . since one fate comes to all, to the righteous and the wicked . . . go eat your bread with enjoyment and drink your wine with a merry heart . . . let your garments be always white, let not oil be lacking for your head. Enjoy life with the wife whom you love, all the days of your vain life which he has given you under the sun because that is your portion in your life and in your toil at which you toil under the sun.*

In so doing, Erasmus introduced his reader directly to Sumerian wisdom, for the lot of mortal man was also the destiny decreed for Gilgamesh, although he was two-thirds god and only one-third man. As he searched the earth frantically for the secret of immortality, Siduri, the ale wife, attempted to console him:

Gilgamesh, whither rovest thou?
The life thou pursuest thou shalt not find.
When the gods created mankind,
Death for mankind they set aside,
Life in their own hands retaining.
Thou, Gilgamesh, let full be thy belly,
Make thou merry by day and night.
Of each day make thou a feast of rejoicing.
Day and night dance thou and play!
Let thy garments be sparkling fresh,
Thy head be washed; bathe thou in water.
Pay heed to the little one that holds on to thy hand,
Let thy wife delight in thy bosom!
For this is the task of (mankind)! (ANET, 90).

Thomas More (1478-1535)

Thomas More was as close a friend to Erasmus, his fellow humanist, as a man could be who yearned for a monastic life that Erasmus had spurned and who was to die for the Church whose shortcomings Erasmus had exposed to the laughter of all Europe. In 1516, More published his *Utopia.* The title may be read "Goodplace" if the Greek root *topos,* "place," is combined with the prefix *eu*, "good," or "Noplace" if combined with *ou*, "no." The *Utopia* described a community inspired expressly by Plato's *Republic.* James Madison, chairman of a committee designated by Congress in 1783 to compile a list of books to be imported for the use of Congress, included More's essay.

As a young man, More had lectured on Augustine's *City of God,* in which his saintly predecessor maintained that in all of ancient philosophy, Plato's conception of the highest good was most akin to fifth-century Christian belief. Later, as Lord Chancellor of England under Henry VIII (named "model monarch" in *Utopia*), More faced down the enemies of the Catholic Church, sometimes with ferocity, until he at last found himself staring, not unexpectedly, into the eyes of his principal. (When, in 1530, before his break with Rome, Henry addressed the Pope in intemperate terms, Clement VII gently reminded him of the virtues that became a Christian king: "We pardon your transport of impatience, exhorting you with a fatherly affection, to keep your temper; and we hope your prudence and piety will prevail upon you to make no resolutions but what are wise.")[27]

More's chief narrator in *Utopia*, Ralph Hythlodaye, learned of the manners and customs of the peoples of many lands when he left an expedition of Amerigo Vespucci to continue a journey around the world. His experience enabled him to evaluate objectively the social injustices troubling sixteenth-century Europe. Hythlodaye tells More that he holds well with Plato and is fully persuaded that all men should have and enjoy equal portions of wealth and commodities, that there will be no happiness in human affairs unless "private property is utterly abolished . . . the one and only road to the general welfare lies in the maintenance of equality in all respects." It is through the king's efforts that his people will be kept safe from injustice and wrong. "For this very reason, it belongs to the king to take more care for the welfare of his people than for his own, just as it is the duty of a shepherd, insofar as he is a shepherd, to feed his sheep rather than himself." As to the defense of the commonwealth, the king of the Macarians, a people who lived not far from Utopia, showed the way, for he maintained only enough treasure "to put down rebellion and . . . meet hostile invasions."[28]

Hythlodaye's recitation taught young scholars in Colonial America the futility and danger of good counsel at the court of an ambitious king. It also foretold, with sad prescience, the circumstances that would lead to More's death twenty years later. Hythlodaye had come to understand that the "indirect" approach, which prompts that things you cannot turn to good, you must at least make as little bad as possible, becomes irrelevant in actual practice. "At court . . . one must openly approve the worst counsels and subscribe to the most ruinous decrees. He would be counted a spy and almost a traitor who gives only faint praise to evil counsels."[29]

Although he had resigned his offices and withdrawn from political activities several years before, in 1535, More refused to swear an oath openly approving Henry's supremacy over the Church. For his refusal, he was indicted, convicted of treason, and beheaded.

The Emergence of Modern States in the Seventeenth and Eighteenth Centuries

Utopian Visions

As a modern system of sovereign states gradually emerged in seventeenth-century Europe, imaginative and Utopian dissertations concerned with the form such states should adopt proliferated, and "very important elements in most of them may be traced to his [*Plato's*] 'Republic.'"[30] Prominent amongst these were Francis Bacon's *New Atlantis,* 1623, James Harrington's *Oceana,* 1656, and Thomas Hobbes's *Leviathan,* 1651. Illustrative of these works is *City of the Sun,* written in 1623 by Thomas Campanella, a Dominican friar. Like the *Republic,* Campanella's model is based upon a city-state organization; rulers and officials are chosen from a select group who are specially trained in the arts and sciences; the Supreme Ruler is served by three Princes, Wisdom, Power, and Love. Education is a function of the state; private property and a natural family are denied the individual as they were Plato's guardians.

The Republic's *Virtues Amended*

English writers and preachers in the seventeenth century's opening decades modified the *Republic*'s virtues. Accepting moderation ("mediocrity"—the avoidance of excess), wisdom, and justice as attributes of the good ruler, they reinstated piety and replaced "courage" with "wealth," as a fifth virtue, believing that possession of a sufficient store of property assured an independent mind, likely to foster spirit and courage.[31] A century and a half later, Blackstone, who had adherents in America, also equated valor and property, and was of the opinion that those who failed to meet existing property qualifications should be denied the right of suffrage, judging them to be "in so mean a situation that they are esteemed to have no will of their own."[32]

A real and immoderate veneration of wealth accompanied the theoretical. On the eve of the American Revolution, bribery and corruption permeated all branches of the English government.[33] No Mesopotamian king would have countenanced the institutionalized pillaging of the estates of widows and orphans that took place there. One observer remarked that the office of Master of Wards "might be worth some thousands of pounds to him who would go, after his death, instantly to heaven; twice as much to him who would go to Purgatory and nobody knows how much to him who would adventure to go to hell."[34]

In the American colonies, royal governors sold public offices, created sinecures for their friends, and established a lucrative trade in political patronage. Fully aware of the sordid motivations that might influence men of affairs, American statesmen, in framing their Constitution, readily accepted the philosopher's dictum that in such an undertaking, for the sake of prudence, it were better to suppose each man a knave, governed only by private interest.[35]

Many of the Fathers of America also believed, however, that man was capable of positive and even noble passions, first amongst them being a desire for an enduring reputation, which might be utilized by a wise government to turn the baser passions to the public good. In his essay on "Honor and Reputation," Sir Francis Bacon had pointed out that the favorable estimation of persons of quality, the revelation of "man's virtue and worth without disadvantage," was the highest honor to which men might aspire. Such fame was to be won, first, by "founders of states and commonwealths," second, by great "lawgivers," third, by those who put an end to civil wars and "deliver their countries from servitude of strangers or tyrants." In fourth and fifth places, Bacon put those who merit a higher ranking, for they are the rulers who most nearly fulfill the objects of the Preamble, i.e., those who "in honorable wars enlarge their territories or make noble defense against invaders" and those who are called fathers of their country, "which rule justly and make the times good wherein they live." [36]

Presumably, when Gouverneur Morris and other members of the Committee of Style approached the task of refurbishing the draft of the Constitution of the United States, they were inspired by a desire for true fame, the approbation and gratitude of future generations. This noble passion prompted them to subordinate the base urgings of ambition, avarice, and self-interest to the common good and caused them, as one author expressed it, "to spend themselves to provide for the common defense, or to promote the general welfare, and even on occasion, to establish justice in a world where justice is extremely rare."[37]

That men will undertake great tasks and brave great perils to gain the approval of later generations is not, however, an improvisation by Bacon or a new discovery of the West. In Sumerian legend, Gilgamesh was similarly motivated as he was about to attack the guardian of the Cedar Forest: "Should I fall, I shall have made me a name; 'Gilgamesh' — they will say — 'against fierce Huwawa has fallen!' (Long) after my offspring has been born in my house . . . .A [name] that endures I will make for me!" (ANET, 79).

John Locke (1632-1704)

In England's "Glorious Revolution" of 1688, when William of Orange, aided by English Protestants, forced the abdication of the king, an ex-don of Oxford, John Locke, published his *Two Treatises of Government* in order "to make good" the title of King William and "to justifie to the World the People of England." Locke's philosophic rationale for the deposition of James II postulated that, by nature, men were free, equal, and independent; that men united in communities pursuant to social contract for their safety and the preservation of their properties; that their governors ruled only with their consent, and that such rule might be abrogated when a government failed to exercise the power entrusted to it for the public good. Revolutionaries of the American colonies seized upon Locke's reasoning a century later to justify their rejection of English rule; his phrasing inspired Thomas Jefferson. The purposes of the Preamble are also discernible in Locke's definition of Political Power:

> *I take to be a Right of making Laws with Penalties of Death, and consequently all less Penalties, for the Regulating and Preserving of Property, and of employing the force of the Community, in the execution of such Laws, and in the defense of the Commonwealth from Foreign Injury, and all this only for the Publick good,*[38]

And in his explanation of how a government may be dissolved:

> *When there is no longer the administration of Justice, for the securing of Men's Rights, nor any remaining Power within the Community to direct the Force, or provide the Necessities for the publick, there certainly is no government left.*[39]

Jonathan Swift (1667-1745)

At the turn of the eighteenth century, Jonathan Swift, dean of St. Patrick's Cathedral in Dublin, placed the ancient platitudes bearing upon just rule in perspective by marking the disparity between classical ideal and the reality of man performing as a political creature. His Mr. Gulliver is seized with melancholy, when, in his travels, he is drawn up onto the flying island of Laputa, and there observes professors in the "School of political Projectors," those unhappy people, who

> *were proposing Schemes for persuading Monarchs to chuse Favorites upon the Score of their Wisdom, Capacity and Virtue; of teaching Ministers to consult the publick Good; of rewarding Merit, great Abilities, and eminent Services; of instructing Princes to know their true Interest, by placing it on the same Foundation with that of their People; Of chusing for Employments Persons qualified to exercise them; with many other wild impossible Chimaeras, that never before entered into the Heart of Man to conceive; and confirmed in me the old Observation, that there is nothing so extravagant and irrational which some Philosophers have not maintained for Truth.*[40]

Citizens of Laputa discussed ingenious proposals for assessing taxes: vices and folly were to be taxed on the basis of a neighbor's evaluation; success with the other sex was to be the measure, according to a man's own appraisal; so too, would wit, valour, and politeness be gauged; "But as to Honour, Justice, Wisdom and Learning, they should not be taxed at all; because they are Qualifications of so singular a Kind, that no Man will either allow them in his neighbor or value them in himself."[41] No man, that is, except Lipit-Ishtar, the "King of Justice, Wisdom and Learning."

Having de-natured God, eighteenth-century philosophers deified nature by seeking in "Nature" the infinite power, wisdom, and goodness that were the attributes of the Puritan God:

Our views of Nature, however imperfect, serve to represent to us, in the most sensible manner, that mighty power which prevails throughout, acting with a force and efficacy that appears to suffer no diminution from the greatest distances of space or intervals of time; and that wisdom which we see equally displayed in the exquisite structure and just motions of the greatest and subtilest parts. These, with perfect goodness, by which they are evidently directed, constitute the supreme object of the speculations of a philosopher.[42]

Emerich de Vattel (1714-1767)

Almost half a millennium after three forest cantons formed the first federal constitution of Switzerland in 1291, Jean Jacques Burlamaqui, a Swiss authority on the principles of jurisprudence, made a direct and major contribution to American constitutional theory. His books *The Principles of Natural Law* and its sequel, *The Principles of Politic Law*, were collected in public, college, and private libraries. Leading colleges of the time used them as textbooks; they were required reading for all law students. Burlamaqui rejected the medieval notion that government was an artificial institution necessary to constrain man and returned to the views of Aristotle and Plato that social and political association were consonant with man's true nature. Plato's thesis that the happiness of a just man lay in the proper performance of his function would not suffice for Burlamaqui. He insisted it was the state's responsibility to assist man in achieving self-perfection, its ultimate goal, his happiness. With Burlamaqui, "happiness" became man's natural and inalienable right.[43]

Emerich de Vattel, a student at the University of Geneva where Burlamaqui taught natural and civil law, wrote a book entitled *The Law of Nations*, published posthumously in 1773, which has been called "one of the great and influential books of the eighteenth century."[44] It provided a comprehensive treatment of the societal purposes subsequently expressed in the Preamble and was constantly cited in America. Vattel wrote:

The end *or* object *of civil society is to procure for the citizens whatever they stand in need of, for the necessities, the conveniences, the accommodations of life, and, in general, whatever constitutes happiness—with the peaceful possession of property, a method of obtaining*

> *justice with security, and, finally a mutual defense against all external violence.*[45]

Vattel's study indicates there was substantial agreement between the ancient Near East and eighteenth-century Europe as to how the purposes of an ideal society were to be realized and particularly how the state was to honor its obligation to provide for the general welfare of its people.

The first of the "Principal Objects of a good Government" set out by Vattel was the duty to "provide for the Necessities of the Nation." (He had already noted the engagement of each individual, by virtue of the act of association, to "promote the general welfare" [16].) It was incumbent upon the nation or "its conductor," he concluded, to provide for "all the wants of the people" by adopting measures calculated to produce a "happy plenty of all the necessaries of Life" (72).

Vattel ranked agriculture the most useful and necessary of all the arts and counseled that the sovereign was to "neglect no means of rendering the land under his jurisdiction as well cultivated as possible" (78). He recommended that the state establish public granaries to prevent scarcity and regulate prices. Centuries earlier, agriculture had also been the source of all Sumerian wealth and the basis of its civilization; the massive irrigation and flood control systems of the ancient Near East testify to its rulers' determination to protect and enhance the productivity of the soil. Magazines built within the temple's enclosure wall were also kept well stocked, used for business purposes, and distributed to the populace in time of need. They contained

> *an immense variety of articles: grain, sesame seed as the raw material for oil, onions and other vegetables, beer, dates, wine (which was rare), fish (dried or salted), fat, wool, skins, huge quantities of reeds and rushes used for ceilings and for torches, temporary structures, mats for floor coverings and hangings, woods of many kinds, asphalt . . . valuable stones.*[46]

Vattel urged the sovereign to encourage commerce, for foreign trade, also critical in Mesopotamia and always supported by its kings, enabled the nation to obtain commodities that could not be obtained at home and to increase its riches. Home trade was also useful, enabling mankind to "resign to others, at a fair price, those things which they have occasion for and which we do not destine for our own use" (86).

We may no longer be accustomed to thinking of highways, bridges, and canals as "Public Ways of Communication," but to Vattel, as it had been to Aquinas, one of the principal things requiring the government's attention, with respect to the welfare of the public in general, was care to make the public ways safe and commodious. "When therefore, the laying out and repairing of highways, bridges and canals would be too great a burthen on the ordinary revenues of the state, the government may oblige the people to labor at them" (102). The "people" of eighteenth-century Europe, therefore, were to be subjected to a forced physical labor from which privileged citizens of Babylon had been exempted thirty-five centuries before. Most of Babylon's inhabitants, however, were no better off than Vattel's contemporaries. Many of Hammurabi's letters to local governors stressed the necessity for maintaining the irrigation system. He ordered them to keep the channels open, install machines for irrigation, and build dams to control flood waters. For these tasks the governors were authorized "to conscript dwellers in any locality where a canal was blocked or overflowed to carry out whatever works of repair might be needed."[47]

Internal improvements undertaken with federal support began in the United States with the first Congress and were numerous and varied despite an apparent limitation on the federal taxing power posed by Art. I, Sect. 8 of the Constitution. That section provides Congress may levy taxes to "pay the Debts and provide for the Common Defense and general Welfare of the United States." For a century and a half the argument was made that improvements accruing to the greater benefit of particular states were unauthorized. Prominent objects of federal grants, nevertheless, made under Congress's power to control navigation, were the roads, canals, rivers, and harbors of the new nation. As James Madison had enthused in No. 14 of the Federalist Papers:

> *. . . the intercourse throughout the Union will be facilitated by new improvements. Roads will everywhere be shortened, and kept in better order; accommodations for travellers will be multiplied and meliorated [*Shulgi and Plato would have approved.*]; an interior navigation on our eastern side will be opened throughout . . . the whole extent of the thirteen States. The communication between the Western and Atlantic districts, and between different parts of each, will be rendered more and more easy by . . . numerous canals (102).*

The Supreme Court of the United States in 1936 brought the debate over the scope of the general welfare provision to an end and affirmed its decision subsequently in reviewing a California case that involved a dispute over water rights. California's Central Valley irrigation system today resembles in many ways the system installed during Hammurabi's time to make use of and control the flow of fresh water. Like the Tigris and Euphrates, California's two great rivers, the San

Joaquin and Sacramento, bisect an arid land. Fed by mountain streams far from the Taurus and Zagros ranges, the California rivers join shortly before passing into San Francisco Bay, as the Mesopotamian rivers meet before entering the Persian Gulf. Numerous dams and reservoirs, hundreds of miles of canals, laterals, and drains carry California's river waters wherever they will serve to greatest effect throughout the Central Valley's vast basin. Millions of irrigated acres produce harvests that are the wonder of the contemporary world, as the harvests of Mesopotamia were legendary in ancient times.

In 1950, the Supreme Court heard the case of riparian landowners on the San Joaquin River who demanded compensation when one of the Central Valley's dams deprived them of the river's natural seasonal overflow. In United States v. Gerlach Live Stock Co., 70 S.Ct. 955, 339 U.S. 725, 738 (1950), Justice Jackson noted that decisions of the Supreme Court after 1936 had finally established the power of Congress "to tax and appropriate for the general welfare, limited only by the requirement that it shall be exercised for the common benefit as distinguished from some mere local purpose," and he added that the power of Congress "to promote the general welfare through large-scale projects for reclamation, irrigation, or other internal improvement is now as clear and ample as its power to accomplish the same results indirectly." Thus Justice Jackson affirmed the power of the Congress of the United States to promote the general welfare of the American people by authorizing the same large-scale projects deemed necessary by Hammurabi to "make good the flesh" of the Babylonians.[48]

After emphasizing the need to provide for the "Necessities of the Nation," Vattel devoted a chapter to "Justice and Polity," in which he writes: "One of the principal duties of a nation relates to justice. They ought to employ their utmost attention in causing it to prevail in the state" (158). By enacting good laws, dictated by wisdom and equity and ensuring their execution, by establishing an independent judiciary, including supreme courts of justice where causes should be finally determined, by appointing judges distinguished for their integrity and knowledge, by rewarding the meritorious and punishing those who transgress, the sovereign, said Vattel, would satisfy his obligation to establish justice in his realm.

"Polity" included the obligation of the prince and magistrates, assisted by the internal police, to preserve everything in order. "Wise regulations ought to prescribe whatever will best contribute to the public safety, utility and convenience," and "by a wise police, the sovereign accustoms the people to order and obedience, and preserves peace, tranquillity and concord among the citizens" (174).

The third object of Vattel's good government was "to fortify itself against external attacks. . . . One of the ends of political society is to defend itself with its combined strength against all external insult or violence" (177). The nation should maintain its strength by increasing its population, as far as possible or convenient, by cultivating military virtues in its citizens, and by sustaining its power through the acquisition of public and private wealth in order to defray the immense expenses necessitated by war (180-82).

The Colonial Search for Precedent

While all other Sciences have advanced, that of Government is at a stand; little better understood; little better practiced now than 3 or 4 thousand years ago.—John Adams to Thomas Jefferson in *The Adams-Jefferson Letters*

When, in 1764, a precocious twelve-year-old Gouverneur Morris applied for admission to King's College in New York, his entrance examination required that he translate selections from Sallust, Caesar, and Cicero and convert portions of the Gospels from the Greek into Latin. Morris was embarking upon a typical Colonial collegiate agenda. Those of America's Founding Fathers who were educated in a formal curriculum were schooled in a tradition that emphasized the authority of Holy Scripture and the preeminence of the classics. Classical Greek and Roman models shaped Colonial minds, tastes, and manners. In American colleges, the language of Livy, Cicero, and Vergil was studied and spoken; prizes were awarded for proficiency in Latin composition. A knowledge of Latin became essential for social acceptance and professional advancement. Quotations from the classics graced and were sometimes forced into the speech and writing patterns of the day.

It was not always easy of course for an active politician to retain his proficiency in the ancient languages. With a candor characteristic of him, if not the age, John Adams described how, in his mature years, he sat down with his "Lexicons and Grammars" to translate "Dionissius Halicarnassis" and amused himself for some time, but found that "if I looked a Word today, in less than a week I had to look it again. It was to little better purpose than writing Letters on a pail of water" (Cappon, 350).

Artists, architects, poets and prose writers, clergymen, and literary stylists nevertheless drew inspiration from the genius of ancient Mediterranean states. Statesmen looked to the lawgivers and philosophers of Greece and Rome for precedent. Jefferson included Aristotle and Cicero as sources in his "elementary books of public right." The principles of the American Revolution, wrote John Adams, were "the principles of Aristotle and Plato, of Livy and Cicero."

If the experience of James Madison, a member of the Committee of Style and Arrangement and "Father" of the United States Constitution, be taken as typical, his early education included the study of Latin, Greek, and Hebrew. Although baptized in the Church of England, he practiced writing dialogues "in the Socratic manner" while attending the Presbyterian College of New Jersey at Princeton. There he also applied himself to theology, philosophy, and principles of government and formed an early acquaintance with the "tradition of political theory from Plato and Aristotle to the moderns."[49]

When Madison attended the College of New Jersey, the renowned Scottish divine John Witherspoon served as its President. A popular preacher, widely influential educator and statesman, member of the Continental Congress, and the only clergyman to sign the Declaration of Independence, Witherspoon taught moral philosophy, a subject that included jurisprudence, the law of nations, civil society, and political science. He lectured on the nature of ideal societies and criticized Plato and Sir Thomas More for implying that a perfect commonwealth might be realized on earth. Witherspoon "followed Aristotle's Politics very closely, distinguishing the noble forms of government dedicated to the public good from the perverted forms devoted to selfish, factional ends. Madison thereby acquired, at the core of his political education, a supreme foundation on the ends, not the means, of government."[50] In all, nine of the twenty-five college-bred delegates to attend the Constitutional Convention were graduates of the College of New Jersey.

Following service in the Continental Congress, the thirty-three-year-old Madison embarked upon a search for precedent to assist him in framing a more effective structure for a new republic. He asked his friend Thomas Jefferson, then in France, to forward "treatises on the ancient or modern foederal republics, on the law of Nations and the history, natural and political, of the New World."[51] As Irving Brant expressed it,

> *Home from his legislative duties in the late winter of 1785-6 he plunged at once into a study of ancient and modern confederacies. What were their elements of strength? of weakness? Why did the old ones fail? Why were the modern feeble? He took them up one at a time—the Lycian Confederacy, the Amphictionic, the Achaean, the Helvetic, the Belgic, the Germanic.*[52]

Madison's studies during this period have been called "probably the most fruitful piece of scholarly research ever carried out by an American."[53]

Weeks before the opening of the Federal Convention, John Adams published the first book, widely circulated, of a three-volume series entitled *A Defence of the Constitutions of Government of the United States of America.* Attempting to defend the various state constitutions against the attack of a former French minister, he reviewed all constitutions, ancient and modern, known at the time. In the course of his survey, Adams observed that in the fourth book of the *Republic,* Plato described a perfect commonwealth where "kings are philosophers and philosophers kings, where the laws govern and justice is established." There the children receive an education that produces "the virtues of fortitude, temperance, wisdom and justice in the whole city." The remainder of Adams's nineteen-page review of the *Republic* described the "revolutions" of the five governmental forms he found there—from the kingly, or aristocratic, through the Cretan, Spartan, or "ambitious" republic; oligarchy; democracy; and tyranny, the "last disease of a city."[54]

Madison had noted Adams's analysis months before the Preamble was drafted. In a letter to Thomas Jefferson, he remarked that Adams's publication had

> *excited a good deal of attention. . . . Men of learning find nothing new in it, Men of taste many things to criticize. And men without either, not a few things, which they will not understand. It will nevertheless be read, and praised, and become a powerful engine in forming the public opinion.*[55]

In the spring of 1787, Madison wrote to George Washington and called for a republic endowed with a strong central authority. He assigned to the militia the function of the *Republic*'s auxiliary guardians, the Akkadian *re/dum*, and the Sumerian *Ukus*: "The Militia ought to be placed in some form under the authority which is entrusted with the general protection and defence"; and "An Article should be inserted expressly guarantying the tranquility of the States against internal as well as external dangers."[56] This was done, and its new Constitution empowered the federal government to undertake the "Enlil functions" for the individual states.

Neither Thomas Jefferson nor John Adams participated directly in the Federal Convention, the former serving as Ambassador to France at the time, the latter as Ambassador to England. Both, in later correspondence, criticized Plato without reserve, unwilling to acknowledge the debt Western civilization and the Colonial American community owed the Greek philosopher. Their unsparing opinions nevertheless demonstrate that Plato's ideas and the concepts of the *Republic* attracted the attention of intellectuals of the Revolutionary era.

Jefferson, who found little that was edifying in Aristotle either, wrote often of Plato using Socrates' name to cover the whimsies of his own brain, of Plato's "mysticism and unintelligible jargon" incomprehensible to the human mind. Writing to John Adams, the sage of Monticello termed Plato's *Republic* the "heaviest task work" he had ever undertaken. He claimed that "while wading through the whimsies, the puerilities and unintelligible jargon of this work" he had often laid it down to ask himself how the world could have given reputation to such nonsense, and he wondered how an able and honest Cicero could have bestowed his eulogies upon Plato. Bringing Plato "to the test of reason," Jefferson concluded that he was a "genuine Sophist," who "has escaped the oblivion of his brethren, first by the elegance of his diction, but chiefly by the adoption and incorporation of his whimsies into the body of artificial Christianity" (Cappon, 433).

Jefferson continued in this vein for another page, and Adams, in his response, rejoiced that Jefferson had seriously read Plato and that his friend's reflections harmonized so perfectly with his own. Adams described his attempts to go through all of Plato's works, laboring through the "tedious toil" armed with Latin, English, and French translations; the result was disappointment, particularly with the *Republic,* astonishment and disgust. Adams admitted he learned two things from Plato: "1. that Franklin's Ideas of exempting Husbandmen and Mariners, etc. from the depredations of War were borrowed from him. 2. that Sneezing is a cure for Hickups" (Cappon, 437).

In their late correspondence, the two ex-Presidents returned frequently to their impatience with Plato's "foggy conceptions," until they died, within hours of each other, on July 4, 1826. It may be they had less to fear from a confrontation with their Maker than with the august shades of Marsilio Ficino, St. Augustine, and Marcus Tullius Cicero.

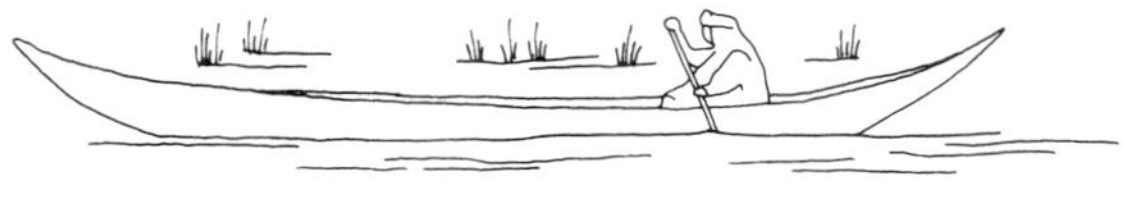

American Colonists of the eighteenth century who had studied the nonsectarian literature of political theory and read Plato's *Republic*, even in translation, were a small elite. Fewer than half the delegates to the Federal Convention were college graduates—however significant that circumstance may be. When Gouverneur Morris graduated from King's College, he was one of only seven students receiving a Bachelor of Arts degree. Those of the colonies' two and a half million inhabitants who were able to trace the Preamble's purposes back to Plato through secular sources constituted a very small minority. Many, however, were able to validate those purposes with Biblical precedents that had been impressed upon their hearts and burned into their consciences from birth.

---

[1] These ideas have been set out in a comprehensive study that lists, in chronological sequence, 27 Western writers, including all major thinkers from Greece of the fifth century B.C. to the European High Renaissance, who have written about the nature and role of a just ruler: Lester K. Born, *The Education of a Christian Prince* (c. 1936; New York: Columbia Univ. Press, 1964).

[2] Sir Ernest Barker, *The Politics of Aristotle* (London: Oxford Univ. Press, 1962), 2-7 n.B. The following citations in the text are from this edition.

[3] "He who commands that law should rule may thus be regarded as commanding that God and reason alone should rule; he who commands that a man should rule adds the character of the beast" (*Pol.*iii, 16.5).

[4] E.A. Speiser, "Authority and Law in Mesopotamia," *JAOS* Supp. 17:8-15, and Speiser, "Early Law and Civilization," 863. No institution or accepted measure short of rebellion was available, however, to restrain the excesses of ambitious Eastern kings. The only lawful means to relieve the people of the heavy curse of a wicked king, were, as James VI, I of England, later helpfully advised, "Patience, prayers to God and amendment of their lives" (*The Trew Law of Free Monarchies* [1598]).

[5] Jacobsen, "Primitive Democracy in Ancient Mesopotamia," 150; Jacobsen also refers to similar institutions amongst Teutonic tribes in Western Europe and the Homeric Greeks.

[6] E. Neufeld, *The Hittite Laws* (London: Luzac & Co. Ltd., 1951), 113 n.92, 115, 161 n.186.

[7] O.R. Gurney, *The Hittites* (New York: Penguin Books, 1966), 69.

[8] Compare Blackstone's description of the grandeur of George III's magistracy. The mass of mankind, he claimed,"will be apt to grow insolent and refractory if taught to consider their prince as a man of no greater perfection than themselves. The law therefore ascribes to the king . . . certain attributes of a great and transcendent nature; by which the people are led to consider him in the light of a superior being . . . .The law ascribes to the king, in his political capacity, absolute perfection . . . .The king is not only incapable of doing wrong but even of thinking wrong; in him is no folly or weakness" (Sir William Blackstone, *Commentaries on the Laws of England* [New York: W.E. Dean, 1850], I:241ff).

[9] Barker, *Politics of Aristotle,* lxi-ii.

[10] Cicero, who wrote of the wisdom and justice of Assyrian and Persian kings, was no stranger to the East. He had studied rhetoric and philosophy on the island of Rhodes when the Rhodian Sea-Law regulated maritime traffic in the eastern Mediterranean. Later, as governor of Cilicia, Cicero put down an insurrection in Cappadocia, where almost two millennia before, Assyrian merchants had established trading colonies.

[11] *The Adams-Jefferson Letters,* ed. Lester J. Cappon (Chapel Hill: The Univ. of North Carolina Press, 1988), 438. Subsequent citations in the text are from this Cappon edition.

[12] Saint Augustine, *The City of God*, ed. Vernon J. Bourke (Garden City, N.Y.: Doubleday & Co., Image Books, 1958), XIX.21.469. The following citations in the text are from this edition.

[13] Barker, *Greek Political Theory*, 445.

[14] W.P. Ker, *The Dark Ages,* cited by Barker in *Greek Political Theory,* 446.

[15] *On the Training of Princes*, Opera Omnia (Parma 1852-71) XVI, 224-90, as cited in Born, *Christian Prince,* 114-16.

[16] Born, *Christian Prince,* 118.

[17] W.D. McCracken, *The Rise of the Swiss Republic* (New York: H. Holt and Company, 1901), 87.

[18] It is not impossible that there was a direct European-Oriental communication. Archaeologists have traced trading connections between Central Europe and Syria back to the beginning of the second millennium B.C. The Swiss were, for certain, introduced to Mediterranean law at the point of the Roman gladius fourteen centuries before. In the thirteenth century A.D., the disclosures of returning Crusaders prompted a more immediate examination of Eastern learning and custom. Devout and landless European princes had for two hundred years gathered at Byzantium and marched through Western Anatolia down into the ancient trading centers of the Levant. Christian noblemen established fiefdoms in Syria and ruled Jerusalem for a period. Knights Templar formed banking institutions on both shores to finance the invasions. Ships that bore Western missionaries and military adventurers to and from the Orient observed Byzantine and Rhodian maritime regulations. When Eleanor of Aquitaine returned from the Holy Land a century before the Swiss League was formed, she ordered that collections of rules she came upon in the East be duplicated to aid Western mariners. Richard I is also reported to have installed a roll of judgments he brought with him from the Near East as law in England. Blackstone claims that all nations of Europe used Richard's laws as a basis of their maritime codes (*Commentaries* I:418).

[19] Edward G. Browne, *A Literary History of Persia* (New York: Charles Scribner's Sons, 1906), 176.

[20] Francesco Gabrielli, *Arab Historians of the Crusades* (New York: Dorset Press, 1957),91.

[21] Ibid., 87ff.

[22] Myron P. Gilmore, *The World of Humanism 1453-1517* (New York: Harper & Row Publishers, 1952), 8.

[23] *The Letters of Marsilio Ficino,* I:xxii.

[24] Baldesar Castiglione, *The Book of the Courtier* (1728), trans. Charles S. Singleton (Garden City, N.Y.: Anchor Books, 1959). Castiglione's treatment was translated and published in England in 1561 and was possessed by early settlers in America.

[25] Born, *Christian Prince*. Further quotes of Erasmus in this section are from the same edition: used by permission.

[26] Erasmus, *Praise of Folly and Letter to Martin Dorp,* 1515, trans. Betty Radice (New York: Penguin Books, 1983),99. The following citations in the text are from this edition.

[27] Jeremy Collier, *An Ecclesiastical History of Great Britain* (London: W. Straker, 1940-1), IX:89-93.

[28] *Utopia,* ed. Edward Surtz, S.J. (New Haven: Yale Univ. Press, 1964), Bk. I:39-48.

[29] Ibid., Bk. I:51-52.

[30] Joyce O. Hertzler, *The History of Utopian Thought* (New York: MacMillan Company, 1923), 99.

[31] Breen, *The Character of the Good Ruler*, 8.

[32] Blackstone, *Commentaries*, I:III:246.

[33] See Jerome Frank's sketch of Blackstone and the corruption of the age in "A Sketch of an Influence," in *Interpretations of Modern Legal Philosophies*, ed. Paul Sayre (New York: Oxford Univ. Press, 1947), 189.

[34] Edmund S. Morgan, *The Puritan Dilemma* (Boston: Little Brown & Company, 1958),25.

[35] A supposition that Hume noted was false (Green and Grose, *Hume's Philosophical Works*, III:117-118). See Forrest McDonald's discussion, *Novus Ordo Seclorum* (Lawrence: Univ. Press of Kansas, 1985), 187ff.

[36] *Selected Writings of Francis Bacon*, ed. Hugh G. Dick (New York: Modern Library, 1955), 137. Bacon learned to his sorrow that the ageless rules of judicial behaviour could not be safely ignored. As Lord Chancellor of England, he was impeached and imprisoned, briefly, for accepting bribes, thus giving offense to the ancient god of Justice: "You [*Shamash*] give the unscrupulous judge experience of fetters, Him who accepts a present and yet lets justice miscarry, you make bear his punishment" (*The Shamash Hymn*, [BWL, 121]).

[37] Douglass Adair, *Fame and the Founding Fathers*, ed. E. Trevor Colburn (New York: W.W. Norton and Co. Inc., 1974), 12.

[38] John Locke, *Two Treatises of Government*, ed. Peter Laslett (New York: Cambridge Univ. Press, 1960), Bk. II:3.

[39] Ibid., Bk. II:219. See quotes from Cicero and St. Augustine, pp. 113-14.

[40] Jonathan Swift, *Gulliver's Travels* (New York: Modern Library, 1958), 149-50.

[41] Ibid., 152.

[42] Colin Maclaurin, *An Account of Sir Isaac Newton's Philosophical Discoveries*, cited by Carl L. Becker in *The Heavenly City of The Eighteenth-Century Philosophers* (New Haven: Yale Univ. Press, 1932), 62.

[43] Ray Forrest Harvey, *Jean Jacques Burlamaqui* (Chapel Hill: Univ. of North Carolina Press, 1937), 16.

[44] William Winslow Crosskey, *Politics and the Constitution in the History of the United States* (Chicago: Univ. of Chicago Press, 1953), 147.

[45] Vattel, *The Law of Nations*, I:sect. 15. Following citations in the text are to section numbers in this edition.

[46] Frankfort, *Birth of Civilization in the Near East*, 61-62.

[47] Driver and Miles, *Babylonian Laws*, I:151 n.2.

[48] Thorkild Jacobsen describes the role of the Mesopotamian king as "defender, guardian of justice and controller of public works" (*Penguin Encyclopedia of Ancient Civilizations*, ed. Arthur Cottrell [New York: Penguin Books, 1980], 76).

[49] *Founding Fathers—Madison*, 20.

[50] Ralph Ketcham, *James Madison—A Biography* (New York: MacMillan, 1971), 43.

[51] *The Papers of James Madison*, eds. Robert A. Rutland and William J.E. Rachal, et al. vol. VIII (Chicago: Univ. of Chicago Press).

[52] Irving Brant, *James Madison—The Nationalist* (New York: Indianapolis: Bobbs-Merrill, 1941-61), 410.

[53] Douglass Adair, *The Lives of Eighteen from Princeton*, ed. Willard Thorp (Princeton: Princeton Univ. Press, 1946).

[54] John Adams, *A Defence of the Constitutions of the United States of America* (Philadelphia: Rudd and Bartram, 1797), 188-89.

[55] *Founding Fathers—Madison*, 132.

[56] Ibid., 110.

VII

THE BIBLE

The Puritans of New England

To the great majority of America's early settlers, the Bible was the Word of God. All truths necessary to man's salvation and the answers to all problems, political as well as doctrinal, were to be found there, expressed in an idiom comprehensible to any devout reader. The Puritans of New England, whose powerful voice was to be heard throughout the American colonies, conceived themselves to be spiritual successors to the Israelites of Exodus. They were a new chosen people, "choice grain," sifted by God from the nation, to be planted in the New World. He had

> *once again Essayed to take a people from the midst of a People and to lead them into a Wilderness to serve him . . . by a mighty Impulse upon their Spirits. [*He had*] moved them to forsake a Pleasant Land and the Native Country, their Father's Houses, their kindred and all that was dear to them therein and at vast Expence and Hazard to Transport themselves, their Wives and Little Ones, over the great and wide Sea, into a waste and howling Wilderness,*[1]

there to rebuild Jerusalem. Puritan leaders proposed to set their City on a Hill upon foundations of a modified Calvinistic theology; to seek express sanction for all daily activities in Biblical teaching, as clarified by John Calvin's *Institution of the Christian Religion.*

In the new land, clergymen called for the establishment of schools to promote and encourage the practice of religion, considering it fit that children given to God in baptism should be educated for him. They immersed the young in the still waters of Holy Scripture; a minimal standard required that children learn to read the Bible and write a legible hand. Zealous theologians prepared catechisms based upon the Ten Commandments, Biblical themes, and prayers. Most children learned at home, many under the tutelage of Scottish teachers respected for their mastery of the classics and their adherence to conservative Calvinistic principles. Higher education included the study of Hebrew, Jefferson's "very language of the divine communication," as well as Latin and Greek.

Religious organizations founded the first colleges, Harvard (1636), William and Mary (1693), and Yale (1701), as seminaries for the training of preachers. By the middle of the seventeenth century, Puritan families in England were beginning to send their sons to Harvard, distinguished early for its godliness, there "to be educated in a purer environment than they could find at Oxford and Cambridge."[2] The College of William and Mary, which later graduated Thomas Jefferson, sought to provide for the Anglican ministry what Harvard had for the Puritan. Yale, a "college remarkable for its persecuting spirit, its republican principles, its intolerance in religion and its utter aversion to Bishops and all Earthly Kings,"[3] was established to restore an orthodoxy from which Harvard was deemed to have strayed. Princeton (1746) produced ministers well grounded in the classics and Calvinist doctrine and could boast James Madison one of its eminent alumni. Dr. Samuel Johnson, father of a second member of the Committee of Style, a graduate of Yale and an ordained priest of the Church of England, served as the first President of King's College of New York (Columbia, 1754), a conservative school whose founders were sometimes charged with seeking to limit the further growth of republican principles.

Graduates of these and other Colonial colleges spread their readings of the Word of God through the colonies. Their sermons, heard from the pulpit or studied in print, had a profound effect upon American religious thought, political organization—and individual sensibilities. Revivalist preachers in the third and fourth decades of the eighteenth century terrified their congregations with graphic accounts of the tortures awaiting the depraved who abandoned God's commandments. It was said of the English missionary George Whitefield, known for his emotionalism, that he "could cause men to weep merely by the way he rolled the syllables of 'Mesopotamia' under his tongue."[4]

Although the fervor of orthodox religion in the founding colonies gradually abated under the persuasion of eighteenth-century rationalism, its influence, and particularly that of Calvin's instruction, remained a strong moral force in the developing wilderness. As New England Congregationalists moved west, through New York and down into the Ohio valley, they brought Calvin's teachings with them; the Scottish-Irish who pressed through the Cumberland Gap and into the present states of Kentucky and Tennessee were guided by his discipline. They were joined by

Germans from the Palatinate and emigrants from Switzerland, members of the reformed, or Calvinistic, branch of Protestantism. Calvin's views inspired the Dutch Reformed Church of New York, French Huguenots in South Carolina, and the believers of numerous smaller sects. "Even Anglicans owned and read Calvin's explanation of the Bible."[5]

Ralph Barton Perry has estimated that the entire population of the thirteen colonies in 1776 was about 2,500,000. Of these, approximately 1,135,000 were adherents of Calvinistic or closely allied sects, and 1,000,000 were Anglicans, half of whom were Negroes, nominally allied.[6] Calvin's discourse, and especially his exegesis of the Decalogue, provided a manual of simple Christian doctrine that shaped Colonial morality and the society erected on its prescriptions.

John Calvin and the Election-Day Sermons

In his *Institution of the Christian Religion*, first published in 1536, John Calvin affixed a short expository statement to each of the Ten Commandments, enlarging upon the bare letter of the provision. His communication was direct, plain, written to be understood, and compelling, in keeping with his belief that bishops and ministers should not adulterate the teaching of salvation, but deliver it pure and undefiled to God's people.

Concluding his analysis of the Tenth Commandment, Calvin explained why justice requires that the people obey and honor secular authority:

> *The rule that forbids us to covet another's possessions ought also to be applied in this way in order that each person may, according to his calling, perform his own tasks, and render to another what pertains to his office (Eph. 4). And he who does not bring forth from the gift of his own calling that which he gives to others, both covets and keeps another's belongings. For this reason a people should hold in honor its kings, princes and magistrates, and others in authority, patiently bearing their government, obeying their laws and commands, refusing nothing which can be carried out under God's will.*

Then Calvin set out the reciprocal obligation of the state and the goals of the Preamble in much the same terms as had Thomas More twenty years before (see p. 124, supra).

> *In turn, let the rulers take care of their own common people, render justice, keep the public peace and tranquillity. . . . In short, let them exercise authority as good shepherds over their sheep.*[7]

To hearten the deputies of God, Calvin reminded them that the judgment of princes must be left to Heaven: "He is God who will stand in the assembly of the gods, and will judge in the midst of gods" (Ps. 82:1), thereby invoking a Biblical passage with roots in the ancient Near East, where the world was traditionally ruled by an assembly of gods.

The Swiss theologian and reformer instituted a practice of delivering an annual sermon before the February election of syndics and other officials. In these sermons he stressed the necessity for choosing magistrates "with a pure conscience and without regard to anything but the honor and glory of God and the safety and defense of the republic."[8] Massachusetts and eventually all American colonies followed Calvin's lead, and stout-hearted speakers reminded chosen magistrates of their civic responsibilities in a stylized sermon preached annually on election day. The sermons were usually published, were studied by those who were literate, and were delivered from the pulpit for the benefit of all.

Election day in Colonial New England was "one of the Weightiest Occasions upon which a People Annually meet Together,"[9] a day likely to be celebrated by solemn processionals, led by the governor and political elite, the clergy, and eminent townspeople. Accompanied by an escort of militia and the music of a military band, these notables wound their way from Council Chamber to Meeting House; they caused cannons to be fired, held collations, and provided elegant entertainments. Gentlemen of rank dined with their Excellencies, the Governors, and drank toasts to their British Majesties.

In the Meeting House, a sermon, often preached by a member of the community chosen for social prominence as much as for religious station, highlighted the preelection ceremonies. The sermon opened with a statement of the Biblical text to be examined, announced a set of proofs for the doctrine under scrutiny and continued to an exposition of the uses and applications of the doctrine. Spokesmen emphasized the necessity and rightness of the civil and ecclesiastical cooperation that made the existing order possible. They reviewed matters of contemporary concern in the light of Biblical parallel; over and over, they described the conduct and attributes expected of civil rulers in terms and with citations from Holy Scripture that varied little in substance from sermon to sermon or year to year.

The following excerpts are from five New England election sermons preached during the first half of the eighteenth century and printed in Ronald Bosco's collection of *Connecticut and Massachusetts Election Sermons*. Extended a hundredfold, they demonstrate how justice, security, and the public welfare as the proper ends of civil government and the long-lived virtues of the good ruler were drummed into the consciousness of Colonial America.[10] Delegates to the Federal Convention, who had heard the sermons spoken and pored over them when published, found little that was unfamiliar in the Preamble presented to them on September 12, 1787.

***Good Rulers a Choice Blessing,* Azariah Mather**

"A good ruler must be a good man. . . . We read 2 Sam. 23:3, 'He that ruleth over men must be Just, Ruling in the fear of God.'" Knowledge and good Understanding, Prudence and Discretion, Courage and Resolution, an Anti-worldly and a Public Spirit, Activity and Zeal were all, according to Mather, qualifications of the Good Ruler. "The great subordinate End of Government is the Public good. . . . A Good Ruler is one that has a Compassionate Regard for those of his charge. Hence they are compared to Fathers and Nursing Mothers. Isaiah 49:23" (Bosco, 85).

***Moses and Aaron,* Thomas Buckingham**

". . . and let it be remembered by all that God is Leading his People to a state of Everlasting Happiness or Misery. GOD leads his people as . . . a Shepherd leads his sheep. . . . GOD is leading them to HEAVEN . . . and while they are in the way thither, they shall want for nothing." God was to provide the three great Ends of Government, "Wisdom and Counsel, Strength and Assistance, Prosperity and Success . . . Government, Protection and Refreshment" (Bosco, 137).

***God's Providence in Placing Men in their Respective Stations and Conditions,* William Burnham**

". . . a sincere aim at God's glory and the good of your people, which are the great Ends of Government." He described the type of men who should lead: "Let them be men of wisdom and good conduct. . . Men zealously bent for Justice, Men of Courage and Fortitude, Pious Godly men of a Generous Public Spirit . . . men who will be faithful to the Public Weal of the people." To the notables assembled he implored: "Let us behold in you not only power but wisdom and a Godlike goodness" (Bosco, 41).

***A Prospect of the City of Jerusalem,* Isaac Stiles**

"Civil Government is a choice and valuable Blessing of very high Importance to the Weal of a Republick. . . . The Government is on his shoulder, who is the Wonderful Counsellor, the Mighty God, the

Everlasting Father, the Prince of Peace. . . . So Moses . . . who had a princely education in the Court of the Pharaoh was inspired with Wisdom, Courage, Meekness, etc.," and all for the common "Safety and Welfare" (Bosco, 141).

***Civil Rulers the Ministers of God, for Good to Men,* Jonathan Todd**

"The publick Good is the great End and original Design of the Institution of civil Government." Power is given to civil rulers from above that they may "promote the Welfare of Mankind. . . . One end and design of civil government is to maintain the publick Peace. . . . Another is to protect men in the Enjoyment of their just Rights and Privileges." The honorable Gentlemen of the General Assembly must "attend upon this very Thing, even to promote the welfare of this People . . . and enact such Laws as shall be the best calculated to preserve the public Peace" (Bosco, 253).

In *The Americans—The Colonial Experience,* Daniel J. Boorstin makes the point that early New England Puritans were the least speculative of theologians. Armed with a rigid orthodoxy, they were determined that accepted doctrine be applied at every stage in the founding of the city, their Zion. The sermon, plain styled as Calvin had recommended, was the principal means of instruction available for their purposes. To the Puritan, Boorstin writes, "The sermon was as important a ritual as the occasions on which ancient Mesopotamians learned from their priests the dooms passed in the legislature of their Gods."[11]

Boorstin's observation prompts an interesting comparison. The ritual of Colonial election-day ceremonies had many features in common with the ancient *akitu* festivals, which saw the public humiliation of proud Babylonian kings. Both events celebrated the reelection or reinvestment of the temporal authority, whose performance, at least theoretically, was reviewed by the priesthood. The standards by which the ruler was judged were similar; he was expected to be wise, just, moderate, courageous, pious, and zealous. Both occasions featured stately processionals, public participation, feasting and rejoicing, but were, in the end, merely formalistic—the Colonial magistrate was reelected, the Babylonian king reinvested. The tone and effect of the two celebrations differed, however, because Colonial clergymen lacked the organization and wealth of Babylonian temples and were dependent for their subsistence upon grants by the community's great men. They usually closed the election sermon with a plea for a more generous allowance.

Mesopotamian Parallels

Impressions of ancient cylinder seals recovered at Susa depict storers of grain standing at the tops of ladders, emptying their sacks into high cylindrical silos. Grain stored in this manner was of necessity commingled, the identity of each deposit being lost in the common mass. So, too, the influences of Mesopotamia upon the thought, customs, literary compositions, and laws of the peoples to the west have been so absorbed into the end product that it becomes a moral impossibility to separate and identify those contributions with certainty. Scholars have nevertheless done much to trace the effects of the earlier civilization upon the later.

"Biblical legend (especially concerning primeval times)," says Yehezkel Kaufmann, "law (especially the Covenant Code, Exod. 20:19-23:33), hymnody and wisdom literature are manifestly indebted to Mesopotamia."[12] Similarities between Babylonian Creation and Flood accounts and the Book of Genesis were first recognized at the end of the nineteenth century, and a large body of authority today testifies to explicit parallels that exist between Mesopotamian writings and portions of the Old Testament. One example is the familiar story of the baby Moses being set adrift upon the river in order to save his life: ". . . she took for him a basket made of bulrushes and daubed it with bitumen and pitch; and she put the child in it and placed it among the reeds at the river's brink" (Ex. 2:3). Its Mesopotamian analogue is a similar tale, long known, told by Sargon the Great (ca. 2300 B.C.), founder of the Dynasty of Akkad, who recalled that when his life was threatened, "My mother, the high priestess . . . set me in a basket of rushes, with bitumen she sealed the lid. She cast me into the river which rose not (over) me. The river bore me up and carried me to Akki, the drawer of water" (ANET, 119).

The Bible reaches back to the most ancient sources. In *The Sumerians,* Kramer discusses in detail fifteen major themes that occur in both Sumerian literature and the Bible. He explains that Sumerian writings made a deep impression upon the literary product of the entire Near East, for, in the very process of learning and adopting the Sumerian cuneiform script, Babylonian, Canaanite, and other western peoples were trained in the Sumerian language and literature.

The ideas and ideals of the Sumerians—their cosmology, theology, ethics and system of education—permeated to a greater or lesser extent the thoughts and writings of all the peoples of the ancient Near East. . . . And the Hebrews of Palestine, the land where the books of the Bible were composed, redacted and edited, were no exception.[13]

Numerous articles, treatises, and books have been devoted to the study of the points of contact between the Old Testament and the inscriptions of Babylon. The Biblical term *torah,* law, corresponds to the Babylonian *kittum u misharum,* Speiser notes, and he emphasizes that the peak of Biblical law was reached, not in Palestine, but in the Babylonian Talmud, which teems with Akkadian and Sumerian loan words.[14]

Winged, human-headed lion and bull figures from Assyria (8th century B.C.)

The books of the Bible adapted Sumerian symbolism as well as its literature and law. Each of the four cherubim accompanying God's chariot-throne in Ezekiel's vision (1:5-10) had four faces, that of a man in front, a lion on the right side, an ox on the left, and an eagle at the back. The man, lion, bull (ox), and eagle were ancient Sumerian symbols, unified by Assyrian sculptors who carved colossal winged and human-headed bulls and lions from single blocks of stone and installed their figures at the gates and palaces of Assyrian cities.

This tetramorph later came to represent the four Evangelists in Christian iconography; Romanesque churches of twelfth-century Europe often used the tetramorph in painting or sculpture to demonstrate the supreme wisdom and power of an enthroned Christ.[15] Christian symbology depicts St. Matthew as the man of the tetramorph, representing "the human nature of Christ, the Incarnation"; Mark as the "winged lion roaring in the desert," the "royal dignity of Christ"; Luke a winged ox or calf as the "sacrifice, the atonement and priesthood of Christ"; and John an eagle "as 'one who can gaze on the sun,' (Jerome), the Ascension and the divine nature of Christ."[16]

symbols of the Evangelists were a popular motif in the early Italian Renaissance. Donatello t magnificent bronze reliefs of the ancient winged figures for the High Altar in the Santo at lua (ca. 1450).

A copper-sheathed wooden lintel from a Sumerian temple (ca. 2500 B.C.). Imdugud, the benevolent lion-headed eagle-god, watches over two stags.

The Christian tetramorph is nowhere more beautifully nor more bountifully illustrated than in the eighth-century manuscript *The Book of Kells* (ca. 750 A.D.), presently maintained at Trinity College, Dublin. *The Book of Kells* is filled with brilliant illuminations of the Evangelist symbols, representing "four stages of the life of Christ; birth, death, resurrection and ascension to heaven . . . a man in his birth, a calf in his dying, a lion in his resurrection, an eagle in his ascending,"[17] i.e., Man represents the Nativity; the Calf, the Crucifixion; the Lion, the Resurrection; and the Eagle, the Ascension.

These animal symbols have been interpreted in many ways throughout the religions and philosophies of the world. If a contemporary

These large baked clay lions, placed at temple entrances in Eshnunna (ca. 1900 B.C.), demonstrate that when it suited their purpose, sculptors of the time fashioned menacing guardian figures.

reading is attributed to ancient Sumer, the man represented rationality, intelligence, and wisdom; the bull or lion, strength and courage; the ox, suffering, patience, labor, and agriculture. The representation of the ox is most significant, for it suggests the means by which early man acquired possessions and, eventually, wealth. The eagle soared and the lion roared, untamed and uncontrolled, beyond the reach of man, but the castrated bull became an animated machine, providing him with the drawing power necessary to cultivate large areas and transport his produce when harvested.

The eagle, prominent in Sumerian and American symbolism, is generally identified with the sun, and as such, is the spiritual, male-fertilizing, father principle, associated with the gods of power and war. A Sumerian chalice shows an eagle with the forepaws of a lion, representing "the firmament—the upper, celestial, ethereal realm . . . the champion of Heaven."[18] Churchmen see the eagle, correspondent between heaven and earth, as prayer ascending and grace descending. (So childless Etana, seeking the plant of birth in Sumerian mythology, rode to heaven on the back of an eagle. His poem fails to disclose the gods' response to Etana's plea, but other records indicate he was, indeed, blessed with a son and heir; Etana's prayer, therefore, may have been answered.)

When Assyrian artisans adopted Sumerian symbology for their imposing stone creatures, were those colossi only guardians, genii, or protectors as they are commonly called?[19] If so, they were remarkably restrained and nonthreatening depictions. As a guardian, a fierce-eyed lion, charging "with wide-open mouth," or bull attacking, head lowered, horns ready to gore, might have been more suitable. It is conceivable that an ancient Mesopotamian, familiar with Sumerian hymnology, on approaching an Assyrian city or palace saw this *lamassu*, or bull-figure, as more than

Human head of winged lion "guardian," p. 146. Guardian-philosopher king?

a mere defending sentinel. To him, the human head, encased in its multi-horned cap, an accepted god-signal, represented divine wisdom; the great bulk of the bull, power; and that same figure, as an ox, great abundance. Even as the bird-god Imdugud had tied together the tails of earthly and heavenly deer, the wings of the bull-figure implied a linking of the terrestrial and celestial, the reconciliation or harmony between earthly powers and forces of the cosmos implicit in his understanding of *kittum u mesharum.* To the Mesopotamian, the stone hybrid-creatures were monumental declarations of political intent, promising justice, security, and welfare at the city gates and announcing the presence of a wise, just, powerful, and pious ruler within the palaces they glorified.

The explanatory text to Henry's *The Book of Kells* raises the distinct and surprising possibility that there may have been an uninterrupted flow of this angel-animal symbology from the most ancient times to the modern era. His commentary makes clear that Near Eastern belief influenced pages of the original *Book of Kells* and other Insular manuscripts, for those documents display "extraordinary similarities" in color, lay-out, patterns, and interlacings, to manuscripts of early Christian Egypt. As Henry explains: "Traces of an extensive [*waterborne*] trade between the Near East and the coasts of Ireland, Scotland, and England [*as early as the fifth century*] have been found in quantity in the last decades."[20]

The Laws

The correspondence between a number of the laws of Moses and sections of the Code of Hammurabi is well known. As the Babylonian conceived that the law had been received by his king from the Sun-god Shamash, the Israelites believed their law was received by Moses directly from God and was revealed by him to them. In Ex. 22:21-27, the God of Israel replaced the familiar figure of the Mesopotamian king as defender of the defenseless, the poor, the widow, and the orphan. In Ex. 22:22-24, He warned: "You shall not afflict any widow or orphan. If you do afflict them and they cry out to me, I will hear their cry; and my wrath will burn, and I will kill you with the sword, and your wives shall become widows and your children fatherless." The origin of the *lex talionis* of Ex. 21:23-25, is often attributed to Hammurabi.

Less well known are the similarities between Biblical law and earlier Mesopotamian legal codes. Drafted perhaps two centuries before Hammurabi's Code, #12 and #13 of the Laws of Eshnunna, dealing with crimes committed at night, #24 with kidnapping, and #36 and #37 with the liability of a bailee have explicit counterparts in Ex. 22:2-3, 21:16, and 22:7-8, respectively. To illustrate the correspondence between the

Laws of Eshnunna and Exodus:

> LE #53: *If an ox gores an(other) ox and causes (its) death, both ox owners shall divide (amongst themselves) the price of the live ox and also the equivalent of the dead ox.*
>
> Ex. 21:35: *When one man's ox hurts another so that it dies, then shall they sell the live ox and divide the price of it; and the dead beast they shall also divide.*

Relatively unknown is the important Sippar tablet, Si 277, discovered in 1979, which revealed for the first time the first six laws of the Law Code of Ur-Nammu. These merit comparison with the last of the Ten Commandments.

Various faiths arrange and enumerate the laws of the great Decalogue differently. John Calvin, the ascendant religious voice of the American Colonial period, justified his designation:

> *The Ten Commandments of the law were divided into two Tables (Ex. 32:15, 34:1, Deut. 10:1). The first table includes the first four commandments, which instruct us in what we owe God; . . . the second table comprises the six remaining commandments which explain love and duties of love to be practiced, for God's sake, toward our neighbor (Inst., 1:16).*

Calvin explained that "beyond the common form accepted almost everywhere," he included four commandments on the first table; i.e., he included idolatry (later punishable by death in New England) as a second commandment and considered as one those numbered ninth and tenth by the Roman and Lutheran Churches. "Honor your father and your mother," the first commandment of the second table, usually numbered fourth, was, to Calvin, the fifth commandment.

In the Prologue, immediately after announcing that he had procured the freedom of the sons and daughters of Sumer and Akkad, Lipit-Ishtar anticipated the command of Exodus 20:12, to honor one's parents: "I made the father support his children (and) I made the children [support their] father; I made the father sta[nd by hi]s children, (and) I made the children stand by their father" (ANET, 159). Lipit-Ishtar did not claim to have prescribed the duty of father and child to support one another; he stated that he enforced an apparently already existing obligation. The tradition of a mutual parent-child obligation to respect one another was deep-seated in the Near East.

An old Babylonian phrase book, composed in Nippur, contains a series of formulas called *ana ittišu,* which were used to train scribes. They are bilingual—Sumerian promulgations, accompanied by Akkadian translations. Their age is uncertain. Four laws included on the seventh tablet of the series read: (i) "If a son says to his father 'Thou art not my father,' he may shave him, he may put the slave-mark on him (and) sell him." (ii) "If a son says to his mother 'Thou art not my mother,' they shall shave half his head and lead him round the city and put him out of the house." (iii) "If a father says to his son, 'Thou art not my son,' he forfeits house and wall." (iv) "If a mother says to her son, 'Thou art not my son,' she forfeits house and furniture."[21]

The offenses dealt with by four of the five (or six) remaining commandments of the second table (Ex. 20:13, 14, 15, and 16) had already been proscribed by the Law Code of Ur-Nammu:

LU #1. *That day* *If a man* *commits a murder* *that man is to be killed.*	Ex. 20:13 *You shall not kill.*

(The principle of *lex talionis,* previously thought to have originated with Hammurabi, may prove to have been the first rule.)

LU #2. *If a man commits robbery*[22] *he will be killed.*	Ex. 20:15 *You shall not steal.*
LU #7. *If the wife of a young man* *of her own inclinations* *goes behind a man* *and sleeps in his lap,* *that woman they shall slay,* *that man, they shall set him* *free.*	Ex. 20:14 *You shall not* *commit adultery.*
LU #25. *If a man came forward* *as a witness (in a law suit)* *and was shown to be a* *perjurer, he shall pay fifteen* *shekels of silver.*[23]	Ex. 20:16 *You shall not* *bear false* *witness.*

Murder, robbery, adultery, and false witness, four of the "moral" commandments of the second table of the Decalogue, as distinguished from the "religious" commandments of the first, were unequivocally condemned in the first Sumerian law code. In Colonial America, interdiction of those very offenses provided a justification for its catechisms and the basis for its laws and way of life they validated. John Calvin explained that "all laws tend to the same end. For together, with one voice, they pronounce punishment against those crimes which God's eternal law has condemned, namely, murder, theft, adultery and false witness" (*Inst.* 6:49). And for the followers of Martin Luther, as well, law, "whether natural, moral or civil," is "all embodied in the ten commandments, and anything else is merely administrative regulation, whether in state or church."[24]

Unlike the provisions of Ur-Nammu's code, which dealt with actions only and did not purport to address state of mind, the last commandment of Exodus, 20:17, sometimes divided into two, reaches into the human heart and condemns evil thoughts and desires: "You shall not covet your neighbor's house; you shall not covet your neighbor's wife." This commandment must be considered in light of a long and evocative hymn to Shamash recovered from Assurbanipal's library at Nineveh. Difficult to date, the composition, containing elements that may be old Babylonian, appears to have been a popular text of the late Assyrian period. It offers a Mesopotamian parallel to Exodus 20:17:

A man who covets his neighbor's wife will (. . .) before his appointed day. A nasty snare is prepared for him. (. . .) Your weapon will strike at him, and there (will be) no one to save him. (His) father will not stand for his defence, and at the judge's command his brothers will not plead. He will be caught in a copper trap that he did not foresee (BWL, 121).

This fundamental catalogue of man's sins against his neighbor was sufficiently novel in Greece during the eighth century B.C. to merit repeating. Although Hesiod apparently felt it unnecessary to counsel his brother that murder was wrong, as Hammurabi had declined to include a general condemnation of murder in his code, the Greek poet in his "Works and Days" denounced other offenses of the second table. He advised Perses to "turn his foolish mind from other men's possessions," that "money should not be seized," that the gods will "blot out" the man who acquires wealth "by force of hands or through his lying tongue," that he who "sleeps with his brother's wife. . . angers Zeus," and that the man who picks quarrels and "attacks his father at the threshold of old age. . . will in the end pay a harsh penalty for his sins."[25]

Turning to man's relationship with the Divine, the subject of the Decalogue's first table, Hesiod urged his brother to resort to the very measures petitioners of Sumer had taken to seek favor with their gods, to "sacrifice to the immortal gods with reverence and ritual cleanliness, and burn the glorious thigh-bones; please the gods with incense and libations . . . that they may favor you"[26]

The True Fatherland

The point has been made lately that those who idealize a ruler as a good shepherd fail to consider why and to what end the shepherd tends his flock. Men from before Gilgamesh, however, have always understood that sheep were to be shorn and eventually slaughtered, a realization implicit in the metaphor, which treats the shepherd simply as guardian, without regard to motive or ultimate purpose. The Babylonian was not thinking of a butcher when he said, "A people without a king (is like) sheep without a shepherd" (BWL, 230).

To call Mesopotamian kings "Warrior-Judges," as is done, is to overlook a major responsibility of the crown. The king who provides security and just decisions alone affords little comfort to a starving population. If we accept the observation of Thomas Aquinas that the state is merely a substitute for the physiological organs of defense and acquisition, the defensive, blocking arm of Prologue and Preamble is readily apparent in their security purposes. The concomitant obligation of the other arm, however, to make good the flesh of the people, carries within it a bluntly aggressive mandate to acquire whatever is needed, however mollified, subsequently, by the "general welfare" phrasing. The paternal duty of the ruler to establish justice terminated at the state's border; his duty to provide did not.

John Calvin, the "Father of America," described the ruler's role as shepherd-father:

> *But since we have been so far describing a magistrate who truly is what he is called, that is, a father of his country, and, as the poet expresses it, shepherd of his people, guardian of the peace, protector of righteousness and avenger of innocence—he who does not approve of such a government must rightly be regarded as insane (Inst.,* 6:54).

Calvin's poet could not have known that by the end of the third millennium B.C., the magistrate-shepherd comparison had been made by the Sumerians. His description of a loving ruler was first symbolically represented by the shepherd's staff held as part of his royal insignia by An, the Sumerian god of Heaven. The metaphor became conventional for An's earth-bound successors.

Etana, the half-legendary Sumerian king, who may actually have ruled at the beginning of the third millennium, has been called "an abiding cultural stereotype whereby the Mesopotamian king is the 'shepherd of the great people' and hence responsible to his own master for the welfare of the flock."[27] The nobles of Uruk voiced their displeasure and alarm when, early in his epic, Gilgamesh failed to display the pastoral disposition they had expected. Gudea of Lagash acquired a wide reputation as the "good shepherd." Shulgi's hymns repeatedly named him *sipa zi*, or righteous shepherd; Lipit-Ishtar's eulogies made him the wise, the leading shepherd; Hammurabi was always the king to whom Marduk committed the shepherding of the black-headed people.

The image of leader as father appears, again and again, in the Old Testament, beginning in Genesis, where Jabal was the father of those who dwelt in tents and of such as had cattle; his brother Jubal, father of all those who played the lyre and the harp. There the Lord God selected Abraham to be the father of a multitude of nations, that he might charge his children to keep the way of the Lord by doing righteousness and justice. He later more than once threatened woe to the shepherd-kings of Israel who neglected the sheep of His pasture and allowed them to be dispersed and destroyed. God was the Good Shepherd who would gather them up. "I myself will be the shepherd of my sheep," said the Lord, "I will seek the lost and I will bring back the strayed and I will bind up the crippled and I will strengthen the weak and the fat and the strong I will watch over; I will feed them in justice. . . . I will set over them one shepherd, my servant, David, and he shall feed them and be their shepherd" (Ezek. 34:15,16,23).

The opening of David's 23rd Psalm, which describes the pastoral-paternal role so eloquently, echoes the voice of the great sovereign of Babylon, when Hammurabi spoke in the prologue and epilogue to his code, not as the raging terror of his enemies, but as the father of his people:

Psalm 23:1-2: *The Lord is my shepherd. . .*
He makes me lie down in green pastures
Hammurabi: *The shepherd called by Enlil am I* (ANET, 164 [50]).
[I] *made the people rest in friendly habitations* (ANET, 178 [36]).
Sum. proverb: *A foreigner's ox eats plants, one's own ox lies in green pastures.*
Akkadian Prophecy: *The cattle* [will lie down] *in green pastures.*[28]
Psalm 23:3: *He leads me in the paths of righteousness.*
Hammurabi: [He] *guides the people aright. . .establishes law and justice in the land* (ANET, 165 [14-18]).

The father-shepherd comparison appears again in the third title of the Messianic king described in the Book of Isaiah, 9:2-7 and 11:1-9. These verses, completed in the middle of the fourth century B.C., although thought to have been begun centuries before as a coronation ode to a Judean king, describe the future king in terms remindful of ancient Mesopotamia. In Isaiah 9:6, the qualities ascribed to the king in his titles make the coming reign of peace possible: "For to us a child is born, to us a son is given; and the government will be upon his shoulder, and his name will be called, 'Wonderful Counselor, Mighty God, Everlasting Father, Prince of Peace.' "

The Reverend J.R. Dummelow interprets the first title, "Wonderful Counselor," as implying "that the future king's rule shall be guided by a divinely inspired wisdom," thus aligning Isaiah with Eastern tradition.[29] The Just, Wise, and Learned Lipit-Ishtar was also the "Counsellor of great judgment," to whom the god Enki gave broad wisdom.[30] The wisdom of Eastern kings as a beneficence of the gods was a staple of royal eulogies, at least from the reign of Shulgi to the sixth century B.C., when the Achaemenid Darius acknowledged Ahuramazda as the source of his wisdom.

Isaiah 11:2 records six "Gifts of the Spirit," characteristics of Israel's great men, which the Messiah will manifest: "And the spirit of the Lord shall rest upon him, the spirit of wisdom and understanding, the spirit of counsel and might, the spirit of knowledge and fear of the Lord." ("Wisdom and Justice were traditionally associated with the ideal king" [RSV note].)

In 1 Kings 3:6-9, Solomon prays to the Lord for guidance: "Thou hast shown great and steadfast love to thy servant, David, my father, because he walked before thee in faithfulness, in righteousness. . . . Give thy servant therefore an understanding mind to govern thy people, that I may discern between good and evil." The Lord replies, bestowing wisdom upon Solomon: "Because. . . you have asked for yourself understanding to discern what is right, behold I now do according to your word, Behold, I give you a wise and discerning mind" (1 Kings 3:11-12). "And God gave Solomon wisdom beyond measure and largeness of mind like sand on the seashore so that Solomon's wisdom surpassed the wisdom of all the people to the east and all the wisdom of Egypt" (1 Kings 4:29-30).

To the Hebrew, as to the Sumerian, it is the ruler's divinely inspired wisdom, manifested in his wise decisions, that assures his domain will be founded in justice. In Solomon's Psalm 72, "Give the king thy justice, O God, and thy righteousness to the royal son! May he judge thy people with righteousness and thy poor with justice!" the wise and just king defends the poor, the needy, and the oppressed. His foes bow down before him. His dominion extends from the Euphrates to the ends of the earth. There is an abundance of grain in the land; its fruit is like Lebanon's; the mountains bear prosperity for the people.

God's wisdom is also seen in Solomon's judgment, 1 Kings 3:28, deciding the fate of the child claimed by the two harlots: "And all Israel heard the judgment which the king had rendered and they stood in awe of the king, because they perceived that the wisdom of God was in him to render justice." So, too, Prov. 1:2-3, "That men may know wisdom and instruction, understand words of insight, receive instructions in wise dealing, righteousness, justice and equity," and Prov. 8:15, "By me kings reign and rulers decree what is just." (A note to this chapter explains that "a divine gift of wisdom is needed by rulers to govern well, do justice and maintain the right" [RSV].)

After pronouncing the divine titles, Isaiah 9:7 declares that the wisdom of the Wonderful Counselor will bring justice "upon the throne of David and over his kingdom, to establish it and to uphold it with justice and righteousness from this time forth and evermore."

Isaiah's second title, "Mighty God," ensures that the future king of Israel will be armed with the strength, made legitimate by divine sanction, to compel the obedience of his subjects when necessary and to defend them from external attack.[31] As Colonial America believed the "Author of Nature" to be the ultimate source of political power, so the Sumerian conceived that the ruler's right to command descended from the gods.

The necessity for divine endorsement of political power became a fundamental acceptance in Mesopotamia. Following mythological precedent, wherein the goddess Inanna sought the blessing of An and Enlil upon her selection of Ur-Ninurta as shepherd over all the people, Sumerian kings, upon their accession to the throne, traditionally sought the benediction of Father Enlil and other gods, either through the intercession of the tutelary deities of their cities, or by direct appeal. In this manner, Shulgi and Ishme-Dagan received the approval of their gods.[32] Ur-Nammu ruled by the grace of Utu, the Sumerian Sun-god, overseer of the moral order. An and Enlil called Lipit-Ishtar, possessed of princely power, to the princeship of the land; he had as his powerful guard Ninurta, god of the south wind; the god Nuska enforced his decisions. So too, lofty Anum, king of the Annunaki, and Enlil named Hammurabi, the powerful son and heir of Sun-muballit, to put into effect the purposes of his government.[33]

Ningišzida, Gudea's personal deity, introduces the prince of Lagash to the god Enki (from Gudea's cylinder seal).

The "shepherd-father" metaphor is omnipresent. This third title connotes a "continuing fatherly love and care," according to the RSV note, and Dummelow explains that the Messiah is called "Father" because of "the protecting care exercised by him over his people." In Babylon, the "shepherd" Hammurabi anticipated countless icons and portraits when he declared that he carried the peoples of Sumer and Akkad in his bosom. The image reappears throughout the Old Testament: Isaiah 40:11, "He will feed his flock like a shepherd, he will gather the lambs in his arms, he will carry them in his bosom." And in Numbers 11:12, Moses complains to the Lord, "Did I conceive all this people? Did I bring them forth that thou shouldst say to me, 'Carry them in your bosom'? "

The last majestic title is "Prince of Peace," or as the RSV notes, "The king who brings peace and prosperity." This title looks to the transcendent reign of the prince who has restored Paradise, when, according to Sumerian mythology, "The lion kills not, / The wolf snatches not the lamb, / Unknown is the kid-devouring wild dog."[34]

The Wisdom, Power, and Love of the coming Messiah presages the advent of Isaiah's idyllic world: a God-given wisdom to administer justice; the power, validated by divine authority, to defend the nation from domestic and foreign violence; and a fatherly love and concern to assure the economic well-being and prosperity of his people. In Colonial America these qualities, and their objectives, descended in an unmeasurable degree from Mesopotamian originals, and, reinforced by the repetitive sermons of the day, inspired devout readers of Holy Scripture, although John Adams, that forthright son of Harvard, struggled with the idea when he wrote to Thomas Jefferson:

Plato's system was 'Agathos' ("good") eternal Self existent, etc. His Ideas, his word, his Reason, his Wisdom, his Goodness, or in one word, his 'Logos' was omnipotent and produced the Universe from all Eternity.

Now! As far as You and I can understand Hersey, Price and Plato are they not of one Theory? What is the difference? I own, an eternal Solitude of a Self-existent Being, infinitely wise, powerful and good is to me altogether incomprehensible and incredible (Cappon, 375).

In the prayer of the New Testament, the state envisioned by the purposes of the Preamble is the Pater Noster fulfilled, the kingdom of God, bringing justice, peace, and plenty, established on earth. "Thy kingdom come" (Matt. 6:10), according to Rev. Dummelow, means, "May justice triumph over injustice, truth over error, kindness over cruelty, purity over lust, peace over enmity." And, he notes, in Matt. 6:11 we are not "taught to pray for luxuries," but rather to ask that God "Give us this day our daily bread"[35]—the American equivalent of the bread made from the blessed pride of the barley, baked in the shrines and tasted in the homes of Sumer when the name of man was fixed.

---

[1] "Moses and Aaron - God's Favor to his Chosen People," A Discourse by Thomas Buckingham, A.M. 1728, in Ronald A. Bosco, *Connecticut and Massachusetts Election Sermons* (New York: Scholar's Facsimiles & Reports, 1978), 137.

[2] Louis B. Wright, *The Cultural Life of the American Colonies* (New York: Harper Torchbooks, 1957), 117.

[3] Thomas Jones, *History of New York During the Revolutionary War* (New York: New York Historical Society, 1879), 5.

[4] Wright, *Cultural Life,* 94.

[5] Ibid., 139.

[6] Ralph Barton Perry, *Puritanism and Democracy* (New York: Vanguard Press, 1944), 80.

[7] John Calvin, *Institution of the Christian Religion,* trans. Ford Lewis Battles (Atlanta: John Knox Press, 1975), Chap. 1: 37. Further citations of Calvin in this chapter are from this edition.

[8] John T. McNeill, *History and Character of Calvinism* (London: Oxford Univ. Press, 1954), 187.

[9] Bosco, "Moses and Aaron," Buckingham, 137.

[10] Daniel J. Boorstin notes that in addition to the Sabbath sermons of New England at which attendance was mandatory, almost any public event—the muster of the Militia, Fast and Thanksgiving days, the hanging of a murderer—provided an opportunity to instruct the faithful by way of an appropriate sermon; he adds that the sermons had additional drawing power for New England Puritans because of the scarcity of other amusements (Boorstin, *The Americans - The Colonial Experience* [New York: Vintage Books, 1964], 12-14).

[11] Ibid., 12-13.

[12] Kaufmann, *Religion of Israel*, 220.

[13] Kramer, *The Sumerians*, 291.

[14] Speiser, "Early Law and Civilization," 876.

[15] André Parrot, *The Arts of Assyria* (New York: Golden Press, 1961), 206.

[16] J.C. Cooper, *An Illustrated Encyclopaedia of Traditional Symbols* (London: Thames and Hudson, 1978), 170.

[17] Francoise Henry, *The Book of Kells* (New York: Alfred A. Knopf, 1974), 198.

[18] Heinrich Zimmer, *Myths and Symbols of Indian Art and Civilization* (Princeton: Princeton Univ. Press, 1992), 73.

[19] The oft-cited authority of Ezekiel 28:14 and 16 will not support the cherubim as guardians. Those verses refer to a single guardian cherub, i.e., one aspect, the power, of the divine nature.

[20] Henry, *Book of Kells*, 213-14.

[21] Driver and Miles, *Babylonian Laws,* II:309.

[22] The nature of the Sumerian offense is, perhaps, more limited in scope than the "stealing" of Ex. 20:15, see Appendix, Exhibit C, "The Earliest Laws of Conversion" (200-201)." As to Biblical terminology for theft and robbery, see Raymond Westbrook, *Studies in Biblical and Cuneiform Law* (London: J. Gabalda, 1988), 15-38.

[23] LU #1, LU #2, and LU #7 are from Yildiz, "Animadversiones"; LU #25 is from J.J. Finkelstein, "The Laws of Ur-Nammu" *JCS,* 22 (Oct.-Dec. 1969):66.

[24] Martin Luther, quoted in J.N. Figgis, *From Gerson to Grotius.*

[25] *Hesiod and Theognis,* Wender edition, ll. 314-34.

[26] Ibid., ll. 334-42.

[27] Speiser, "Authority and Law in Mesopotamia," 17:9.

[28] Grayson and Lambert, "Akkadian Prophecies," 14.

[29] *A Commentary on the Holy Bible,* ed. The Rev. J.R. Dummelow (New York: Macmillan Publishing Co. Inc., 1936), 421.

[30] As noted, Good counsel and Wisdom are equated by Plato in *The Republic.* "And what is Plato but Moses speaking in Attic Greek?"—Numenius.

[31] An always realistic John Adams wrote to Thomas Jefferson: "I have long been settled in my own opinion that neither philosophy nor Religion, nor Morality, nor Wisdom, nor Interest will ever govern nations or Parties against their Vanity, their Pride, their Resentment, or Revenge, or their Avarice or Ambition. Nothing but Force and Power and Strength can restrain them" (Cappon, 375).

[32] Samuel Noah Kramer, *In the World of Sumer* (Detroit: Wayne State Univ. Press, 1986), 113.

[33] The ancient god Dagda was the nearest Celtic mythology had to a universal god. No Prince of Peace, he shared the remaining Messianic attributes with his son. He was the *Ruad Rofhessa,* or "Lord of Perfect Knowledge," possessed of powers of wizardry, the *Eochaid Ollathair,* or "Father of All." His power was symbolized by the club his son bore, so heavy it had to be carried on wheels, and with it he slew nine men at one stroke (Nora Chadwick, *The Celts* [London: Penguin Books, 1971], 170).

[34] *Enki and Ninhursag: a Paradise Myth,* trans. S.N. Kramer (ANET, 38).

[35] Dummelow, *Commentary on the Holy Bible,* 646-47.

VIII

CONCLUSION

Is there anything whereof it may be said, See, this is new? it hath been already of old time which was before us. —Ecclesiastes I:10

In the distant half-light of Sumerian legend, the attributes of just rule may be made out in the sacred symbols—scepter, crown, tiara, and shepherd's crook—which lay before Anu when Etana of Kish ascended to heaven on the back of an eagle and learned how to be King and Counselor to the people.

By the close of the third millennium B.C., in the prologue to the Laws of Ur-Nammu, traces of the Prologue's structure, like the spinal column of a foetus, begin to cohere. Then, the king, the mighty warrior, by the power of Nanna and by the true command of Utu, established justice in the land, abolished malediction, violence, and strife, and ensured order and tranquility in his realm. By exempting the seafarers from the exactions of their overseer, the herdsmen from the levies of the oxen, sheep, and donkey takers, as Urukagina had done centuries before, he established the freedom of Sumer and Akkad and other settlements oppressed by Anshan. He installed a system of standard weights and measures and planted gardens, which became the province of the supreme royal gardener, thereby encouraging commerce and agriculture and enhancing the people's well-being. He lent his support to the widow, the orphan, the man of one shekel, the man with one lamb; settled his generals, his mother, brother, and sister, his relatives and their loved ones. Finally, the king repeats that he made "hatred and violence, outcry for justice," disappear, and declares again, "Justice I established in the land."

In 2094 B.C., Shulgi, the son of Ur-Nammu and perhaps the true author of the first law code, succeeded his father as king of Ur. The city's hymnal poets called Shulgi the "righteous man," the "righteous lord," the "righteous shepherd." He was the great protector of Sumer, the lofty wall who locked the front door of the homeland, the "great door" of the city. He was a "net, spread over heaven and earth" to capture criminals and foes. He subdued the fortified lands and filled Sumer with abundance.

In fact, many of the remarkable legal decisions of the neo-Sumerian period, reflecting the sound logic of his judges, were recorded in the closing years of Shulgi's righteous term. His military campaigns were successful and purposeful, assuring a steady flow of essential materials into his kingdom. He joined the Tigris and Euphrates with a strong wall to defend his people, erected splendid temples and palaces, established scribal schools—and resting places. His judicious trading policies and efficient administration procured more nourishment for the flesh of the Sumerians than had ever before been possible. It is small wonder that Lipit-Ishtar, whose father, Ishme-Dagan, had been a great admirer of Shulgi, looked to his wisdom and accomplishments for stimulation and direction.

Sixteen decades later, the Prologue to the Law Code of Lipit-Ishtar identified justice, security, and welfare as the proper objectives of government, for the first time, in a considered and deliberate statement of political purpose.[1] The repetition of those objects in the epilogue to his law code testifies they were more than fortuitous when set out in the Prologue:

> *Verily, in accordance with the tr(ue word) of Utu, I caused (Su)mer and Akkad to hold to true justice. Verily, in accordance with the pronouncement of Enlil, I, Lipit-Ishtar, the son of Enlil, abolished enmity and rebellion; made weeping, lamentations . . . tabu* [Lit. "turned to something forbidden"], *caused righteousness and truth to shine forth; brought well-being to the Sumerians and Akkadians* [Lit. "made well the bodies of the Sumerians and Akkadians"].

Then, to make certain the provisions of his law code were put into effect, the prince of Isin built a hall of justice, happily called a "place of reconciliation," on a site assigned by the gods, where litigants might resolve their disputes.[2] Everyone spoke of his righteousness; he protected Isin from the loud strife of foreign countries, made pleasant the life of everybody in the land.

The exalted objectives of the state proclaimed by Lipit-Ishtar express a vision common to all men. That vision emerges in their prayers and hymns of praise, as introductory passages to bodies of law, myths to explain the origin of cities, goals of imaginary and utopian societies, and in the promises of priests and politicians in every age, in every land. In the second millennium, those purposes and the time-honored attributes of a perfect ruler, familiar to all peoples of western Asia who shared the Mesopotamian heritage, received endorsement and widest circulation when they appeared in the prologue and epilogue to the Laws of Hammurabi. Through that medium alone, knowledge of their significance may be imputed to every nation of the ancient world that had access to his stele, or to one of its numerous copies, from the Babylon of the eighteenth century B.C. to the Achaemenid administration of Darius in the sixth. After the twelfth century, rulers of Susa in their eastern territories possessed the famous stone upon which Hammurabi's political ideals had been inscribed. By then they were part of a continuous written record almost a thousand years old.

These are the choice words of a great and powerful king, concerned for the welfare of his people and their posterity, as he called upon the god of justice to bless those of his successors who followed his instruction, honored his ordinances, observed his laws, and instituted just and compassionate government:

In the days to come, for all time,
let the king who appears in the land observe
the words of justice which I wrote on my stela;
let him not alter the law of the land which I enacted,
the ordinances of the land which I prescribed;
let him not rescind my statutes!
If that man has intelligence
and is able to guide his land aright,
let him heed the words which I wrote on my stela,
and may this stela show him the road (and) the way,
the law of the land which I enacted,
the ordinance of the land which I prescribed;
and let him guide aright his black-headed (people)!
Let him enact the law for them;
let him prescribe the ordinances for them!
Let him root out the wicked and the evil from the land
let him promote the welfare of the people!
I, Hammurabi, am the king of justice,
to whom Shamash committed law.
My words are choice; my deeds have no equal;
it is only to the fool that they are empty;
to the wise they stand forth as an object of wonder.
If that man heeded the words which I wrote in my stela,

and did not rescind my law,
has not distorted my words,
did not alter my statutes,
may Shamash make that man reign
as long as I, the king of justice;
may he shepherd his people in justice! (ANET, 178).

By the sixth century of the third millennium B.C., armies from Sumer and Akkad had already overcome Assur, the old capital of Assyria, and penetrated into Anatolia, opening the way for their merchants to bring cedar, diorite, and silver from the northwest and marking Assur as the hinge of a subsequent Anatolian-Babylonian trading system. Early in the second millennium, an ancient trade route ran from Susa and the east, through Eshnunna, Assur, Nineveh, and along the "Cappadocian Road" to Kanish, where an Assyrian network of commercial centers flourished. That route later marked the eastern course of the Persian Royal Road from Susa to Sardis (see map, p. 64).

Assyrian rulers, always impressed by the accomplishments of the south, became untiring imitators of its highly developed culture. Assyrian laws of the second millennium, drafted after Hammurabi's, resemble the Babylonian in text and in the casuistic "If a man" formulation, as do Hittite laws of the same period. During the second and first millennia, Assyria imposed an intermittent sovereignty upon Babylon; Assyrian conquerors carried north its cuneiform literature and the statue of Marduk itself; they adopted the Babylonian system of weights and measures and the Babylonian calendar.

In the first millennium, Assurbanipal, last great Assyrian monarch, whose grandfather had destroyed Babylon, claimed he could read the "dark" Akkadian characters. He sent emissaries to search the archives of ancient Sumerian cities for precedent, and recast Hammurabi's Code under its Assyrian title, *Judgments of Hammurabi.* Assurbanipal's library has yielded a tablet that warns a Mesopotamian king of the divine retribution awaiting him and his people should he fail to establish justice. This tablet employs a literary form utilized throughout the West in its *speculum* writings to define the perfect prince, beginning, at least, with Isocrates' advice to Nicocles. Late Assyrian manuscripts were wont to extol Shamash, protector of Sumerian cities, sometimes as a warrior god, always as the god of light and justice, the god who "shepherded whatever had breath," the shepherd who cared for the people of all lands.

Assyrian stonemasons tried to represent religious and philosophical abstractions in a real and difficult medium by cutting likenesses of fantastic beasts for display in their cities. They thus reproduced in stone political ideals that Sumerian poets had inscribed on clay. The prophet Ezekiel and Christian theologians later appropriated the Assyrian combination of four Sumerian animal symbols and gave them meaning according to their own beliefs. In the early Middle Ages, Irish monks copied and adorned the same symbols with intricate and beautiful illuminations, elaborate tracery, and ornamentations. These symbols address us today.

A Hittite nation, whose armies had taken Babylon in the sixteenth century B.C., bearing home the much-traveled statue of Marduk, remained the dominant power in Anatolia for another four hundred years. In western Anatolia, Hittite kings wed their daughters to princes of the Arzawan province, whose capital city appears to have been the original site of Ephesus, settled later by a son of Codrus, the Athenian king so admired by Erasmus and Vattel. Carian women of Hittite descent married early Greek settlers, according to Herodotus. In the east, dynastic marriages linked Hittite rulers to Hurrian, Assyrian, and Babylonian royal families; excavators have recovered copious evidence of their correspondence.

Legal historians have subjected Hittite laws to close analysis and noted numerous parallels to Babylonian enactments. Hittite scholars used a Babylonian script and studied the Sumerian language in their capital city; bilingual Sumerian-Hittite texts and the identification of a Sumerian ideogram helped decipher the Hittite language in this century. Hittite prayers addressed a "Sun God of Heaven, shepherd of man," a god who gave justice to the entire animated world.

Most Biblical scholars now believe that Abraham was born in the city of Ur (Biblical Ur of the Chaldees—ca. 140 miles south of Babylon) and that he lived there with his family, perhaps as late as the end of the eighteenth century B.C. By then, major Sumerian and Akkadian literary and legal works had articulated the purposes of the Prologue for at least three centuries, and the Code of Hammurabi itself had been newly promulgated. It is possible, as Kramer suggests, that ideas Abraham and his forefathers came to know through the important academy maintained at Ur "gradually became part of the traditions and sources utilized by Hebrew men of letters in composing and redacting the books of the Bible."[3]

Significant correspondences between the books of the Bible and earlier Mesopotamian writings are numerous, striking, and well documented. Later Hebrew prophets, looking to the advent of a wise and just, mighty, but loving king, awaited a ruler whose virtues included the divinely ordered wisdom, the divinely sanctioned power, and the pastoral concern always claimed by Hammurabi and other shepherd kings of the East.

The kingdom of the best Persian god, Ahura-Mazda (Lit. "Wise Lord"), was attained through Righteousness; his prophet, Zoroaster, became the Judge of holy Righteousness, set by Ahura-Mazda to be shepherd of the poor. Ancient writers, including Herodotus, Isaiah, Xenophon, and Cicero, agreed that "Father" Cyrus, whose power, evidenced by soldiers of unknowable numbers, had reduced Ionian cities and allowed him to occupy Babylon itself, brought prosperity to his people and cared for them in justice and righteousness. His inscriptions appropriated Hammurabi's titles, as "King of Babylon," "King of Sumer and Akkad," "King of the world quarters." Darius, the pious king, granted wisdom and friendliness by Ahura-Mazda, repeated Shulgi's words when he professed to love what was right and to hate what was not right. Darius owed his reputation amongst the Greeks as lawgiver largely to men from Babylon, expert in the laws of Mesopotamia. His legislators studied Hammurabi's virtues; his imitative Ordinance of Good Regulations, proclaimed everywhere throughout his far-flung empire, guided Greek colonies in western Asia.

Greek literature before Plato teems with concepts and images of good government adumbrated by Oriental scribes, some suggesting contacts before a post-Mycenaean darkness descended upon the eastern Mediterranean. Wide-thundering, far-seeing Zeus began as a mountain god, associated with the Zagros range east of Mesopotamia. Also, like Enlil, a Storm-god, Zeus developed from a credulous Cretan deity (he swam there) into an all-knowing, all-powerful, and just ruler of gods and men. His daughter, Athene, benefactress of Plato's city, identified by Plato with a Libyan goddess, by others with an Eastern deity, was goddess of counsel and wisdom, champion of justice and defender of the law. She cast the deciding vote at Orestes' trial, making his matricide justifiable. As a warrior goddess, Athene was invincible in battle; Ares himself could not match her fury. Industries she nurtured helped sustain the Greek people. Many of the implements she claimed to have invented were known, and the arts and sciences she is said to have taught—architecture, mathematics, and metallurgy, among others—were well advanced in Sumer when it flourished and Greece had yet to begin its rise.

Homer, probably an Aeolian-Ionian if such a person ever existed, described a steadfast and many-wiled hero in the *Odyssey*: a sceptered king, schooled in justice, whose wisdom was like a god's, who spoke no word within his country that was unfair, and was never outrageous to any man, but was kind, like a father, and gave, beyond all others, sacrifice to the gods. Although untrained, Odysseus displayed most of the virtues of Plato's guardians and resembled, in many ways, the Sumerian Gilgamesh, whose epithets he shared. In singing of the rich abundance enjoyed by a people blessed with a strong, just, and pious ruler, Homer repeated an ancient Mesopotamian melody.

Hesiod, descended from Cadmeians of Asia Minor, wrote of temperate barons who reached straight and unfaltering decisions, as had Lipit-Ishtar, and of shining Themis, goddess of sacred law, order, and harmony, who bore to Zeus "Order, blooming peace and justice." Hesiod introduced into Western secular literature the canon of moral laws upon which the Third Dynasty of Ur had been founded. When Solon, employing an Ionian style, produced a written law for his native city, he followed a practice favored by Mesopotamian kings from Ur-Nammu to Nebuchadnezzar II. Solon's effort to establish an equitable system of weights and measures repeated a course first deemed essential by the Sumerian. He warned Athens there could be no tranquility for a city whose people were immersed in corruption and impiety, as Esarhaddon, several decades before Solon's birth, had blamed the downfall of Babylon on the greed, profanity, and overreaching of its citizens. Solon's attempt in his *Seisachtheia* to establish justice by adjusting economic inequities that were corroding Athenian society was similar, in purport, to the *mesharum* acts of numerous Babylonian kings; his law dealing with the nocturnal thief had its counterpart in the city of Eshnunna.

Pythagoras, who may have absorbed some measure of Babylonian learning on his much heralded but ill-documented voyages, identified three classes of men attending the Olympic games. The observation attributed to him reprised an ideal Mesopotamian society made up of classes who ruled wisely, fought bravely, and produced abundantly. It also suggested a similar tripartite division of Reason, Spirit, and Appetite in the human psyche and provided a matrix for the construction of Plato's perfect commonwealth.

Democritus, greatest of the Greek physical scientists, whose Babylonian researches are best recorded, conceived an atomist theory for the structure of the soul, which augmented the three divisions of Pythagoras.

Herodotus of Halicarnassus placed the goals of the well-ordered state in a Persian society that existed seventy-five years before he wrote. Greek statesmen and philosophers debated his findings in Athens shortly before Plato's birth.

Plato ascribed to Protagoras, whose roots were Asian, the theory of the three stages in the development of human society: from the primitive state, in which, as recipient of the stolen gifts of Prometheus, man was enabled to secure his basic needs; to his association, out of terror and solely for his preservation, in a city that lacked the art of polity and so could not endure; and finally, to a moral society founded on justice and regard for the rights of others. Zeus's direction to Hermes, accustomed to travel abreast of the wind, to institute a law establishing justice, furnishes a specific analogue to Anu's instruction to the wind god, Enlil, to *mishara shakana,* the traditional divine command to Mesopotamian rulers to establish justice in the land. That very phrase was still used in Babylon during the second half of the sixth century B.C., and inspired Persian kings when Protagoras lived. Whether or not Plato borrowed extensively from Protagoras, as his detractors claimed, in this dialogue he states unequivocally that the aims of the *Republic*, visible in the epithets of the city's patroness, were those taught in Athens by a philosopher schooled in Persian beliefs, rules, and customs, which incorporated Babylonian ideas and practices.

In his *Laws,* Plato used the same three-sectioned prologue-corpus-epilogue organization employed by Lipit-Ishtar and Hammurabi in presenting their codes. Plato's insistence that preambles, religious in tone and poetic in form, were indispensable to a cheerful acceptance of the laws by the citizenry, expanded upon the approach initiated by the two Mesopotamian kings. His argument that justice consists in giving every man his due "states the logic of his [*Hammurabi's*] code," says Muller, in not giving "equal rights to men naturally unequal."[4] Indeed, Plato's definition of justice provides a single, comprehensive rule broad enough to encompass the first Laws of Ur-Nammu.

Certain of Plato's laws, in manner of expression and substantive detail, resemble provisions of Hammurabi's collection, particularly those dealing with trespassing cattle; damages caused by a defendant's negligence in failing to control large volumes of water; theft and receipt of property stolen from holy places; homicide, involuntary and justifiable; warranties on the sale of a slave, notably that against epilepsy; adverse possession, and the right of one in possession whose title is challenged to claim over against his seller. Death is once more the prescribed punishment for the footpad who comes in the night. The ritualistic sacrifices, prayers, and votive offerings to various deities, which played so large a role in shaping Mesopotamian civilization, become again, in the *Laws,* the best and noblest policy that a wise and good man can follow. In the *Republic,* Plato assigned the virtues he found in Persian kings to its men of gold, silver, and brass—professionals charged by him to give effect to political goals mandated by Lipit-Ishtar's gods.

There can be little doubt that the purposes of the best state, as expressed in Eastern literature, and especially by Hammurabi's panegyrists in introducing the most advanced and enduring jurisprudential accomplishment of the ancient world, were known to Ionian settlers and to travelers, traders, and teachers from Greece who sought knowledge in the East before Plato. If Iamblichus was correct and Pythagoras was studying as a disciple of Zaratas in Babylon when Darius commandeered its priests to interpret Hammurabi's inscriptions, he could scarcely not have known something of their commission. Later, when Darius presented the stele bearing his laws to Babylon, Pythagoras could not have been unaware of its contents or its source.

If, as many claim, Herodotus actually visited Babylon, he had a unique opportunity to learn of the origin of the Persian laws when he conversed with the Babylonian priests in their temple, men who were first-generation descendants of the scholars who had assisted Darius in the preparation of his Ordinance. It is not easy to believe that a reporter and trader as observant and inquisitive as Herodotus, who had promised to write a history of Babylonia and who had presumably accumulated a body of information on the subject, would have remained ignorant of the existence of the legal framework that had sustained the civilization of western Asia for a thousand years.

Xenophon and Plato expressed their great admiration for Darius's laws. Both Greeks understood that legislators do not invent a completely new body of law without reference to what has gone before, but utilize existing concepts and modify them as necessary to deal with issues in need of immediate resolution. To conclude that they and other Greek wise men of the time assumed that Darius's Ordinance sprang from the lucubrations of sixth-century Persian jurists, whose native language was then being reduced to writing for the first time and whose king proudly proclaimed himself "King of Babylon," without consulting the obvious antedating authority, would seem to do them less than complete justice.

Certain it is that until the time of the American Revolution, students of government inquiring into the character of the just prince and the objectives of the state he might be expected to administer accepted without substantial emendation the virtues of Eastern rulers—wisdom, justice, temperance, piety, and fortitude—which Plato and Xenophon had admired in Persian society. Beginning with the cardinal precept of Isocrates that the office of king "demands the greatest wisdom," there is scarcely a specification of ideal rule or of the reciprocal obligation of ruler and subject in Western political literature that cannot be matched against an Eastern theoretical, if not actual, authority. Constantly cited were the age-old propositions that monarchy is the best form of government, that the just ruler should be subject to the law, educated from childhood to obey and so to rule, shepherd of his flock, father to his family, pilot of the ship of state, godlike in appearance, magnanimous and high-minded; that he should know and love the truth, hate falsehood, silence the malcontent and seditious man, defend his people in time of distress, protect the widow and the orphan, curb the malice and oppression of public officials, heed the counsel of older men, avoid flatterers, take the straight way, and order his life and actions on those of God, or gods, enact good laws, appoint honest magistrates, take little sleep, and labor through the night for the well-being of his people.

A century before the first of the thirteen colonies was settled in America, learned men in the universities of Europe studied the structure and goals of Plato's *Republic,* available, again, to the West with the translation of Byzantine manuscripts. Half a millennium before that, some princes of Islam organized their governments about the theories of the Greek philosopher. Renaissance courtiers wondered how best to acquaint their rulers with Plato's constraining virtues. They debated whether the rule of a good prince or the government of a good republic would more surely restore the golden age to earth.

The kingly qualities to be sought in those to whom kingly powers were to be entrusted, which Erasmus explained at length to Charles, were in large part the virtues of the *Republic*'s guardians. Perfection of those qualities in the character of the prince, achieved by his careful education under the guidance of skilled tutors, as Plato had recommended, would make him a paragon for his people, and they, with pleasure, would imitate his conduct. Thus ameliorating the character and morals of the citizenry by his own good example, the just prince would transform the social order and redress the social and political wrongs that Erasmus deplored. (Erasmus's teachings had as little effect upon Charles V as Plato's had had on Dionysius or More's were to have on Henry VIII. A society founded on Erasmus's "good example thesis" nevertheless was established in Mexico by a contemporary judge and later bishop, Vasco de Quiroga, whose integrity, kindness, and blameless life earned him the respect of his Indian followers).[5]

Thomas More shared many of Erasmus's views and sought to achieve in *Utopia*, through customs, laws, and institutions, the blessed state Erasmus expected to result from the exercise of the good prince's powers. More's essay, acknowledging the *Republic*'s guidance, foreshadowed the objects of the Preamble, as he charged the king to keep the people safe from injustice, to care for their welfare, to protect them from the threat of rebellion from within and invasion from without.

Students in Colonial American colleges read the works of Homer, Plato, Xenophon, Aristotle, Cicero, St. Augustine, Erasmus, More, and the speculative tracts of Europe's seventeenth-century philosophers who drew from the *Republic* in shaping their idealistic governments. At Princeton, Witherspoon criticized the *Republic* and *Utopia* for intimating, however indirectly, that a perfect commonwealth might be achieved on this sinful and imperfect earth. He taught his students, well represented at the Federal Convention in Philadelphia, what the proper ends of government should be.

The preamble to the Massachusetts Constitution, prepared by John Adams, and numerous other political writings of the time borrowed extensively from Cicero and St. Augustine, whose Latin may have been more readily comprehensible to Western students of classical languages than were the complexities of Plato's Greek. Within weeks of the opening of the Constitutional Convention, Adams had excited a great deal of attention in publishing the first book of his *Defence*, which, in briefing the *Republic*, reviewed the cardinal virtues and reaffirmed the necessity for establishing justice in the ideal city. Men of learning, said James Madison, found nothing new in his recitation.

Although the philosophical and religious consciousness of the Western world had absorbed the ideas of the *Republic* by the time of the American Revolution, its political goals seem to have been so taken for granted by some men of learning that the part the *Republic* played in their promulgation was forgotten, and two of America's wisest and most literate statesmen, John Adams and Thomas Jefferson, could roundly disparage the *Republic*'s contribution to Western thought.

The influence of the Bible in the New World was immediate and pervasive. Puritans of New England believed that Moses had delivered from the Lord a "form and pattern of Government" in the Old Testament, and they initiated a Colonial way of life based upon rules of communal behavior that were first set out in the Laws of Ur-Nammu. Close and continuing study of the Bible caused its imagery to become familiar to far more Americans than had ever penetrated the "puerile and unintelligible jargon" of the *Republic*. In the Bible, the qualities of the Good Shepherd and the characteristics of the future king made the goals of the ideal state achievable. Good Counsel, Wisdom, and Justice; Authority, Power, and Security; Love, Concern, and Welfare; these, expressed in countless ways, were the great stones upon which the government of the Preamble was to be established.[6]

To members of the Federal Convention who had read the Bible, studied Calvin and his *Institution,* taken part in election proceedings, listened to and read the sermons, pamphlets, and religious tracts of the time, the text of the Preamble accepted by them on September 12, 1787, could have occasioned little surprise. The Bible's precepts were a component of their religious and political heritage; its verses enriched their common vocabulary. The throne of David had been established in justice. The wisdom of God was in Solomon to render justice. Civil government, Calvin said, pertained to the establishment of civil justice; its end was to promote general peace, prosperity, and tranquility. Todd preached that civil government was ordained as a means to protect men in the enjoyment of their just rights and privileges and to promote the peace and welfare of the people, peace and quietness being absolutely necessary to the well-being of any people. The Miltonian description of "Liberty" as a "blessing" was repeated in the sermons of the Reverend Samuel Davies, one-time President of Princeton and founder of the Hanover Presbytery in Virginia, who called for religious freedom in the heart of the Anglican Dominion and urged his followers to "secure the inestimable blessings of liberty." The Virginia Declaration of Rights, on June 12, 1776, declared, "No free government or the blessing of liberty can be preserved to any people but by a firm adherence to justice, moderation, temperance, frugality and virtue."

The phrase "domestic tranquility" was so well known in the American colonies that it became a source of amusement to fellow members of the Federal Convention when Elbridge Gerry of Massachusetts, during the course of a debate on the desirability of maintaining a standing army, pointed out that a standing member might indeed ensure domestic tranquility, but that it might also lead to foreign entanglements.

Finally, in a book consulted often by the First Gentlemen of America, Emerich de Vattel popularized the objectives of the blessed state within a generation of the Convention in his *Law of Nations*. He specified, although not in the following order, that a nation must (i) cause justice to prevail in the state, (ii) maintain an internal police to preserve tranquility among the citizens, (iii) defend itself with its combined strength against all external insult and violence, and (iv) provide for the necessities of the nation. The purpose of the act of association by which a multitude of men come together to form a nation, according to Vattel, was "to promote the general welfare," a phrase James Madison said was well known at the time in America.

Madison might have included the other phrases of the Preamble as well. When the Convention appointed the Committee of Five to revise the style and arrange the Articles of the Constitution on September 8, 1787, the proceedings referred to the Committee still bore the preamble of August 6th, which merely listed the States ordaining and establishing the Constitution. On Monday, September 10, at least three members of the Committee of Style were engaged in active debate on the wording of various Articles. The whole Committee, therefore, had one day, September 11, to revise and arrange the entire Constitution, which it reported in the following day. The Committee could hardly have begun a discussion at the time as to what the proper purposes of their new government should be. Its members came to their task with the purposes of an ideal commonwealth firmly fixed in their minds. The Preamble need not have been "deliberately and carefully" drawn by "skilled lawyers of the time," as Crosskey maintains; it might as readily have been fashioned by any moderately read man of the cloth.[7] By the time of the Federal Convention, the business of designating the ends of government and human polities, had, as Randolph said, been exhausted; the objectives of the Preamble had become commonplace.

The Chief Use of History

But what is government itself but the greatest of all reflections on human nature? —James Madison, *Federalist* No. 51

If the immediate sources of Preamble and Prologue are to be found in the legal, literary, philosophical, and religious traditions of their times, the wellspring of both arises from man's basic desire to return to the nurturing warmth and protection of his first sanctuary, the womb, where the Sumerian, curiously, had also located the origin of his freedom—*amargi*, "a return to the mother." This desire for security and nourishment compels men to enter into political associations that must subscribe to at least a minimal standard of justice in order to endure. Most legislators and philosophers herein, who sought to devise real and imaginary societies where men might live together harmoniously, agreed that politics and morals are inextricably linked. They attempted to predicate an ethical basis for their communities and establish a consensus as to those actions to be deemed right, true, and good, and those to be condemned as wrong, false, and evil.

In the American colonies, the majority of those who had endorsed the ideals of the Preamble professed to believe in a Supreme Being of infinite power, wisdom, and goodness, a Creator who had revealed, in the Decalogue, abiding principles of right and wrong. The Sippar tablet, Si 277, demonstrates that moral principles underlying Sumerian culture were very much the same as those that inspired the Founding Fathers of America. The idea of a one God, a God of Justice, whose Will was the law, who loved his people and entered into a covenant with them, is a Hebraic innovation, but laws anticipating five of the six commandments of the second table of the Decalogue, dealing with purely human relationships, had served as beacons of morality in Mesopotamia from the reign of Ur-Nammu; the sixth, which searched the covetous heart of man, has its parallel in a Babylonian hymn of the second millennium. The Commandments, said St. Paul, are summed up in the sentence "You shall love your neighbor as yourself." Paul's admonition had conceptual roots in Babylonian wisdom literature.

Underlying the moral order of the American Colonial period was a belief in a Natural Law, its origin sometimes ascribed to Stoic philosophy, where "man, through his divinely given capacity of reason was directly participant with the gods themselves. Nature, human nature and reason were one."[8] It was Cicero's *recta ratio*—

> *right reason, in agreement with nature; it is of universal application, unchanging and everlasting; . . . and there will not be different laws at Rome and at Athens, or different laws now and in the future, but one eternal and unchangeable law will be valid for all nations and all times, and there will be one master and one ruler, that is, God, over us all, for he is the author of this law, its promulgator, and its enforcing judge* (*Rep.*, III. xxii.)

It was Blackstone's and Colonial America's law:

> *. . . for as God, when he created man . . . laid down certain immutable laws of human nature . . . gave him also the faculty of reason to discover the purport of those laws. . . . This law of nature, being coeval with mankind, dictated by God himself . . . is binding over all the globe, in all countries and at all times* (*Commentaries,* Bk. I. Intro. Sect. II. [40-1]).

If not the law of Thomas Jefferson:

> *He [*man*] was endowed with a sense of right and wrong. . . . This sense is as much a part of his nature, as the sense of hearing, seeing, feeling; it is the true foundation of morality, and not the* to kalon, *truth, etc. as fanciful writers have imagined. . . . This sense is submitted, indeed, in some degree to the guidance of reason; but it is a small stock which is required for this* (*Papers* 12:15).

The law of reason, which would be the same for Rome and Athens, immutable, governing the people of all ages, was, by definition, the law of ancient Ur. The Akkadian *kittum*, with its Sumerian antecedents, had, it appears, long before postulated a higher law, part of the cosmic design, ultimately the gift of the forces of the universe. This law existed, eternal and universal, an order beyond the reach of gods and men, although its Mesopotamian adherents had not as yet named Reason its author.

Perhaps it is inevitable that the declared intentions of political associations based upon ethical principles and elementary notions of equity and fairness that proceed from the very nature of reasoning, or merely intuitive man, should have come to resemble each other, however far apart in space and time and however remote may be the prospect of their realization. The songs and laws of early Mesopotamia first laid out a plan for the heavenly city of the *Republic,* an antecedent of the City of God later envisioned by European settlers in America. All derive, in part, from a Mesopotamian legal tradition that was "living and life-giving . . . because in the final analysis, it sprang from man's hope to achieve harmony with the cosmos."[9]

The Mystery of the Preamble

Remaining unexplained is the unique form used by Preamble and Prologue to frame their purposes. The thirty-six centuries that separate the two have produced no independent writing whose structure resembles either so much as does that of the other. Although the entire purport and some of the vocabulary of the Preamble were available to its author, or authors, from other sources, its purposes might have been expressed in countless ways without repeating the distinctive style and formulation of the Prologue as it did.

The prologue to the Laws of Ur-Nammu, the hymnology of Shulgi, the self-adulatory hyperbole of Hammurabi, Hittite and Assyrian writings, the Persian accounts of Herodotus and Xenophon, the philosophies and poetry of Greece, the prophecy of the Old Testament, the prayer of the New, the rich fabric of Cicero's prose, the teachings of the Church Fathers, the blessed state of Erasmus, the dogma of John Calvin, the creations of More and seventeenth-century philosophers, the recapitulation of Vattel and the careful reasoning of many others, all adjudged justice, order, defense, and provision of the necessities of life for its citizens to be the ultimate goals of good government. No writer, however, focused upon the manner in which those essential purposes were to be set out as did the draftsmen of Preamble and Prologue. Each concisely summarized his ideas in a series of infinitive phrases that followed in the same sequence in a single sentence and served to introduce, in one case, the code of laws of an ancient Eastern kingdom, and in the other, the fundamental laws of a new Western republic.

One can only wonder how the Prologue, which had lain so long forgotten, should have been reconstituted almost wholly by the Committee of Style and Arrangement within a few decades of the rediscovery of the language in which it was first written. The mystery posed by the near identity of these two introductory declarations of national resolve, one scratched on parchment with a quill pen in Philadelphia in the late hot summer of 1787, the other pressed into wet clay by a reed stylus in Sumer almost four millennia earlier, each by an unknown hand, remains unresolved.

If, however, any measure of the acclaim commonly accorded the Preamble be deserved,[10] how may we gauge the achievement of the forgotten Sumerian who first identified the objectives of the Prologue, whether that be Lipit-Ishtar, an advisor, or, as is most likely, an ancient even more remote, whose perception was memorialized by the Sumerian king? Somewhere in the earth of the Near East there remains a scattering of dust that once was a man who had the wit to recognize and the genius to express sentiments of universal and timeless appeal in a manner that has not yet been surpassed. In forming his perfect outline of the functions of government, he enabled those who came after him to better understand themselves and to appreciate the catholicity of man's aspiration, his common, contentious humanity. As Chief Justice John Jay wrote of the Preamble:

. . . let us turn to the Constitution. The people therein declare their design in establishing it comprehended six objects: 1. to form a more perfect union; 2. to establish justice; 3. to ensure domestic tranquility; 4. to provide for the common defense; 5. to promote the general welfare; 6. to secure the blessings of liberty to themselves and their posterity.

Jay added:

It would be pleasing and useful to consider and trace the relations which each of these objects bears to the others, and to show that collectively, they comprise everything requisite, with the blessings of Divine Providence, to render a people prosperous and happy.[11]

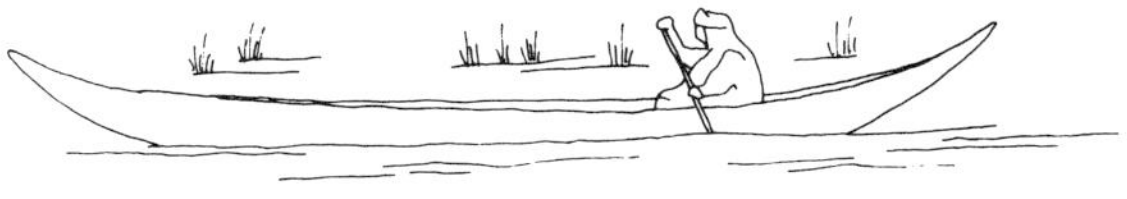

[1] Lipit-Ishtar himself was a king of an Amorite or a West Semitic dynasty, "but the fact that he reigned less than a century after the great Sumerian Third Dynasty of Ur and compiled his code in the Sumerian language makes it highly probable that his laws stem in large measure from the Sumerian cultural heritage" (Steele, "The Code of Lipit-Ishtar," 425).

[2] Ferris J. Stephens, "Lipit-Ishtar's Hall of Justice," *JAOS,* 70, no. 3, 179.

[3] Kramer, *The Sumerians,* 292.

[4] Herbert J. Muller, *Freedom in the Ancient World* (New York: Harper & Brothers, 1961), 59.

[5] Ross Dealy, *The Politics of an Erasmian Lawyer, Vasco de Quiroga* (Malibu Beach: Undena Publications, 1976).

[6] Preachers talked of "Wisdom and Counsel, Strength and Assistance, Prosperity and Success," "Discretion and Counsel, Protection and Assistance, Refreshment," (Buckingham); "Power, Wisdom and a Godlike goodness" (Burnham) in Bosco, *Election Sermons,* 137, 141. Cf. the epilogue to the Laws of Hammurabi: " . . . with the insight that Enki allotted to me, with the ability [def. *'sufficiency of power,'* O.E.D.], that Marduk gave me, I rooted out the enemy above and below; I made an end of war; I promoted the welfare of the land" (ANET, 178).

[7] Crosskey contends the Preamble was so drawn as to "*assure to the government* that the Constitution was creating powers fully adequate, on a national scale, to all the 'objects' for which governments commonly were formed"; by insisting that his is the only "rational conclusion," a "manifest certainty," Crosskey overstates (*Politics and the Constitution,* 375).

[8] Corwin, "The 'Higher Law' Background," 156.

[9] Speiser, "Cuneiform Law and The History of Civilization," 540.

[10] "It would be difficult - if not impossible - to form a more complete or perfect outline of the functions of government than is to be found in the Preamble. The concept is lofty and pure and the enumerated purposes the noblest to which a government can commit itself" (Watson, *The Constitution of the United States,* 105).

[11] Dallas v. Georgia, 2 Dall. 419.

APPENDIX

The Exhibits following, with the exception of Exhibits E and J, compare legal concepts and procedures of modern Anglo-American jurisprudence with those found in the most ancient records of the Near East. Those records include the four earliest known collections of laws and case reports of litigation that took place before Sumerian and Akkadian courts.

Exhibit E attempts to show that Mesopotamian law codes, and especially that of Hammurabi, were more than academic or religious exercise. It suggests that through Hammurabi's work much of Mesopotamia's legal and political tradition became available to the West.

Exhibit J contains a contemporary's evaluation of the delegates who sat on the Committee of Style and Arrangement at the Constitutional Convention of 1787.

Exhibits

The principal authorities cited and abbreviations used are:

The Laws

(a) The Laws of Ur-Nammu (ca. 2100 B.C.). Citations are from J.J. Finkelstein, "The Laws of Ur-Nammu," *JCS*, 22, nos. 3-4, (Oct./Dec. 1969):66-82. The first six laws of Ur-Nammu had not been published when Finkelstein wrote. They have since appeared in Fatma Yildiz, "Animadversiones—A Tablet of Codex Ur-Nammu from Sippar," *Orientalia*, 50 (1981): 87-97.

(b) The Laws of Eshnunna (ca. 2000 B.C.). Trans. Albrecht Goetze. Citations are from *Ancient Near Eastern Texts*, ed. James B. Pritchard, 3rd ed. (Princeton: Princeton Univ. Press, 1969) (ANET).

(c) The Law Code of Lipit-Ishtar (ca. 1900 B.C.). Trans. Samuel Noah Kramer. Citations are from ANET.

(d) The Code of Hammurabi (ca. 1765 B.C.). Trans. Theophile J. Meek. Citations are from ANET.

The Cases

Unless otherwise noted, cases cited are from Adam Falkenstein's *Die neusumerischen Gerichtsurkunden* (NG), dating from about 2000 B.C., and M. Schorr's *Altbabylonische Rechtsurkunden* (AR), dating from the eighteenth century B.C. References to the Babylonian Laws are from G.R. Driver and J.C. Miles *The Babylonian Laws* (Oxford: Clarendon Press, vol. I, 1952; vol. II, 1955).

EXHIBIT A

LEGAL PARALLELS
ANCIENT AND MODERN

Mayhem

California Penal Code 203:

[Mayhem defined.] Every person who unlawfully and maliciously deprives a human being of a member of his body, or disables, disfigures, or renders it useless, or cuts or disables the tongue, or puts out an eye, or slits the nose, ear, or lip, is guilty of mayhem.

In the debate taken up from time to time as to which objective of the Preamble to the United States Constitution is most important, justice is, more often than not, deemed paramount. But it was not by chance that the Laws of Ur-Nammu, the first law code ever committed to writing, were almost exclusively penal in nature. When the clamor of anarchy rises, the cries of the widow, orphan, and man of one shekel are likely to be lost in the din. Domestic tranquility may not guarantee justice, but without some assurance of internal order, justice cannot last. Coalescing aggregations of people must consent to regulation and subscribe to laws meant to curb the passions and violence of the worst amongst them. "Forceful hurt to the body, forceful damage to property" are indeed the forms of harm that appeal "most directly to the quickening legal conscience."[1]

Thus, the principal task confronting the French-speaking kings of England after the Norman conquest was maintaining order and inhibiting the violence which marked that fierce and turbulent age. Grievous woundings were not unusual; fearful injuries were expected and accepted with equanimity. William Marshal, a professional tourney champion and the noblest knight of Christendom, more than once placed his head upon the blacksmith's anvil in order that his dented helmet might be removed.

Offenses causing serious bodily injuries—woundings, cuttings or disfigurings, the deprivation of a limb—were common enough to find their way into the early statute books of England. Henry de Bracton (d.1268 A.D.), author of the first systematic treatise on the laws of England, carefully distinguishing injuries to foreteeth and molars, defined "mayhem" in the following manner:

Mayhem is when anyone is rendered in any part of his body disabled from fighting, as when portions of the bone have been extracted from his head. Likewise, if a bone be broken, or a foot, or a hand, or a finger, or any other member be cut off, or the nerves of some limb have become contracted by the wound so made, or the fingers have been rendered crooked, or if an eye has been scooped out, or anything else has been done to the body whereby a man is rendered less able and competent to defend himself. If foreteeth are broken, it is mayhem, for teeth of this kind assist much to victory. Castration is also adjudged to be mayhem, but not if an ear or a nose is cut off.[2]

Before the Normans came, the Laws of Alfred invoked the ancient *lex talionis* "eye for eye, stripe for stripe" rule of Exodus to punish acts of mayhem and homicide. A killer became an outlaw, a friendless man, a wolf to be hunted down and destroyed by the community. His punishment might be left to the kin of his victim, and the law would not chastise kinsmen who took life for life. Gradually, a table of pecuniary compensations for serious injuries superseded *talion*, outlawry, and blood feud. The offender might pay a price, make "bot," or betterment (compensation or reparation), to the injured person, pay a "wite" (fine or penalty) to the king and so buy back the peace. Homicide became emendable; a statutory sum, the "wergild," could atone for the death:

A complicated tariff was elaborated. Every kind of blow or wound to every kind of person had its price, and much of the jurisprudence of the time must have consisted of a knowledge of these pre-appointed prices.[3]

In Sumer, at the end of the third millennium B.C., the freshly anointed Ur-Nammu, faced with the same need to establish and maintain order as that which challenged William the Conqueror, moved to "banish malediction, violence and strife" in his lands as well. He also provided compensation in his laws for woundings similar to those described by Bracton, in accordance with his own graduated schedule:

15. If a man, by . . . , cut off the foot [var: 'limb'] of another man, he shall pay ten shekels of silver. 16. If a man shattered another man's limb with a club in a deliberate attack, he shall pay one mina of silver. 17. If a man cut off the nose of another man with a knife [?], he shall pay two-thirds mina of silver. 18. If he cut off his . . . [finger?

ear?] with a . . . , for each [finger? ear?] he shall pay x shekels of silver. 19. If he knocked out his teeth, he shall pay two shekels of silver [per tooth].[4]

Scholars have frequently questioned whether early Mesopotamian legal compilations were meant to be observed in actual practice. What reason is there to believe, however, that the schedule of fines and reparations proposed by Ur-Nammu's lawmakers would have been any less useful to their contemporaries than the tariff described by Pollock and Maitland was to the English?

Burglary

To Sir Edward Coke (1552-1634), Chief Justice of England and the ultimate common lawyer, a burglar was

by the common law a felon, that in the night breaketh and entreth the mansion house of another, of intent to kill some reasonable creature, or to commit some other felony within the same, whether his felonious intent be executed or not.[5]

Of burglary's origin, legal commentators Pollock and Maitland write:

The thought that crimes committed at night are to be punished more severely than similar crimes committed by day was not far from our ancestors but we can as yet give no precise account of the genesis of burglary.[6]

Man first expressed his dread of the prowler who invades his home at night in the thirteenth of the Laws of Eshnunna (ca. 2000 B.C.), which sealed the fate of the culprit with resounding finality:

A man who is caught in the house of a muskenum, [one of lesser rank, a "commoner" perhaps] *in the house, during daytime, shall pay 10 shekels of silver. He who is caught in the house at night, shall die, he shall not get away alive* (ANET, 162).

In the United States, the common law defined burglary as "a breaking and entering of the dwelling house of another, in the nighttime, with intent to commit a felony therein," a crime that was formerly punishable by death. In 1915, the Supreme Court of North Carolina affirmed the conviction of a defendant sentenced to be electrocuted for first degree burglary.[7]

The ancient fear of the nocturnal intruder persists and finds voice in today's criminal statutes. In California, a breaking and entering of an inhabited building in the nighttime still distinguishes first from second degree burglary. California Penal Code 460:

1. Every burglary of an inhabited dwelling house . . . or the inhabited portion of any other building committed in the nighttime is burglary of the first degree.

2. All other kinds of burglary are of the second degree.

A well-known columnist, and man of peace, recently shot an intruder who had entered his backyard at 2 A.M. He explained, "The first overriding fact was that my home was violated, my family was threatened by strangers who came in the darkness."[8]

"Criminal" Procedure

For the past thirty years, the Police Department of Central Falls, Rhode Island, conducted its own legal proceedings at police headquarters; police officers there routinely issued summonses and presided at hearings of traffic and misdemeanor cases. Persons suspected of lesser offenses were ordered to report to the Police Chief and "show cause" why warrants should not be issued for their arrest. Local officials explained that the usurpation of the court's function by the police of Central Falls, in issuing orders, holding hearings, and rendering decisions, went unchallenged simply because the practice had been in effect for so long.[9]

Legal commentators expressed disbelief and dismay at their temerity, but, all else failing, the police of Central Falls might have cited ancient Babylonian precedent as authority for their assumption of jurisdiction. In M. Schorr's *Altbabylonische Rechtsurkunden,* the *abû-šabim,* or "Fathers of the People" ("Fathers"), who, Schorr suggests, were probably police officials, appear several times. Their title indicates they were not considered *daiyānu,* or "judge," and Driver and Miles confirm that "it seems a mistake to regard the *abū sābē* as forming a court."[10] Nevertheless, in at least one instance the Fathers appear to have usurped the function of a court, i.e. to hear, consider, and determine controversies and to make binding orders and judgments.

During the reign of Ammisaduqa (1646-1626 B.C.), five head of cattle belonging to the herdsman Ilusi-ibni at Asar-mama had "gotten lost" and were found in the possession of three persons, Ibni-Marduk, Ibni-Emahtila, and Atamu. The Fathers dispatched two emissaries, with written instructions to bring the three suspects to Babylon. There the Fathers heard the report of the arresting officers (or defendants—the tablet is not clear) and ordered the defendants to replace the cattle (AR #309). In this instance, the Fathers clearly functioned as judges, presiding over a court exercising a "criminal" jurisdiction. When they wished to examine the three suspects, they issued written instructions to their two officers, directing them to take the three into custody and bring them to Babylon. There the Fathers heard testimony, considered the matter, rendered a decision, and imposed a penalty, all functions of a court of law.

It would seem the Babylonian Fathers were as intent upon expediting the administration of justice as were the police officials at Central Falls. If they charged the three defendants in their instructions, they may lay claim to having issued one of the first arrest warrants in recorded history, a warrant being defined as a

> *judicial order or command, in writing, in the name of the People, signed by an authorized judicial officer, commanding the arrest of the defendant named for the crime charged therein.*[11]

Security Interests in Personal Property

The Uniform Commercial Code, which has been adopted in all of the United States except Louisiana, is a modernization of statutes relating to important commercial transactions. It was drafted by more than twelve hundred of the most experienced commercial lawyers in the nation, working together for the greater part of the decade after 1955.

The most significant innovation of the Uniform Commercial Code is its Article 9. That Article supersedes legislation dealing with chattel mortgages, conditional sales contracts, trust receipts, and other similar security devices. Each of these had developed independently with its own specialized forms, rights, and filing requirements, all meant to grant A a lien on personal property of B as security for a debt. Article 9's comprehensive scheme, which seeks to simplify and unify the law, applies to all transactions intended to create a "security interest" (1-201 [37]) in personal property; it rejects traditional nomenclature and calls an agreement to create such an interest a "security agreement," (9-105 [1] [h]) regardless of its form. If the security interest is taken by the seller of the collateral, or by the financer of the purchase, it is a "purchase money security interest" (9-107). Today, the security agreement is the basic document that supports the billions of dollars spent annually in the purchase of consumer goods, equipment, farm products, inventory, and other personal property.

Such agreements are not, however, new. One of the oldest tablets yet unearthed, a fragmented text discovered at Tello, site of the ancient city of Lagash, is the best preserved of four similar tablets. Dating from the Third Dynasty of Ur, it describes the successful foreclosure by a creditor of his lien upon a slave. At trial, the creditor presented the "relevant" document, in which the debtor had declared under oath before the king that if he failed to return a sum of money to the creditor within two years, he would give Ninkusu, his slave, in payment of the full purchase price. The court thereupon awarded the slave to the creditor (NG #116). In the language of the Uniform Commercial Code, the debtor had executed a security agreement, granting the secured party a purchase money security interest in the slave. When the debtor defaulted, the creditor utilized the available judicial procedure and exercised his right to foreclose upon his security interest. Clearly, the Sumerian financed the acquisition of his slave using jural conceptions and documentation very much like those employed by an American consumer today in purchasing an automobile or an item of equipment.

A security agreement, under the Uniform Commercial Code, must be signed to be effective. The tablet from Tello does not indicate how this debtor "signed" his document, although it was customary for him to do so. The usual method was by the debtor impressing his seal in the wet clay or by pressing his fingernails or the corner of his garment on the edge of the tablet in the presence of witnesses.

The brevity of the text tells us much of the Sumerian scribe's perspicacity in analyzing and presenting the essential features of the litigation. The terms of the security agreement, its execution under oath, its presentation at trial, the judgment of the court and its order are all recorded in less than fifty words.

A Water Easement 4000 Years Old

An easement is an interest in land in the possession of another which entitles the owner of such interest to a limited use or enjoyment of the property.[12]

It is a curious fact, but perhaps because the land has always possessed an abundance of water, little English authority may be found relating to easements in water until well into the nineteenth century:

Neither sanitary nor gastronomic demands required large amounts of water and industrial requirements were limited to mill ponds and fishing. Colonial America embraced somewhat the same conditions. No proper study of the historical precedents of water law has yet been made. That water rights were developed in ancient times we know from fleeting glimpses in Genesis. . . . Irrigation in the Tigris-Euphrates valley is shown both by ruins of irrigation canals and by references in the limited Sumerian and Semitic literature available to us.[13]

The case of *Zimmerman v. Union Paving Company* (4 A2d—Superior Court of Pennsylvania, Jan. 31, 1939) shows how an American court dealt with the subject of water easements. There, a grantor conveyed a portion of a larger tract of land by warranty deed. The deed gave the grantee the express right to conduct water from a spring on the grantor's remaining land. When the grantor subsequently conveyed excavation rights to a third party, the exercise of which destroyed the spring and the grantee's easement, the latter successfully sued for damages. In holding for the grantee, the court declared:

> *The deed created an easement, without question, by its very wording, an easement appurtenant to the land conveyed by the deed . . . certainly all his [*grantor's*] land which was close to the spring and necessary to support its base became a servient estate and the appellee's [*grantee's*] land, for this purpose was the dominant estate.*[14]

Almost four millennia ago, at Sippar, the northernmost of the cities of lower Mesopotamia, in the reign of Zabium (1844-1831 B.C.), three brothers, Bela, Gimil (?) Irra, and Gimil (?) Šamaš, the sons of Nanna(r)-mansum, sold part of a field to Ši-Lamázi, the Sal.Me-Priestess of Shamash. The document of conveyance provided that "From the Tränkanlage [*watering place*] of Nanna(r)-mansum may she water it [*her portion*]" (AR #94). It appears that by the express terms of the grant, Ši-Lamázi acquired an interest that entitled her to a limited use or enjoyment of the vendor's land, an appurtenant easement, making hers the dominant and the vendor's the servient estate.

Before an easement by express grant may be effected, however, it is essential that the grantor have the legal capacity to do so. In this case, the three brothers did not own the Tränkanlage. Fortunately for Ši-Lamázi, who may have relied upon the fact, the true owner of the Tränkanlage, the father of the vendors, Nanna(r)-mansum, appears as the first witness on the document of conveyance. His consent, acquiescence, or ratification of the grant may be presumed.

---

[1] 1 Thomas Atkins Street, The Foundations of Legal Liability, 6 (1906).

[2] Henry de Bracton, Law and Customs of England, Twiss' Trans. II:469, 471.

[3] F. Pollock and F. Maitland, The History of English Law, 451 (2d. ed.1898).

[4] Finkelstein, The Laws of Ur-Nammu, 70.

[5] Coke, Third Inst. 63. Hale, P.C. i 547.

[6] Pollock and Maitland, History of English Law, 493.

[7] State v. Allison, 169 N.C. 375, 85 S.E. 129 (1915).

[8] San Francisco Chronicle, June 17, 1988, reprinted from the Washington Post.

[9] San Francisco Chronicle, Sept. 7, 1987, reprinted from the New York Times.

[10] Driver and Miles, Babylonian Laws, I:488 n.

[11] Bienstock v. McCoy, 88 N.Y.S. 2d. 279, 194 Misc. 927 (1949).

[12] Restatement of Property, Sect. 450.

[13] Thompson on Real Property, 1a:289. A document executed in the reign of Samsuiluna, King of Babylon (1749-1712 B.C.), reads: "The year in which King Samsuiluna had squared stones of one and one half gar, four ellen and ten zoll in length *[ca. thirty-five feet]* hewn in the mountains of the land of the Ammurru [*Upper Syria*] channelled the floods of the Samsuiluna canal into a reservoir, caused them to flow over the broad land, made the arable land rich and produced great wealth and abundance." P. Koschaker and A. Ungnad, *Hammurabi's Gesetze* (Leipzig: Verlag von Eduard Pfeiffer, 1924), 148.

[14] Easements may be appurtenant or in gross. An appurtenant easement is one which is attached to and passes with the dominant tenement (the interest of the owner of the easement) as an appurtenence thereof. An easement in gross is not appurtenant to any estate in the land, but is a mere personal interest in, and right to use, the land of another. Cadwalader v. Bailey, 17 R.I. 495, 23 A. 20, 14 L.R.A. 300 (1891); Pinkum v. Eauclaire, 81 Wisc. 301, 51 N.W. 550 (1892); Restatement of Property, Sect. 454.

EXHIBIT B

THE NEGLIGENT SUMERIAN—MISFEASANT AND NONFEASANT

The notion that a person who should have realized his careless behavior posed an unreasonable risk of harm to others ought to compensate those directly injured by such behavior has had a long and difficult gestation period in English law. It was not until the nineteenth century that the law came to acknowledge negligence as a discrete cause of action.[1] Actions sounding in negligence occur not sooner than the fourteenth century and then only with respect to certain relationships.

Before then, the writ of trespass was the appropriate remedy for all direct injuries to person and property. Trespass provided relief for the intentional offenses—assaults and batteries, thefts of chattels, and trespasses upon real property—that constituted the bulk of noncontractual or tort liabilities recognized at the time. The action of trespass was semicriminal in character. If the appellant-plaintiff failed to allege the appellee-defendant had caused his injuries *vi et armis et contra pacem,* that is, by force of arms and against the king's peace, the royal court obtained no jurisdiction.

Early forms of trespass and other available writs were rigidly construed. Courts frequently denied recourse to appellants whose complaints fell within generally accepted legal principles because they were unable to bring their causes within the letter of the available writs. In 1285, clerks of the Chancery therefore were authorized to issue additional writs,

> *whensoever . . . it shall fortune in the Chancery that in one case a writ is found and in like case, falling under like law and requiring like remedy, is found none.*[2]

The form of action so authorized, to deal with wrongs analagous to but not identical with those covered by trespass, was called trespass "on the case." Because it mitigated the rigidity of its parent action and greatly expanded the remedial process, trespass on the case came to be used "to enforce every species of legally recognized duty to protect every kind of legally recognized right for which no precisely applicable writ could be found or where the appropriate writ had unduly burdensome procedural incidents."[3]

Most importantly, the writ of trespass on the case became the proper remedy for dealing with activities that would today be characterized as negligent. Cases began to appear, toward the middle of the fourteenth century, requiring those involved in trades or common callings to use care in pursuing their occupations:

The original notion of a tort to one's person or property was an injury caused by the act of a stranger, in which the plaintiff did not, in any way, participate. . . . If . . . one saw fit to authorize another to come into contact with his person or property and damage ensued, there was no tort. The person injured took the risk of all injurious consequences, unless the other expressly assumed the risk himself or unless the peculiar nature of one's calling . . . imposed a customary duty to act with reasonable skill.[4]

In 1348, an English court imposed an obligation to act with reasonable skill upon a ferryman who had undertaken to transport the plaintiff's horse across the river Humber. The plaintiff claimed the animal had drowned because the ferryman overloaded the boat.[5]

The action was sustained on the idea that there was a misfeasance on the part of the defendant in the performance of a lawful undertaking, to wit, in his improperly overloading the boat, and that he was liable for the consequences of his misfeasance. The action was in substance based on the defendant's negligence.[6]

Three millennia before the English court reached its decision, the first written law of the ancient Near East dealing with the concept of negligence addressed facts surprisingly similar. The fifth of the Laws of Eshnunna imposed a liability upon a Mesopotamian boatman for his misfeasance as well:

If the boatman is negligent and causes the sinking of the boat, he shall pay in full for everything the sinking of which he caused (ANET, 161).

The Babylonian verb *egûm,* meaning "to be negligent," occurs six times in the Laws of Hammurabi, and the substantive "neglect," or "negligence," (Bab. *mēgūtum*) once.[7] Another phrase denoting laziness or negligence, more or less equivalent, appears in Hammurabi's 53rd law. There, the man who has a dyke in his field must maintain it so as to prevent a breach and damage to his neighbor's crops. If the man "has let his hand be slack" (Bab. *ahšu iddi*) and his neighbor's grain is destroyed, he must "make good" the loss.[8]

The difficulty of grasping and expressing precisely, in twentieth-century terms, a concept of "negligence" that existed, with its countless nuances and colorings, in the mind of an experienced jurist living forty centuries ago in a foreign land is obvious. Conduct is currently held to be negligent in the United States only when some unreasonable risk of danger to others could have been foreseen by an ordinarily prudent person. If the man who lets his arm drop, or his hand be slack, does so under circumstances in which the danger is unforeseeable, he incurs no liability. Inasmuch as the ultimate test of liability is currently one of the reasonableness of the defendant's conduct, it may be that the standard of care required by the eminently reasonable Babylonian, who recognized force majeure defenses still available, was not too far from the modern.[9]

Hammurabi's legal advisors who had framed CH #53 would surely have found unreasonable, if not absurd, a decision reached by the Supreme Court of North Carolina a few years before the outbreak of the American Civil War. In that case the defendant mill owner repeatedly shut down his gates, particularly on Sundays and at night, until he had accumulated a large head of water. He released the water from time to time in immense volumes and with great force and violence so as to damage the plaintiff's dam, constructed below on the same stream.

The plaintiff brought his action "on the case," i.e., sounding in negligence, but the Court, following the inflexible system of common law pleading inherited from English practice, held for the defendant. It explained that because the defendant's act was intentional and the plaintiff's damage immediate, his proper remedy was an action of trespass, *vi et armis,* and not on the case for negligence. Such a result was not infrequent in Anglo-American jurisprudence, where an arcane procedure might require that substance give way to form and an intentional transgressor escape a liability that one merely negligent would have borne.[10] It is very likely that under the circumstances of the North Carolina case, a Babylonian court of Hammurabi's time would have reached a decision most men would regard as more "just" than that rendered by the Supreme Court of one of the United States shortly before Abraham Lincoln became President.

Misfeasance and Nonfeasance

Early Western jurisprudence drew a fundamental distinction between acts of misfeasance, active misconduct on the part of the defendant that caused the plaintiff's injuries, and nonfeasance, the defendant's failure to take positive action to protect another from harm not caused by his own wrongful act. A misfeasance resulted in new harm to the plaintiff; he was positively worse off as a result of the wrongful act. In cases of nonfeasance, the plaintiff was in reality no worse off; he was merely deprived of a protection that would have benefited him had the defendant afforded it.

The obligation to take action to aid others is not general to the highly individualistic common law of England. In his study "The Moral Duty to Aid Others," Francis H. Bohlen examines those noncontractual relationships to which Anglo-American case law has attached a duty of positive action and identifies the common attributes shared by those relationships in order to ascertain their underlying basis. He concludes that the class of positive obligations remaining after removal of those based solely on the consent of individuals comprises four groups: (i) obligations created by statute, wherein the Sovereign imposes the obligation upon its subjects in order to ensure the safety of the community; (ii) obligations arising from family relationships; the duty of a father or husband to provide the necessaries of life to his wife and children; (iii) duties incident to the tenure of real estate—the occupant being bound to take care in the construction and maintenance of all artificial structures and conditions upon his land, that they do not become the cause of injury to those who are forced, in the exercise of their independent rights, to come into contact with the property; and (iv) duties annexed by policy of law or custom to relations voluntarily assumed. These are akin to contract since every man is taken to know the law. By entering into such a relationship, he is deemed to have agreed to its legal incidents.

Having identified the relations to which the duty to take positive steps for the protection of others has adhered, Bohlen emphasizes that such obligations are imposed only when absolutely necessary. He sums up the basis for the rule:

> *Finally, it may be said that these obligations only attach where one party, having exclusive control of a condition, has the entire power to prevent harm arising from it and where the other, from the very nature of the relation, must be altogether helpless and incapable of protecting himself and so is forced to rely completely upon the care of his associate for safety.*[11]

Bohlen's conclusions, based solely upon an analysis of Western case law, are consistent with the attitudes of ancient Mesopotamia, for the idea of positive obligation, which was "slow to receive recognition in [*Western*] law,"[12] may be found in the earliest laws from that region and inferentially, at least, in a Sumerian court decision of the twenty-first century B.C.

In the ancient Near East, private houses, usually one- or two-story buildings constructed of mud brick, were highly vulnerable to the action of the elements. The ravages of wind, rain, and flooding had to be redressed constantly by the diligent house owner. Properties that adjoined depended for their mutual security upon the integrity of their walls, and the land owner who allowed his property to fall into a state of disrepair exposed his neighbor as well as himself to the incursion of the trespasser. It is not surprising to find, therefore, that Sumerian courts charged the property owner with a duty to maintain his grounds.

A *ditilla* tablet (recording a completed legal proceeding) prepared in 2032 B.C. during the reign of Su-Sin, king of Ur, reports that a witness named Urmes testified under oath concerning damage done to the house of Ahu'a by the house of Urlama. Urigilama, the son of Urlama, appeared before the court and declared:

I will not compensate him for the damage caused. Let him take this house (for that)!

The court thereupon awarded the house of Urlama to Ahu'a (NG #143).

Falkenstein suggests the damages described in NG #143 had been assessed in an earlier case. The present action was presumably brought to enforce the judgment against the heirs of the defendant, Urlama, who had died. As a possible basis of liability, Falkenstein alludes to the eleventh law of Lipit-Ishtar, which sets out the obligation to repair in the following manner:

If adjacent to the house of a man the bare ground of (another) man has been neglected and the owner of the house has said to the owner of the bare ground, "Because your ground has been neglected someone may break into my house; strengthen your house," (and) this agreement has been confirmed by him, the owner of the bare ground shall restore to the owner of the house any of his property that is lost (ANET, 160).[13]

The rule of LI #11 may accurately state the common law of ancient Mesopotamia at the time of the 2032 B.C. *ditilla,* and may restate the basis for the award in that case (or in that of its predecessor). LI #11 was promulgated, however, a century and a half after the judgment was recorded. Moreover, LI #11 described a duty expressly undertaken by the defendant to strengthen his house. His liability might on that account have stemmed from breach of the express agreement. Whether such an agreement was involved in NG #143, or its predecessor, and whether the obligation to repair would have been imposed without such an agreement, cannot be determined. Sounding either in contract or tort, however, the gist of the plaintiff's action appears to have been the nonfeasance of the defendant. If true, NG #143 represents the earliest record of a duly constituted court recognizing a private right arising from breach of a duty, contracted or imposed, and awarding damages for injuries sustained by its breach.

The draftsmen of LE clearly required no agreement or acquiescence in order to impose a duty to act upon the ox owner, the dog owner and the owner of the wall threatening to fall, the parties burdened by LE #54-58:

54. If an ox is known to gore habitually and the authorities have brought the fact to the knowledge of its owner, but he does not have his ox dehorned, it gores a man and causes (his) death, then the owner of the ox shall pay two-thirds of a mina of silver.

56. If a dog is vicious and the authorities have brought the fact to the knowledge of its owner, (if, nevertheless) he does not keep it in, it bites a man and causes (his) death, then the owner of the dog shall pay two-thirds of a mina of silver.[14]

58. If a wall is threatening to fall and the authorities have brought the fact to the knowledge of its owner, (if, nevertheless) he does not strengthen his wall, the wall collapses and causes a free man's death, then it is a capital offense, jurisdiction of the king (ANET, 163).[15]

These provisions required only that the defendant be given notice of the dangerous agency or condition in order to charge him with a duty of positive action to prevent injury to others. The modern rule also requires that before an individual may be charged with a duty of care with respect to a dangerous agency or condition, he must first know that the peril exists. A leading case in the United States, decided by the Supreme Court in 1872, involved the shipment of three hundred and twenty-nine pounds of nitroglycerine from New York to California in an unmarked box. Nitroglycerine had been discovered in 1847 and its use for blasting first suggested by Nobel in 1864. Its properties were little known when an expressman in California attempted to open the leaking box with mallet and chisel. Held: The defendant was not liable for injuries caused by the ensuing explosion because he had no reason to know of the nature of the shipment or to suspect its dangerous character.[16]

The procedures instituted in Sumer to deal with the notice issue testify to the ingenuity of the ancient lawmakers, for the difficulty of prosecuting such an action is greatly increased if the true nature of the defendant's belief in the existence of a particular fact must be proved before his duty to act with due care arises. In Eshnunna, receipt of notice from the authorities established the owner's belief beyond question.

No official notice was necessary, however, to impose a positive, noncontractual liability upon the land occupier in the 53rd provision of the Laws of Hammurabi:

If a seignior was too lazy to make (the dike of) his field strong and did not make his dike strong and a break has opened up in his dike and he has accordingly let the water ravage the farmland, the seignior in whose dike the break was opened shall make good the grain that he let get destroyed (ANET, 168).[17]

Litigants continue to argue the age-old issue of the riparian owner's obligation to prevent injury to others by taking positive measures to control the flow of water. In a recent leading California case, the plaintiff alleged the defendant flood control district had failed to maintain and repair a breach in its levee, despite repeated notices by the plaintiff of the dangerous condition. As a result, large quantities of water inundated the plaintiff's land through the breaches, causing damage to his greenhouse and growing plants. The court observed:

It seems to be the basic thought of the district that it was under no affirmative duty to act even after notice of the defective condition of the levee and of the danger to adjoining landowners. This is the basic fallacy of its case. Under the Restatement, which sets forth in succinct form the common law rule, there is such a duty. After having constructed the levee, the district was under the same duty to maintain it in a reasonable manner as a private landowner would be, at least after notice. Thus the plaintiffs have stated a good cause of action for negligence.[18]

CH #53 satisfies Bohlen's criteria for imposition of a positive duty, for the land occupier, in complete control of the potential cause of harm, has the ability by the use of due care to protect his neighbor. The neighbor, unable to protect himself, must of necessity rely upon the land occupier for his safety and the preservation of his property. The following description of the irrigation and flood control system that evolved in ancient Mesopotamia demonstrates why it was necessary for the authorities to impose an affirmative duty to act where, as in CH #53, a vital community interest was involved:

The country . . . has always depended for its fertility . . . almost entirely on perennial irrigation, i.e. irrigation all year round. . . . In a flat land which is almost entirely dependent on an elaborate system of canals for a proper supply of water, constant care is necessary to ensure that this is kept at a proper level and so flows through the whole length of the main channels and down its tributaries; thus a moment's careless-

ness may result not only in leaving crops and cattle dry and parched in one part but also in widespread floods in another part of the district. . . . The tenants of the irrigated lands . . . had each to do his share in the making and maintenance of the dykes and embankments. Further, it appears that each of the riparian owners had a duty to see that he neither flooded his neighbor's lands nor left them high and dry.[19]

In LI #11 and LE #54, 56, and 58, the interest threatened by the nonfeasance of the owner is the person or property of an individual. Ancient lawmakers readily imposed a duty to take positive action in those instances, although the community as a whole would not have been sorely inconvenienced if the recalcitrant ox or dog owner or the owner of the threatening wall escaped liability. The necessity for imposition of the rule was far more acute, however, under the circumstances of CH #53. There, in a society founded upon an intricate web of watercourses maintained by adjoining land occupiers, the magnitude of the injury to the community at large caused by a land occupier's "laziness" or "negligence" would have been intolerable.

Inasmuch as the affirmative obligation is founded in necessity, it follows that the rule was first established when, or soon after, the necessity first arose. CH #53 (and possibly LU #28—see note 17) likely ratified a custom or unwritten law that developed over a course of time, concurrent with development of the irrigation system itself, rather than having risen, full blown, from the inspiration of early lawmakers. Archaeologists have traced the beginnings of the irrigation system along the Tigris and Euphrates back to the late sixth millennium B.C., three full millennia before the first law codes were written. Imposition of a liability for passive inaction, or nonfeasance, which came so late to Anglo-American law, may well, in the East, have antedated recorded history.

---

[1] Negligence is "conduct which falls below the standard established by law for the protection of others against unreasonable risk of harm." Restatement of Torts 282 (2nd ed.). The elements necessary for a cause of action in negligence include: a legal duty to use due care; a breach of that duty; and a reasonably close connection between the conduct and the resulting injury.

[2] Statute of Westminster II.

[3] Francis H. Bohlen, The Moral Duty to Aid Others as a Basis of Tort Liability, 56 U.Pa. L.Rev. 222 (1908).

[4] James Barr Ames, The History of Assumpsit, 2 Harv. L. Rev. 1 (1888).

[5] Y.B. 22 Ass. 94, pl. 41.

[6] 3 Street, The Foundations of Legal Liability, 251 (1906). Holmes explains why the rule probably developed as it did; "One adversely inclined might say that it was one of many signs that the law was administered in the interest of the upper classes." Oliver Wendell Holmes, Jr., The Common Law, 203 (1923).

[7] Driver and Miles, Babylonian Laws, I:461.

[8] Ibid., I:465.

[9] Assuming the reasonable Babylonian was speaking of laziness or negligence at all, for, on its face, the Babylonian phrase of CH #53 may be read as having imposed a strict liability.

[10] Kelly v. Lett, 13 Iredell Law 50 (1851).

[11] Bohlen, Moral Duty, 244.

[12] Prosser, Torts, 191 (1941).

[13] Translation by S.N. Kramer. Bohlen states that the voluntary entry into a relationship, without which an individual may not be charged with a burden of positive action, is incidental, as well, to the occupancy of real estate. "The occupancy of real estate, is, save perhaps in the case where it comes into one's possession by inheritance, a conscious, voluntary act" and "it is possible even to presume a willingness to take the benefit of an inheritance" (243 and n.6). In NG #143 above, Urigilama, who had presumably taken the house by inheritance, burdened with a duty to maintain it so as to prevent injury to his neighbor, severs the "voluntary" relationship and relieves himself of the obligation by divesting himself of his interest.

[14] The general common law rule was that the owner of a dangerous animal was absolutely liable for injuries caused by it, if he knew, or should have known, of the dangerous propensities of the animal. Restatement of Torts, 507, 509. "Dog-bite" statutes today may impose a stricter duty. Cf. Calif. Civil Code 3342.

[15] Cf. Bohlen, Moral Duty, 228: "An occupant of real property is bound at the least to see that care is taken in the maintenance and construction of all artificial structures and conditions upon his land, that they shall not become a source of injury, either permanently or on some particular occasion, to those who, as abutting property owners or persons using adjacent highways, are forced in the exercise of their own independent rights into contact with the property. The duty goes no further than to afford to such persons this species of protection. This lies exclusively within the power of the occupant, he having the exclusive control of the premises; as to this, the abutting owner or wayfarer, being helpless to protect himself, must and is allowed to rely upon the occupant."

[16] The Nitroglycerine Case, 15 Wall 524, 21 L. Ed. 206 (1872).

[17] A similar duty may have been intended in the 28th of the Laws of Ur-Nammu. The basis of the liability in that provision, however, is not clear. The man might have committed an intentional offense, acted carelessly, or been held to a standard of strict liability, making him, in effect, an insurer of his portion of the waterway.

28. If a man caused water to flood the cultivated field of a(nother) man, he shall measure out (to him) three kur of barley per iku of field. Finkelstein, The Laws of Ur-Nammu, 70.

[18] Hayashi v. Alameda County Flood Control, 167 C.A. 2d. 584; 334 P.2 1048 (1966).

[19] Driver and Miles, Babylonian Laws, I:151.

EXHIBIT C

THE EARLIEST LAWS OF CONVERSION

A conversion is any distinct act of dominion wrongfully exercised over another's personal property in denial of or inconsistent with his rights therein.[1]

The tort of conversion recognized in the United States today evolved from the English common law action of trover (Fr. *trouver,* "to find"), which permitted recovery of a lost chattel from a finder who refused to return it upon demand. The original thirteenth-century English writ was enlarged in the sixteenth century to include chattels that had been stolen or bailed. By the beginning of the eighteenth century, the action of trover had come to redress almost all serious interferences with the possessor's right.

The traditional view held that trover and conversion accomplished a "forced sale" of the converted property to the defendant, who thereby became an involuntary purchaser liable for its full value.[2] The defendant was usually barred from tendering the property's return in mitigation of damages.

Contemporary texts list the following as the principal acts of interference with the personal property of another that will be deemed a conversion:

I. A wrongful taking with intent to exclude the owner
II. An unauthorized transfer or disposal
III. A wrongful withholding from one entitled thereto
IV. Destruction, serious damage, or material alteration
V. A purported transfer by one without title or right

Thirty-five centuries before the action for trover and conversion evolved into its final phase in English jurisprudence, the earliest court decisions and legal compilations of the ancient Near East had identified and made actionable the specific acts of interference with the possessor's right included within all of the above categories. The "forced sale" rationale that determined damages awarded pursuant to the English writ, and guides American judges today, also underlay similar awards of the older period.

Contemporary law distinguishes tort from crime. The former is a legal wrong, other than a contract breach, redressable in an action for civil damages. The action is begun and pursued by the person injured. A crime is "a violation of or a failure to perform a legal duty of such importance to the protection of society that the state takes notice thereof and imposes a penalty or punishment for such violation or neglect."[3] A criminal proceeding is instituted and prosecuted by the state, as representative of the public. Its object is to safeguard the common interest by punishing those who break its laws. A criminal prosecution is concerned with the injury done the state; compensation for the victim is usually beyond its purpose.

In addition to giving rise to civil or tort liability, most conversions are today denominated crimes. There is no evidence that jurists of ancient Mesopotamia attempted to distinguish tort from crime. Pertinent sections of the California Penal Code are noted herein, nevertheless, as typical of modern statutes in which contemporary legislators have defined, in current terms, the sins of the sons and daughters of Sumer and Akkad.

The Principal Acts of Conversion

I. A Wrongful Taking with Intent to Exclude the Owner

. . . a conversion generally consists of a wrongful, tortious or unlawful taking of property from the possession of another by fraud, duress, trespass, theft or force and without the other's consent or approbation, express or implied.[4]

A. Robbery

Cal. P.C. 211:

Robbery is the felonious taking of personal property in the possession of another from his person or immediate presence, and against his will, accomplished by means of force or fear.

The first written law dealing with robbery is the second of the Laws of Ur-Nammu: (LU #2)

If a man commits robbery, he will be killed.[5]

Three centuries later, the twenty-second law of Hammurabi repeats the provision: (CH #22)

If a seignior committed robbery and has been caught, that seignior shall be put to death.

Information relating to the prosecution of "criminal" offenses in the neo-Sumerian era is scant. A tablet prepared in the year 2038 B.C., however, provides a fleeting glimpse of the investigation of a "criminal" complaint in which the State played a leading role. When the complainant, Nann-aki'gga, reported to the governor that he had been robbed, the governor dispatched the *mashkim* Urmami,[6] together with an inspector, to investigate the facts. Urmami heard the testimony of the accused and determined that the robbery had not been proved. In a confused recital that follows, a State official apparently took the accused to appear before the judges (NG #121).

In a second case from the same period, the State imposed what punishment it could upon Urmes, a fisherman who robbed Sulgilugal, another fisherman, and fled. Urmes' wife, daughter, and slave were awarded as slaves to the victim (NG #42).

B. Theft

Cal. P.C. 484:

(Theft defined; . . .) (a) Every person who shall feloniously steal, take, carry, lead, or drive away the personal property of another, or who shall fraudulently appropriate property which has been entrusted to him . . . is guilty of theft.

It is curious that the Laws of Ur-Nammu contain no provision devoted expressly to theft, although most of its laws are penal in nature and a number of contemporary case reports describe thefts of various sorts.

At Eshnunna, the sixth law read:

If a man . . . takes possession of a boat (which is) not his, he shall pay 10 shekels of silver.

The taking of the boat is an apparent theft and conversion, but Albrecht Goetze, who translated this provision, advises that the gap in LE #6 might have read: *(who finds himself) in great peril.* If so, the man taking the boat might have been privileged to do so and incurred no liability. The law today recognizes a defense based upon private necessity that permits a person threatened by serious danger to use, or even destroy, the property of another if necessary to save himself. It is the theologian's argument that a starving man may take, without moral guilt, whatever is necessary to sustain life. The test is one of reasonableness; the harm threatening the defendant must be weighed against the harm to the property of the plaintiff. When the threat no longer exists, the defendant must pay for the use of the plaintiff's property. The description of the "man" in LE #6 as being "in great peril" and the charge of ten shekels, possibly for use of the boat, suggests the Sumerian allowed a defense of privilege to a conversion and that his sense of reasonableness was not far from contemporary understanding.

LE #12 and #13 raise a presumption that the man caught in the field or house of a *muskenum*[7] is a thief, without any requirement of an actual taking.

LE #12: A man who is caught in the field of a muskenum in the crop during daytime, shall pay 10 shekels of silver. He who is caught in the crop (at ni)ght, shall die, he shall not get away alive.

LE #13: A man who is caught in the house of a muskenum, in the house, during daytime, shall pay 10 shekels of silver. He who is caught in the house at night, shall die, he shall not get away alive.

Unlike LE #12 and LE #13, where his mere presence in the field or house of a *muskenum* raises a presumption of theft, LI #9 requires that the man be caught stealing:

If a man entered the orchard of (another) man (and) was seized there for stealing, he shall pay 10 shekels of silver.

The Laws of Hammurabi provided the following penalties for thefts of personal property: CH #6—theft of church or state property, the penalty is death for thief and receiver of the stolen goods; CH #8—theft of an ox, sheep, ass, pig, or boat belonging to church or state, restitution is thirtyfold; if owned by a citizen, restitution is tenfold; if the thief is indigent, death; CH #25—appropriation from a house on fire, the culprit is thrown into the fire; CH #94—short weight by a merchant, he forfeits loan; CH #108—short weight by woman wine seller, the water ordeal; CH #254—theft of seed or fodder, mutilation. Thefts of agricultural implements are treated more lightly: CH #259—a plow, 5 shekels; CH #260—a seeder or harrow, 3 shekels.

Modern statutes deal with the offenses addressed by Hammurabi's 25th, 94th, and 108th laws in the following manner:

Cal. P.C. 500:

[Larceny of goods saved from fire in San Francisco: Punishment.] Every person who, in the City and County of San Francisco, saves from fire or from a building endangered by fire, any property, and for

two days thereafter corruptly neglects to notify the owner or Fire Marshal thereof, is punishable by imprisonment in the state prison.

California B. & P.C.A. 12020:

(Use of incorrect weight or measure or instrument.) Misdemeanor. It shall be unlawful for any person, by himself, or through or for another, to use for commercial purposes any weight or measure or weighing, measuring or counting instrument, knowing it to be 'incorrect' as this term is defined. . . . Every person who violates this section is guilty of a misdemeanor.

Although the written Laws of Ur-Nammu were silent on the subject of theft, a case decided in 2031 B.C. indicates the courts of the time punished the wrongful appropriation of another's property. In NG #126, restitution by the thief failed to forestall her prosecution or her loss to her master. Luhuwawa, a slave, stole a garment from Bazi, but later returned it. She was tried, nevertheless, and testified that a slave of Bazi had given it to her. The slave took the oath to support his denial and Luhuwawa was awarded to Bazi. Luhuwawa might have fared better under today's law:

Cal. P.C. 512:

[Intent to restore property: Effect as defense or in mitigation of punishment.] The fact that the accused intended to restore the property embezzled, is no ground of defense or mitigation of punishment, if it has not been restored before an information has been laid before a magistrate, or an indictment found by a grand jury, charging the commission of the offense.

The remaining neo-Sumerian reports are too fragmented to furnish significant details. In NG #202, a collective tablet (one recording more than one decision), two men accused of having stolen a donkey produce two character witnesses to vouch for them. A constable leads them away to appear before the judges. NG #219 describes a theft of onions; NG #203 (a), the theft of a bed; NG #203 (d), simply notes that a party found guilty was awarded as a slave to the victim.

C. Wrongful Dispossessions

Dispossessing another of a chattel by assuming physical control over it, with the intention of exercising such control to the exclusion of the former possessor, is a conversion.

In LU #5 (Finkelstein), #8 ("Animadversiones"), the wrongdoer assumes physical control and manifests a dominion inconsistent with the owner's right:

If a man, in high-handed fashion, deflowered the virgin slave-girl of another man, that man must pay five shekels of silver.[8]

The 31st of the Laws of Eshnunna addresses the same offense:

If a man deprives another man's slave-girl of her virginity, he shall pay one-third of a mina of silver; the slave-girl remains the property of her owner.

LE #22 and #23 describe dispossessions clearly wrongful, where the distraint is without color of right.

LE #22:If a man has no claim against a(nother) man, but (nevertheless) distrains the (other) man's slave-girl, the owner of the slave-girl shall (decla)re under oath: 'Thou hast no claim against me' and he shall pay (him) silver in full compensation for the slave-girl.

LE #23: If a man has no claim against a(nother) man but (nevertheless) distrains the (other) man's slave-girl, detains the distrainee in his house and causes (her) death, he shall give two slave-girls to the owner of the slave-girl as a replacement.

Complete destruction of another's chattel is an obvious conversion and in LE #23, the distrainor, who causes the death of the slave-girl after the original wrongful dispossession, commits a second conversion.

The creditor in CH #113, who resorts to self-help, is guilty of an unlawful taking:

If a seignior held (a debt of) grain or money against a(nother) seignior and he has then taken grain from the granary or threshing floor without the consent of the owner of the grain, they shall prove that that seignior took grain from the granary or threshing floor without the consent of the owner of the grain and he shall return the full amount of grain that he took and he shall also forfeit everything else that he lent.

In CH #241, the distraint of an ox is a conversion, presumably because the ox represents the only means the debtor has of providing for himself, and his only hope of ever repaying the debt:

If a seignior has distrained an ox as a pledge, he shall pay one-third mina of silver.[9]

Two tablets, one from Sumer and the other from Babylon, record the prosecution of lawsuits by private individuals for the unlawful taking of personal property from their possession. These are comparable to modern civil actions in tort for conversion. The first (NG #128), which describes the wrongful asportation of sheep, is equivocal. It is a *ditilla* tablet, the record of a completed legal proceeding, which states that

Urigalima, the son of Urbaba, had "taken away" six *bargalla* sheep from Uralla, for his father. At trial, Urigalima admitted Uralla's testimony was accurate and Urlama, the governor, ordered Urbaba to compensate Uralla for his loss.[10]

More detailed is a later action, brought in 1646 B.C. by a warehouseman, Warad-Sin, who, on the order of Iluni, had received sixty *kur* of grain from Gimillum, the steward of Marduk-musallim, for "further lending." Warad-Sin did as requested and loaned out the grain.[11] Thereafter, and before the loan had been repaid, king Ammisaduqa declared a *mesharum*, an act granting relief to hard-pressed debtors, which appeared to include the debtors to whom Warad-Sin had granted credit. Iluni and Gimillum, concerned for the safety of their investment, demanded return of their grain, but received only Warad-Sin's assurance that the debtors would pay "as they are able." Unsatisfied, Iluni and Gimillum forcibly removed a quantity of grain from the warehouse.

Warad-Sin thereupon brought an action before the judges at Babylon, who assigned the case to the court at Sippar. At trial, Iluni claimed that Gimillum, and not he, had taken the grain, but after imposition of the cleansing oath on the defendant, a settlement was reached. Iluni was to deliver the thirty *kur* of grain taken from the warehouse to Marduk-musallim and pay Warad-Sin sixteen *kur* as a penalty. Warad-Sin's document, found in the portfolio of Marduk-musallim, was canceled, leaving Marduk-musalim thirty *kur* short. This became the obligation of Iluni (AR #273).

Noteworthy in this case is the court's ready acceptance of the bailee Warad-Sin as plaintiff in the action. Roman, English, Continental European, and American lawyers have since debated whether bailor or bailee is the proper party to institute such a suit and what should be the measure of recovery for the one who prevails. California aligned itself with the judges at Sippar and the weight of authority in the United States in 1922, allowing recovery of full damages by the bailee.[12]

II. An Unauthorized Transfer or Disposal

Possession of the defendants in the previous section, "A Wrongful Taking," was always unlawful. This section deals with conversions that occur when the original possession of the defendant bailee is pursuant to contract and therefore lawful, but where a subsequent action of the bailee is inconsistent with the owner's right.

A. Appropriation to own use

An appropriation by a storage-bailee to his own use is a conversion. In 2033 B.C., Kamu received two containers of silver from Urmes and gave a sealed document for them. Kamu then appropriated the contents, claiming that Urmes had taken three hundred and thirty *kur* of barley which belonged to him from the official warehouse. Urmes brought suit and testified the warehouse records showed he had received nothing. He took the purification oath and was awarded damages in an undisclosed amount (NG #205).

Kamu's appropriation of Urmes' silver was an embezzlement under today's law:

Cal.P.C. 503:

"Embezzlement" defined. Embezzlement is the fraudulent appropriation of property by a person to whom it has been entrusted.

Cal. P.C. 507:

When bailee, tenant, or lodger guilty of embezzlement. Every person entrusted with any property as bailee, tenant or lodger, or with any power of attorney for the sale or transfer thereof, who fraudulently converts the same or proceeds thereof to his own use or secretes it or them with fraudulent intent to convert it to his own use is guilty of embezzlement.

Kamu's attempt to justify his conversion and offset his claim against Urmes would not be allowed today:

Cal. P.C. 511:

Claim of title a ground of defense: (Unlawful retention of property as offset not authorized). Upon any indictment for embezzlement, it is a sufficient defense that the property was appropriated openly and avowedly, and under a claim of title preferred in good faith, even though such claim is untenable. But this provision does not excuse the unlawful retention of the property of another to offset or pay demands held against him.

A carrier who appropriates to his own use is also a converter. In the year following the case above, the enterprising Sumerian Adaga failed to turn over four *kur*, ninety *sila* (ca. 30 bu.) of fresh fish which had been given to him for delivery to the palace. He was held liable and assessed sixty *kur* as a penalty (NG #189). The carrier's liability for misappropriation appeared as part of a collection of laws three centuries later in CH #112:

When a seignior was engaged in a (trading) journey and gave silver, gold, (precious) stones, or (other) goods in his possession to a(nother) seignior and consigned (them) to him for transport, if that seignior did not deliver whatever was to be transported where it was to be transported, but has appropriated (it), the owner of the goods to be transported shall prove the charge against that seignior in the matter of whatever was to be transported, but which he did not deliver, and that seignior shall pay to the owner of the goods to be transported fivefold whatever was given to him.

California's statute is specific. Cal. P.C. 505:

When carrier or other person having property for transportation, for hire, guilty of embezzlement. Every carrier or other person having under his control personal property for the purpose of transportation for hire, who fraudulently appropriates it to any use or purpose inconsistent with the safekeeping of such property and its transportation according to his trust, is guilty of embezzlement.

CH #253-55 pose difficulties in translation because of uncertainties in the text and doubt as to the precise meaning of terms used to describe various types of fodder.[13] The seignior hired in these sections is a contract employee, a bailiff in charge of the cultivation of the owner's field.

CH #253: If a seignior hired a(nother) seignior to oversee his field, and lending him feed grain, entrusting him with oxen, contracted with him to cultivate the field, if that seignior stole the seed or fodder and it has been found in his possession, they shall cut off his hand.

CH #254: If he appropriated the feed grain and thus has starved the oxen, he shall make good twofold the grain which he received.

Part of the difficulty in the translation disappears if the concluding clause of CH #253, beginning with *if that seignior*, is regarded as a transposition with CH #254. The latter follows naturally after the protasis of CH #253 ending *cultivate the field* if the suggested transposition is reversed. CH #253 would then read:

If a seignior hired a(nother) seignior to oversee his field, and lending him feed grain, entrusting him with oxen, contracted with him to cultivate the field, if he appropriated the feed grain and thus has starved the oxen, he shall make good twofold the grain which he received.

The feed grain entrusted to the bailiff, after the reversal, is the subject of both protasis and apodosis of CH #253, and CH #254 stands by itself, describing a different offense, a clear theft where the bailiff is caught red-handed:

CH #254: If that seignior stole the seed or fodder and it has been found in his possession, they shall cut off his hand.

Cal. P.C. 508 describes the offense of the unfaithful servant in the following manner:

When clerk, agent or servant guilty of embezzlement. Every clerk, agent or servant of any person who fraudulently appropriates to his own use or secretes with a fraudulent intent to appropriate to his own use, any property of another which has come into his control or care by virtue of his employment as such clerk, agent or servant, is guilty of embezzlement.

The thefts and misappropriations of CH #253-54 are conversions, as are the alternate offenses of CH #255:

If he has let the seignior's oxen out on hire or he stole the seed grain and so has raised nothing in the field, they shall prove it against that seignior and at harvest-time he shall measure out sixty kur of grain per eighteen iku. (i.e., double the normal yield.)

The shepherd or herdsman who sells or changes the brand on sheep or cattle entrusted to him acts in derogation of the owner's right and is guilty of a conversion. CH #265:

If a shepherd, to whom cattle or sheep were given to pasture, became unfaithful and hence has altered the cattlemark or has sold (them), they shall prove it against him and he shall make good in cattle and sheep to their owner tenfold what he stole.

B. Denial of Deposit—Refusal to Return

A bailee who refuses to acknowledge the deposit or to redeliver, after a lawful demand by the owner, is guilty of conversion. During the reign of Su-Sin, in 2031 B.C., Nadi advised Mani that he had taken away five she-donkeys and swore under oath that he would give a receipt for them. When Nadi failed to fulfill his promise, Mani filed a complaint. After the witnesses testified, and one took the oath, the court held for Mani. The specific judgment is not recorded (NG #146).

CH #124 later fixed the liability of a storage-bailee who denied the deposit:

If a seignior gave silver, gold, or any sort of thing for safekeeping to a(nother) seignior in the presence of witnesses and he has denied (the fact) to him, they shall prove it against that seignior and he shall pay double whatever he denied.

CH #120 is ambiguous on its face, but Driver and Miles read it as stating the liability of the storage-bailee in the alternative, (i) for appropriation to his own use and (ii) for denial of the deposit:

If a seignior deposited his grain in a(nother) seignior's house for storage and a loss has then occurred at the granary or the owner of the house opened the storage-room and took grain or he has denied completely (the receipt of) the grain which was stored in his house, the owner of the grain shall set forth the particulars regarding his grain in the presence of god and the owner of the house shall give to the owner of the grain double the grain that he took.

C. Misdelivery

When a bailment terminates, the bailee is bound to return the property deposited to his bailor, or to the holder of a paramount title, if he has knowledge of that interest. Delivery to one not entitled to possession is a conversion and it is immaterial that the bailee acted in good faith or exercised reasonable care to avoid mistake; he delivers at his peril.[14] A prudent bailee, therefore, and especially one faced with the possibility of competing claims, or aware that a third party may possess an interest, will either obtain a court order authorizing the delivery, or procure suitable indemnities from the person to whom he makes delivery. The indemnity may not save him from liability, but will serve as a buffer between him and loss. Two bailees of Old Babylon well understood the wisdom of the latter course.

In a case recorded during the reign of Samsuiluna (1749-1712 B.C.), Sinabusu deposited documents concerning the office of *kalu* priest[15] and his share of an inheritance with the *nisakku*-priest, Nann(r)tum. Two years after the death of Sinabusu, Nann(r)tum delivered the documents to Aba-Ellil-Gin, but only after that gentleman had agreed to settle any claims arising from delivery of the documents to him (AR #236).

A second decision, rendered in Hammurabi's reign, dealt with the pledge of a slave owned by Marsitim to secure a debt owed to Erib-Sin, by his wife, Mazabatum, and himself. Later, Mazabatum and her brother came before the judges, seeking return of the slave after the debt had been paid. The judges ordered that their tablet be broken (their note destroyed) and that the slave be delivered to Mazabatum for return to Marsitim, who was not present at the hearing. The order also provided that Mazabatum and her brother would be responsible to the creditor, Erib-Sin, should any claim be made by Marsitim on account of the slave (AR #27).

The Babylonian judges anticipated a problem that recently caused a major California bank difficulty when it repossessed a boat subject to its security interest. The boat had been sold by its debtor, through a bankrupt dealer, to a third party, who had acquired rights as an owner.

When the debtor paid off the loan, the bank returned the boat to him and was successfully sued for damages by the third party, whose equity had been overlooked.[16]

III. A Wrongful Withholding from One Entitled Thereto

The finder who comes into possession of another's property obtains a special property interest that will usually prevail against everyone except the owner. Upon demand, however, the finder must surrender the property to the owner and his refusal to do so constitutes a conversion. These are the cases that first gave rise to the English writs of trover.[17]

The early laws of Mesopotamia imposed a positive burden upon some finders of attempting to ascertain the owner of lost property, and held a finder delinquent in that duty guilty of theft. In Eshnunna, the law allowed the finder of lost chattels belonging to the palace or to a *muskenum* six days within which to surrender the lost property; after that, a wrongful intent was presumed and he was subject to prosecution for theft.

LE #50:

If the governor, the river commissioner (or) an(other) official whoever it may be seizes a lost slave, a lost slave-girl, a lost ox, a lost donkey belonging to the palace or a muskenum and does not surrender it to Eshnunna, but keeps it in his house, even though he may let pass only seven days, the palace shall prosecute him for theft.

And so shall the State of California prosecute such a finder. Cal. P.C. 485:

(Appropriation of lost property by finder: When theft.) One who finds lost property under circumstances which give him knowledge of or means of inquiry as to the true owner, and who appropriates such property to his own use, or to the use of another person not entitled thereto, without first making reasonable and just efforts to find the owner and to restore the property to him, is guilty of theft.

CH #16 and #19 contained similar provisions concerning the harboring of fugitive slaves and imposed the death penalty for failure to comply.

CH #16: If a seignior has harbored in his house either a fugitive male or female slave belonging to the state or to a private citizen and has not brought him forth at the summons of the police,[18] *that householder shall be put to death.*

*CH #19: If he [*a seignior who has caught a slave in the open*] has kept that slave in his house (and) later the slave has been found in his possession, that seignior shall be put to death.*

In NG #189, Adaga, the audacious Sumerian who had failed to deliver the consignment of fresh fish to the palace, was tried on the same day for the offense of having harbored a bowman absent without leave for four years from service in a troop of the king's archers. The court charged Adaga a "rental" of forty shekels of silver for his use of the king's bowman.

Later, in the reign of Ammisaduqa, three defendants were found in possession of five head of cattle which had "gotten lost" from the herd of another. The *abû-šabim* (police officials?) summoned them to appear and after a hearing ordered them to replace the cattle. The police officials also awarded one head of cattle to their secretary as a penalty (AR #309).

Retaining the found chattel for an unreasonable length of time also gave rise to a "statutory" liability in Sumer. LI #12 deemed the man who harbored a runaway slave for one month a converter:

If a slave-girl or slave of a man has fled into the heart of the city (and) it has been confirmed that he (or she) dwelt in the house of (another) man for one month, he shall give slave for slave.

IV. Destruction, Serious Damage, or Material Alteration

. . . conversion is limited to the more serious forms of interference with the control of property. . . . If the defendant, by his intentional conduct completely destroys the chattel, there is obviously a complete interference and a conversion; and the same must be true if he so radically alters it that its character is substantially changed.[19]

Reference has already been made to the conversions committed by the abuse and ultimate death of the slave-girl held wrongfully by the distrainor (LE #23, p. 204). The award of twofold damages suggests the death was considered an additional offense, after the initial conversion. CH #116 deals with a similar death by abuse, however, where the original taking by the creditor was lawful, and a double penalty is also assessed:

If the pledge has died from beating or abuse in the house of his distrainor, the owner of the pledge shall prove it against his merchant, and if it was the seignior's son, they shall put his son to death; if it was the seignior's slave, he shall pay one-third mina of silver and also forfeit everything else that he lent.[20]

The bailee in CH #245, who beats a hired ox to death, is held liable for the chattel's destruction:

If a seignior hired an ox and has caused its death through carelessness or through beating, he shall make good ox for ox to the owner of the ox.

The brander who removes the slave-mark of a slave not his own commits a distinct act in derogation of the owner's right and is guilty of conversion. CH #226 described the offense and its penalty:

If a brander cut off the slave-mark of a slave not his own without the consent of the owner of the slave, they shall cut off the hand of that brander.

V. A Purported Transfer From One Without Title or Right

A buyer, pledgee, or other transferee of an interest in property whose transferor is a thief or other person without right gets nothing by the transfer. Hence his possession of the true owner's goods under a claim of title or interest is a conversion.[21]

The proposition that one who possesses no proprietary interest can convey none is of ancient origin. Grant Gilmore sums up its recent progress:

It has been said to be a rule rather of logic than of law that a man cannot transfer title to property he does not own, or, as the Latin tag has it: "Qui non habet, ille non dat."

In a footnote Gilmore continues:

. . .the rule appears to have had a long life in the law. It appears in Perkins Profitable Book 14 (15th ed. 1827) first published in 1532 in Law-French. Perkins' version, translated, is ". . . it is common learning in the law, that a man cannot grant or charge that which he hath not. . . ." Another Latin version is Nemo dat quod [qui] non habet. *. . . It appears to have become fashionable to quote the rule in one of its Latin versions only in the nineteenth century. The antique dress may have been thought to be more respectable and more impressive (as well as, perhaps, more comprehensible) than Perkins' Law-French.*[22]

A hollow, cone-shaped tablet from Lagash, presently stored in the Iraq Museum, dates back to the middle of the third millennium B.C. Its inscription lists in detail the foodstuffs paid for the purchase of a piece of real property. The cone tablet is identified with a peg which, according to the tablet, was "driven into the wall." The last portion of the cone's inscription warns that if someone other than the purported seller has possession of the property, the cone "will be driven through the (*seller's*) mouth."[23]

This tablet indicates the would-be purchaser in Sumer four thousand five hundred years ago acquired no more from the fraudulent seller than his counterpart does today in the West. We can only wonder what the reaction of the judges of Lagash would have been could they have known that a rule of logic so obvious to them would be considered more respectable or more impressive by students of the law living four millennia later because it was expressed in a language that would flourish twenty-five centuries after their deaths.

An early case, if not one of first impression, considering the status of a purchaser from a seller without right was heard in the year 2039 B.C. Suili, whose sheep had been stolen, accused Anamu of the theft. Anamu appeared and claimed he had purchased the sheep from Lugalezen. Lugalezen denied the sale, but at trial, seven witnesses testified that Anamu had indeed, "measured out the barley." This tablet is of the *dinutilla* type, in which judgment is suspended until the witnesses and the accused take the formal oath. It does not provide the final decision. Presumably, if the witnesses swore, confirming their testimony, Lugalezen would have been prosecuted as a thief, Suili would have recovered against Anamu, as a converter, and Anamu would have looked to Lugalezen, or his estate, for satisfaction (NG #128).

The lawgivers of Eshnunna first fixed the general rule a century later in LE #40:

If a man buys a slave, a slave-girl, an ox, or any other valuable good, but cannot (legally) establish the seller, he is a thief.

Two documents from Old Babylon demonstrate that the plea of the defendant buyer in possession of lost or stolen property had become fixed by this time. The first is a letter from an unnamed source addressed to a high official in Saduppum, which required the sellers accused to appear and answer the charge brought against them:

Cattle belonging to Badidum were lost and they seized them in the hand of Dukunum and Sarrum-Adad, the tamkarum. This is what they said: "There are the sellers who sold to us. Warad Sin, son of Sa-ilum and Lustamar, son of Sin-X, who sold to us dwell in Saduppum." Having heard (this letter), send Warad-Sin and Lustamar here, so that they may answer their opponent.[24]

The pertinent part of the second document reads:

Sin-eribam, the son of Ilima-aki, they seized in (possession of) stolen property belonging to Ilsu-nasir. He spoke thus: "There is (someone) who sold to me, (namely) *my associate;* (but) *he has fled to Babylon."* [25]

During the reign of Hammurabi, the procedure for similarly testing the chain of title was set out in detail in CH #9-13. In CH #9, a seignior (owner) has found his lost property in possession of another, who claims to have purchased it from a third party. Both produce their witnesses, the purchaser his seller, and the judges consider their statements, made *in the presence of god.* If the seller proves to be the thief, he is put to death, the owner recovers his lost property and the purchaser recovers the purchase monies from the seller's estate. CH#10—If the purchaser fails to produce the seller and his witnesses and the owner has produced his witnesses, the purchaser is put to death as a thief and the owner recovers his lost property. CH#11—If the owner fails to produce his witnesses, he is put to death for making a false claim. CH#12—*If the seller has gone to his fate,* the purchaser recovers fivefold from his estate. CH#13—sets a six-month limit for that seignior to produce his witnesses.

The foregoing provisions invite comparison with the "vouching to warranty" procedure utilized in medieval England to establish the identity of the thief. There, in the twelfth century, if the person having possession of stolen goods was not freshly taken, the owner who wished to reclaim the chattel was obliged to bring an "appeal" in the king's court. The possessor-appellee might defend by claiming to be the vendee of a third person, in which case he would "vouch the third person as warrantor" to appear and defend the action:

If the warrantor failed to appear, or appearing, successfully disputed the sale . . . by wager of battle, the appellor recovered the chattel and the appellee was hanged. If the appellee won in the duel with the vouchee, the vouchee was hanged. If the warrantor came and acknowledged the sale . . . the chattel was put temporarily in his hands, the appellee withdrew from the appeal and the appellor thereupon appealed the warrantor as the thief or with words that he knew no other thief than him. The warrantor might in his turn vouch to warranty or dispute the appellor's right. If the appellor was finally successful against any warrantor, he recovered the chattel. If he was unsuccessful, the chattel was restored to the original appellee.[26]

It is notable that issues involving title to stolen goods resolved by armed combat eight centuries ago in England (a resolution sometimes accomplished by the substitution of a hired champion, falsely vouched as warrantor) were decided in Hammurabi's administration, and before, by courts of law conducted by judges of integrity, who heard the testimony of sworn witnesses, considered the weight to be accorded documentary evidence, and rendered their judgments accordingly. After great argument, England abolished trial by battle in real actions in 1819.

CH #6, CH #7 and CH #35 later dealt with conversions resulting from transfers without right. CH #6 deemed the receiver of stolen goods as culpable as the thief and punished him as severely:

If a seignior stole the property of church or state, that seignior shall be put to death; also the one who received the stolen goods from his hand shall be put to death.

California deals with receipt of all stolen property in Cal. P.C. 496:

(Receiving or concealing stolen property; . . .) 1. Every person who buys or receives any property which has been stolen or which has been obtained in any manner constituting theft or extortion, knowing the property to be so stolen or obtained, or who conceals, sells, withholds or aids in concealing, selling, or withholding any such property from the owner, knowing the property to be so stolen or obtained, is punishable by imprisonment in a state prison, or in a county jail for not more than one year.

The offense of the transferee in CH #7 was aggravated because, in addition to disregarding the requirement that a contract be executed before witnesses, he was charged with notice that the would-be transferor lacked authority to transfer:

If a seignior has purchased or he received for safekeeping either silver or gold or a male slave or a female slave or an ox or a sheep or an ass or any sort of thing from the hand of a seignior's son or a seignior's slave, without witnesses and contracts, since that seignior is a thief, he shall be put to death.

Acquiring some items of property from minors today may also be unlawful. Cal. P.C. 501:

(Purchasing or receiving in pledge junk, etc., of minors, misdemeanor.) (a) Every person who purchases or receives in pledge or by way of mortgage from any person under the age of 16 years, any junk, metal, mechanical tools, or implements, is guilty of a misdemeanor.

In CH #35, the seignior who purchased livestock given to a soldier by the king got nothing.

If a seignior has bought from the hand of a soldier the cattle or sheep which the king gave to the soldier, he shall forfeit his money.

Penalties and Damage Awards

I. Corporal Punishment

In the ancient Near East, punishments prescribed for conversions resulting from robbery, theft, or fraud were frequently corporal, i.e., death, mutilation, or the water ordeal—at least on clay. The few reports available indicate the harsh letter of the law was at times ameliorated by court decision. The punishment meted out where the robber had escaped was the enslavement of his wife, daughter, and slave. Thieves apprehended in the neo-Sumerian cases were usually awarded as slaves to the victims of their offenses. The thief who stole a bed in NG #203 was assigned to the *erén,* a quasi-military support force, a step removed from enslavement. If NG #128, the taking of the six *bargalla* sheep, does involve a theft, as Falkenstein suggests, the penalty for the wrongful taking is merely compensatory. The embezzlement by Adaga of the fresh fish consigned to the palace and his detention of the king's bowman for four years brought him only a monetary penalty, although one probably large enough to ensure his enslavement. If any law seems to have been settled in Mesopotamia, it was that the man in possession of property without convincing proof of ownership was a thief. Nevertheless, when three defendants were found in possession of cattle which had "gotten lost," they were simply ordered to replace the cattle and subjected to a twenty percent fine.

II. Punitive Damages

Many courts recognize that exemplary or punitive damages, which in most jurisdictions are recoverable in tort actions involving ingredients of malice, fraud or wanton and reckless disregard of the plaintiff's rights in addition to compensatory damages for the injury done, are properly recoverable in an action for the conversion of personal property.[27]

This limited sampling of ancient Near Eastern law suggests that courts of the time also allowed punitive damages in actions for conversion. In the code provisions and decisions of Sect. II, above, dealing with the following conversions, where the original possession was pursuant to contract and therefore lawful, the damages assessed contain a punitive element, including mutilation. CH #124 (p. 208, deposit); CH #120 (pp. 208-9, grain); CH #253 and #254 (pp. 207-8, fodder); CH #255 (pp. 207-8, seed grain); CH #265 (p. 208, cattle); NG #189 (p. 206, by carrier); CH #112 (p. 206, same), and CH #116 from Sect. IV (p. 211, death of pledge). The punitive element appears to be lacking, however, even in some outright thefts and forcible dispossessions, i.e. LU #5 (pp. 203-4, rape of slave-girl); CH #259 (p. 202, theft of a plow); CH #260 (p. 202, theft of a seeder), and NG #128 from Sect. I (pp. 204-5, the "taking" of cattle). The punitive awards reflect a Mesopotamian belief that a contractual breach constituted an offense not only against the other contracting party but against the royal and divine authorities from whom the law derived as well. The breach of a promise to behave as a proper and trustworthy bailee was an offense, in and of itself, which compounded the effect of the conversion.

III. The "Forced Sale" Rationale

In the absence of special circumstances, the general modern rule is that the plaintiff may recover the fair, reasonable value of the property converted and may refuse to accept a tender of the property in mitigation of damages:

> *He who interferes with my goods and without delivery by me and without my consent, undertakes to dispose of them as having the property, general or special, does it at his peril to answer to me for the value in trespass if I choose to demand the value.*[28]

The equities that underlie today's "forced sale" rule appear to have guided the judges and legislators of Mesopotamia as well. The court, in NG #128, assessing damages to be paid for the carrying off of the six *bargalla* sheep, required the defendants to "replace," not return, the sheep. The court's award suggests the conversion was regarded as a forced sale, although it is possible the defendants in this case no longer had possession of the sheep and could not have returned them had they been ordered to do so.

The issue arose again when the defendants in AR #309 were found in possession of cattle that had "gotten lost." They, too, were ordered to replace the cattle or compensate for them, although it appears the cattle were on hand and could have been returned; one was awarded as a penalty to the scribe of the presiding official.

The man who harbored a runaway slave in LI #12, was not required to return the slave but after one month had to give "slave for slave."

The version of LE #22 published in ANET provides that the unlawful distraint of the slave-girl requires payment, *in full compensation,* not the return of the slave-girl. It should be noted, however, that a hiatus occurring in LE #22 between the Akkadian words, *mala* and *amtim,* has caused a controversy described by Yaron in *The Laws of Eshnunna,* 183:

> *The sanction laid down in LE #22 for the distress of the slave woman has been the subject of contention between Goetze and Von Soden. In the opinion of the former, the convicted distrainor has to pay silver* mal tahhi amtim—*"in full compensation for the slave woman." Von Soden has repeatedly insisted on reading* mala idi amtim—*"as much as is the hire of a slave woman."*

The difficulty with this tablet could hardly have occurred at a more critical point for the present discussion, nor does the hiatus pose the only difficulty with LE #22, for the section does not specify who is to get possession of the slave woman. If the convicted distrainor retains possession, Goetze's reading of full compensation is consistent with the forced sale theory of damages, although the owner, under those circumstances, should also receive a rental for the slave woman during the time he was deprived of her services. If the distrainor remains in possession, Van Soden's reading would suggest that the owner was to be satisfied with a continuing hire of the slave woman and the denial of her possession as a result of an illegal act by the distrainor, an unlikely result. Conversely, if the slave woman is returned to the owner, Van Soden's reading would appear to be appropriate and equitable, and the full compensation reading unwarranted, unless viewed as a penalty.[29] It may be that either the damage or possession problem of LE #22 will have to be resolved before a reasonable inference may be drawn with respect to the other.

LE #31 expressly rejected the forced sale theory in the circumstances stated, but demonstrated by its denial that the concept was one understood by Mesopotamian lawgivers. There, the man who deprived another man's slave of her virginity was assessed one-third mina of silver, and *the slave-girl remains the property of her owner.*[30]

Whether passage of title to the attacked slave was implicit in LU #5, the Sumerian counterpart of LE #31, is not apparent. The damage award of five shekels allowed by that section was, however, a fair price for a female slave at that time.[31]

It is not possible to determine whether the award of ten shekels for the conversion of the boat in LE #6, if indeed it was a conversion, was based upon a forced sale theory. In light of the flat negation of that rationale in LE #31, however, it might be argued that the same draftsmen who made no comment on the issue in LE #6 intended by their silence to distinguish that section from LE #31, and considered the boat converter to be, in effect, a purchaser.

---

[1] Kaufman v. Provident Sav. Bank & Trust Co. 23 N.Y.S. 2d. 637 (1940) *aff'd.* 263 App. Div. 703, 31 N.Y.S. 2d. 664 (1941).

[2] As a general rule, the highest intermediate value from the date of the conversion until the expiration of a reasonable time after the owner knows, or should have known, of the conversion.

[3] State v. Bundy, Mun. Ohio 154 N.E. 2d. 924 (1956). California Penal Code (herein "Cal. P.C.") 15: "'Crime' and 'public offense' defined. A crime or public offense is an act committed or omitted in violation of a law forbidding or commanding it, and to which is annexed, upon conviction, either of the following punishments: 1. Death;

2. Imprisonment; 3. Fine; 4. Removal from office; or 5. Disqualification to hold and enjoy any office of honor, trust or profit in this state."

[4] 18 Am. Jur.2d. Sect. 25-26.

[5] Animadversiones. Yildiz questions whether Falkenstein's translation of the Sumerian *sa-gaz-šè . .aka* as "to commit robbery" is sufficiently precise. Falkenstein had written, "the neo-Sumerian term for robbery, *sa-gaz-aka,* contains in *sa-gaz* a loan word from the Akkadian, śakkaś-um, which means the same as *habbatum,* 'robber'." NG I:133. Driver and Miles in Babylonian Laws, I:110 explain: "The verb used for 'robbing' (Bab. *habatum*) has elsewhere the meaning of raiding, plunder or pillage so that the offense is closely akin to the English 'robbery' which means stealing by violence or intimidation from a person who is present at the taking."

[6] A court official who served as bailiff, notary, and judge.

[7] A *muškēnum* was a member of a lower social class which at Eshnunna seems to be closely connected with the palace or the temple (ANET 162 n 5).

[8] Finkelstein's view is that the gravamen of the offense is not the rape of the slave-girl, but the "unilateral and unauthorized usurpation of someone else's property." Laws of Ur-Nammu, 73.

[9] "The need for a law prohibiting the distraint of a farmer's oxen is illustrated by a letter of Hammurabi to Sin-idinnam, governor of Larsa, instructing him to investigate a complaint that one of the royal herdsmen has seized three oxen in distraint and kept them for three years and to see that justice is done." Driver and Miles, Babylonian Laws, I:435, citing Ungnad, *Babylonische Briefe aus der Zeit Hammurabi-Dynastie* (va. B1).

The prohibitions of CH #113 and CH #241 against the seizure of grain and distraint of an ox are notable in light of CH #115 and CH #116, which implicitly sanction distraint of the debtor's son or slave.

[10] Falkenstein queries whether a theft was involved in this case, but there is no indication that a preliminary investigation had been undertaken by state officials, and the award lacks a punitive character.

[11] The interest rate on loans of barley, in Hammurabi's reign, was $33^1/_3$ percent; the economic incentive to "lend again" is apparent.

[12] Whitworth v. Jones, 38 C.A.D. 601, 11 Cal. L. Rev. 29 (1922), and Bode v. Lee, 102 Cal. 583, 36 Pac. 936 (1894), a warehouse case.

[13] Driver and Miles, Babylonian Laws, I:446.

[14] "The foundation for the action of conversion rests neither in the knowledge nor the intent of the defendant. It rests upon the unwarranted interference by the defendant with the dominion over the property from which the injury to the latter results. Therefore, neither good nor bad faith, neither care nor negligence, neither knowledge nor ignorance are of the gist of the action." Poggi v. Scott 167 C.372, 139 p. 815 (1914).

[15] The chief function of the *kalu* priest was the singing of lamentations, with instrumental accompaniment, at funerals.

[16] Security Pacific National Bank v. Goodman, 10 U.C.C. Rep. 529 (1972).

[17] 1 Harper and James, The Law of Torts, Sect. 2.29.

[18] Lit. "at the proclamation of the herald."

[19] Prosser, Torts, 107 (1941).

[20] The law treats today's lender more gently. In First National Bank of Seattle v. Gidden, 175 App. Div. 563, 162 N.Y. Supp. 317 (1st Dept. 1916), aff'd. N.Y. 698, 122 N.E. 880

(1919), the bank was unable to redeliver a warehouse receipt for five thousand cases of salmon, upon tender of payment of the debt which it secured. The court held, nevertheless, that "a failure to surrender the warehouse receipt did not constitute a defense to an action on the acceptance." Gilmore comments: "That proposition can be taken as a fixed rock in security law. The bank's behavior may be characterized as negligent, perhaps as grossly negligent. But the same result would follow if the bank willfully refused to return the collateral—or indeed if the bank's officers had eaten the salmon at a great salmon party. There have been a few scattered suggestions in the literature to the effect that a pledgee, guilty of peculiarly outrageous behavior with respect to the collateral should be held to have discharged the debt. The overwhelming weight of authority, however, is that nothing the pledgee can do results in a discharge." Grant Gilmore, Security Interests in Personal Property II: Sect. 42:12 (1965).

Article 9-207 (1) of the Uniform Commercial Code, entitled "Rights and Duties When Collateral is in Secured Party's Possession," imposes a duty upon the pledgee in possession to "use reasonable care in the custody and preservation of collateral in his possession," and 9-207 (3) imposes liability "for any loss" caused by his failure to observe such a duty. See discussion by Gilmore as to whether 9-207 (3) changes the "ancient rule of damages" afforded by "the remedy of trover." Ibid. 42:13.

[21] 4 Witkin, Summary of California Law, 2622 (8th ed. 1974).

[22] Gilmore, Security Interests, I:Sect. 7.10

[23] Piotr Steinkeller and J.N. Postgate, Third-Millennium Legal and Administrative Texts in the Iraq Museum, Baghdad (Winona Lake, Indiana: Eisenbrauns, 1992), 21.

[24] A. Goetze, Fifty Old-Babylonian Letters from Harmal, 28 Sumer 14 (1958), 54ff.

[25] S.D. Simmons, Early Old-Babylon Tablets from Harmal and Elsewhere, 60 JCS 14 (1960) 28ff. The phrase "there is (someone) who sold" may have become "an almost stereotype formula, employed whenever it was desired to shift responsibility to a third person." Reuvon Yaron, The Laws of Eshnunna, 180 (1968).

[26] James Barr Ames, History of Trover, 11 Harv. L. Rev. 279 (1897) .

[27] 18 Am. Jur. Sect. 92.

[28] Gibbs v. Chase, 10 Mass. 125, (1813). Also, " . . .when a wrong complained of amounts to a conversion, the injured party has the right to so treat it and sue for the value of the property so taken and also to refuse to accept it when the wrongdoer offers to return it." Hicks Rubber Co. v. Stacey, 133 S.W. 2d. 249 (Tex. Civ. App. 1939).

[29] Cal. Civ. Code 3336: "(Damages for conversion of personal property). The detriment caused by the wrongful conversion of personal property is presumed to be: First - The value of the property at the time of conversion, with interest from that time, or, an amount sufficient to indemnify the party injured for the loss which is the natural, reasonable and proximate result to the wrongful act complained of and which a proper degree of prudence on his part would not have averted; and Second - A fair compensation for the time and money expended in pursuit of the property."

[30] The high measure of damages awarded by this provision is inexplicable—twenty shekels of silver at a time when a female slave might be purchased for a fraction of that sum—"and the slave-girl remains the property of her owner."

[31] The average price of twelve female slaves sold in discrete transactions recorded in NG was 4.8 shekels.

EXHIBIT D

THE SALE AND LEASE-BACK OF SUMERIAN SLAVES

In a typical "sale and lease-back" transaction, an owner who wishes to withdraw the capital invested in a piece of equipment, but retain its use and enjoyment, sells the equipment to another, frequently a bank or leasing company. The seller receives the purchase price and simultaneously leases the equipment back for a definite term at a specified rental. As with a loan, the rent payments, based upon the value of the chattel and the credit of the lessee, are calculated to repay the full purchase price and provide the lessor with an agreed-upon return on his investment.

Many considerations, including tax advantages, balance-sheet effect, and cost of financing may make a sale-leaseback preferable to a conventional mortgage. A critical issue is whether the indicia of ownership retained by the seller are so numerous or compelling that the arrangement will be viewed by a court as a financing device rather than a lease and the anticipated advantages thereby lost.

At the end of the third millennium B.C., the courts of Sumer readily accepted the sale-leaseback form as conclusive and granted it literal effect. In the fifth year of the reign of Su-Sin, king of Ur (2037-2029 B.C.), a completed legal proceeding (*ditilla*) was recorded which stated that Urenki had purchased a slave, Burmama, from Langa, but that Langa took the slave from Urenki and "brought him again into his hand." The judgment entered required repayment of the purchase price of fourteen shekels of silver and payment of eighteen shekels of silver as a "rental" for three years from the time of purchase (NG # 204[a]). If we assume no appreciation or depreciation in the value of the slave, the lessor Urenki in this case received an annual return in excess of forty percent, uncompounded, on the silver he advanced. The legal rate of interest on a loan of silver at the time of Hammurabi, a somewhat later period, was twenty percent.[1]

Nor is NG #204(a) anomalous. In at least three similar neo-Sumerian cases, the "seller" retained possession of the slave and was later successfully sued by the "buyer" for rentals due. In two instances, the seller provided a guarantor of his obligation to make the requisite lease payments. The high rate of interest involved suggests no true sales were intended in these transactions, but that they were structured as they were simply to avoid legal lending limitations.

Another *ditilla* recorded in Su-Sin's reign reported that Ludingarra had purchased a slave for ten shekels of silver ten years before from the defendant, Urbaba, but had never received possession of the slave. At trial, Urbaba denied he had sold the slave, but the court held against him and awarded the slave to Ludingarra. Because Urbaba had use of the slave for ten years, he was charged a rental of three shekels per year (NG #65).[2]

In NG #66, Andaga kept a slave for four years after the sale and was ordered to pay the buyer a rental for that period at the rate of three shekels per year. In NG #70, the seller Ba sold Dati, the daughter of free parents, to a buyer whose name cannot be determined. Several years later, the buyer demanded the slave and it was discovered that Ba had sold her abroad, an illegal act. The court ordered Ba to provide another slave for the buyer and because the second sale was illegal, to furnish an additional slave to the parents of Dati. A guarantor, Lulisin, had underwritten Ba's obligation to make lease payments. He was ordered to pay the rental of twelve shekels of silver.[3]

In NG #63, Lugal-Ka-gina bought a slave from Urbaba for eight shekels of silver, but the slave at that time "was not settled with Lugal-Ka-gina." When Urbaba died, apparently in the same year, Lugal-Ka-gina rejected the widow's offer of a slave of lesser value in settlement and after trial the judges awarded Lugal-Ka-gina the slave he had purchased. In this case, a guarantor also paid the "guarantee amount," but the tablet is broken and the amount of his payment cannot be determined, nor is the interest rate or amount given.

The lessors' demand for guarantors in NG #63 and #70 is understandable, for a slave who may die or escape offers little comfort as collateral to a lender, especially when the term of the loan has not been fixed and interest accumulated may eventually exceed the value of the slave.[4] It seems likely these investments were unsecured loans garbed as sales merely to avoid interest restrictions and that the true value of the slave was of secondary importance.[5]

The cases set out above share the following characteristics: (i) The subject of the sale is a slave. (ii) The medium of exchange is silver. (iii) The loan is of indefinite duration. (iv) The interest rates, or rentals, are in excess of the legal limit. (v) No document is produced at the trial to confirm the sale. (vi) The plaintiff-lessor prevails.

Centuries later, in the thirty-ninth year of Hammurabi's reign (1753 B.C.), a variation of the sale-leaseback device appears in two transactions involving real property. In AR #141, Silli-istar built a house for the children of Pirhum and leased it back for a period of ten years to recover his building costs. After the term of the lease had expired he was to have no further claim for his costs against the house. Again, four years later, in 1749 B.C., Silli-istar built a house for Sin-imgurrani and leased it back for a period of eight years, again ostensibly to recover his building costs.[6]

Silli-istar's purpose in not taking title to these properties in his own name is unclear, but it was obviously not to his advantage to do so. It is possible his motive was purely financial and that he had factored interest rates into his "building costs" that would have allowed him to circumvent interest limitations. It is also possible he was attempting to avoid royal ordinances aimed at restricting ownership of real property. There is evidence that Rim-Sin, king of Larsa, had sought to limit the acquisition and retention of houses and landed estates by men of great wealth. By distributing such properties he was able to reward his victorious warriors, whose continued support was necessary to face the military threat posed by Hammurabi in the north. It may be that towards the end of his reign Hammurabi experienced similar pressures, prompting him to emulate the measures adopted by the defeated Rim-Sin a few years earlier.

---

[1] CH #88: "*If he [*a merchant*] lent money at interest, he shall receive one-sixth (shekel) six se (i.e. one-fifth shekel) per shekel of silver as interest.*" (Since there were one hundred eighty se in a shekel, the interest rate was again twenty percent. ANET, 169 n.77.)"*The rate on interest fixed in . . . the Laws i.e . . . 20 percent on loans of money, is high, though not excessive in view of the high value of money and it accords more or less with those found in documents of this and other periods.*" Driver and Miles, Babylonian Laws, I:176.

[2] Interest rate estimated by Falkenstein based on NG #204(a).

[3] The sale prices of the slaves in NG #66 and #70 are not given, but the text lists the sale of thirty slaves whose average price was seven shekels. If the slaves of NG #66 and #70 were of average value, the interest rate would be in excess of forty percent.

[4] It strikes a modern reader as curious that the lessors made no attempt to collect rentals as they accrued. Driver and Miles explain: "*It must be remembered that the Babylonians usually . . . seem to have meant only a single sum repayable at the repayment of the capital sum and not a series of payments to be made at stated intervals until the original loan is repaid.*" Babylonian Laws, I:174. Nor was it unusual for the duration of the loan to be left indefinite: "*In the Laws, too, nothing is said of the duration of the loan and this is generally very vaguely expressed in the documents. Thus, while every*

document is exactly dated and so fixes the date of the making of the loan, the time of its repayment together with interest is fixed indefinitely, for example, 'at harvest time,' in such and such month, or in the month calling for payment . . . or on demand or when the creditor comes for payment or the time for it falls due." Ibid., 175.

5 Slaves were, however, frequently used as collateral for loans. NG #116 records the successful foreclosure by a creditor of his lien upon a slave. His loan was of a definite, two-year duration. Moreover, the creditor was awarded the slave after he produced the "relevant document." It is interesting, particularly in view of the jurist's penchant for supporting a dubious legal position with an abundance of documentation, that in none of the lease-back arrangements was a document memorializing the sale introduced at trial, although it was the very cornerstone of cuneiform law that the details of every business transaction be reduced to writing.

6 AR #142. Silli-Istar was a contractor who apparently built houses on speculation. He appeared frequently with his brother, Ibku-Sin, in litigation regarding the purchase of building lots. In AR #284A, Silli-Istar was accused of having purchased a lot with "society funds." He prevailed by testifying that the lot was bought with his mother's money. "No way have society funds purchased the lot," he insisted.

EXHIBIT E

THE MESOPOTAMIAN LAW "CODES": IN REAL LIFE, MEANT TO BE IGNORED?

Many Assyriologists express the view that the Laws of Hammurabi and other ancient law codes of the Near East were part of a religious or academic literature, given little effect in practice. That possibility is raised by Driver and Miles in their review of a case decided during the reign of Samsu-iluna (1749-1712 B.C.). There, a woman named Takkubi married for the second time and brought the son of her first marriage with her to the house of Marduk-nasir, her second husband. Later, she suffered a "stroke of god" (a serious illness, the precise nature of which is unknown) and went before the court with Marduk-nasir, where they were granted a divorce, presumably because of her illness.[1]

In light of section 148 of the Laws of Hammurabi, which provides:

If a man has married a wife and ague attacks her (and) he sets his face to marry another woman, he may marry her. He shall not divorce the wife whom ague has attacked; she shall dwell in the house which he has built and he shall continue to maintain her so long as she lives.

Driver and Miles conclude:

It looks as if the judges can disregard provisions of the Laws, and this case supports the view that the Laws lay down rules of a general character and have not the force of a modern code or of an English statute,[2]

CH #148, however, only denies the husband his traditional right to proceed unilaterally and divorce his wife by saying, "Thou art not my wife." It does not preclude divorce by mutual agreement. In the reported case both parties were before the court when it reached its decision. It may be the heart of Takkubi was satisfied by a settlement from Marduk-nasir and the divorce was consensual. Such a result would be consistent with the rationale of CH #149, the following section, which allows the sick wife to demand return of her dowry and leave the house of her husband if she so chooses. The scant reported facts of this one Babylonian case do not support a sweeping inference that the judges of the time might disregard provisions of the royal law.

Cyrus H. Gordon reasons that the law codes were disregarded in actual life because the business contracts and court decisions of the day omit any reference to them. He reaches the stunning conclusion that "the rediscovery of Hammurabi's code would have come as a complete surprise to most kings of Babylon after Hammurabi."[3] A. Leo Oppenheim advises that such codes represent "interesting formulations of social criticism and should not be taken as normative directions in the manner of post-biblical and Roman law."[4] Jacob J. Finkelstein writes that Mesopotamian law codes are not to be evaluated as law, but as "royal inscriptions of the apologia genre," noting there is never "any adjuration of judges and officials to pay heed to these 'Codes.'"[5]

Little authority is offered to support these surprising statements. Gordon relies upon the fact that contemporaneous contracts and court decisions fail to refer to the kings' codes. However, documentation of the time is notably sparse, little given to surplusage, and reference to laws that had undoubtedly been committed to memory by legal scribes and judges would have been unnecessary. Because the kings' codes were not specified does not mean they could be, or were, disregarded. English decisions did not cite statutes and case law before the last decades of the seventeenth century—A.D.—but few would argue they were ignored before that time. Although applicable law is seldom cited in today's business contracts, no responsible lawyer would begin to draft a contract without having consulted all pertinent statute and case law to ensure that the agreement afforded his client every right and protection available.

Oppenheim refers to Finkelstein's treatise on Ammisaduqa's Edict as his only authority. There, Finkelstein stresses that the purpose of the lower Mesopotamian law codes was "decidedly not legislative, if indeed it is not altogether anachronistic to speak of 'legislation' in the Mesopotamian context." Certainly, if legislation is the "action of making or giving laws" by a legislature, which is "a body of persons invested with the power of making the laws" (O.E.D.), and the power to make the laws in the ancient Near East devolved upon and was retained by the king, it is clearly anachronistic to speak of "legislation" in that period.

Finkelstein also claims that the "stylized prologues and epilogues" of the law codes had a "purely 'historical' and religious import." The prologues and epilogues of Mesopotamian law codes, however, had a greater significance and practical purpose than Finkelstein indicates. In a society where the personal prestige of the ruler was of paramount importance, the constant recital of his virtues and the elaboration of his excellences were vital to the projection of a powerful public image. The prologue to his law code was a panegyric intended to impress his superior qualities upon the consciousness of his people and persuade them that the laws of a wise, powerful, and benevolent king were worthy of being obeyed. The prologue constituted the king's covenant with his people as well, for it implied a limitation upon the royal authority. By acknowledging the need to establish justice and provide for the well-being of his subjects, the king promised those who lived by his laws that he would be a just and merciful ruler.

If the prologue to the great Code of Hammurabi provided the carrot, the epilogue to that collection of laws wielded the stick. The dread sanctions Hammurabi invoked upon successors who failed to heed his instruction furnish powerful evidence of his determination that his laws should endure. Could Hammurabi have intended, when he compiled his lengthy catalogue of maledictions and curses in the epilogue, to cow posterity into observing laws his contemporaries were free to ignore?

As noted, experienced jurists of ancient Mesopotamia had undoubtedly committed its laws to memory. Those men were also fully aware of the formidable power of the crown. The mere failure of recovered documentation to specify that judges and officials had been "adjured" to pay heed to the royal laws hardly justifies an inference that the laws were therefore without legal effect.

I. Justice Was To Be Established

The provisions of Mesopotamian law codes were observed and were the law of the land. The kings' mandate was to establish justice. It was not enough for those rulers to demonstrate they were aware of the chasm between the real and an ideal order or that they were capable of constructing a hypothetical slate of perfect laws. It was the rulers' divinely ordained charge and the pledge they undertook upon assuming the throne to "establish" (Akk. *šakânu*, Sum. *gar*) justice in the land. To establish is "to fix, settle, institute or ordain permanently," "to set up on a secure or permanent basis," "to found (a government, an institution)" (O.E.D.).

Mesopotamian rulers were bound to "make *misaru*," i.e., to implement *kittum,* the eternal and universal truth, on earth. Their actions, institutions, and administrations indicate they well understood their duty. They promulgated just laws, appointed and supervised a judiciary consisting of judges, scribes, bailiffs, archivists, runners, heralds, and other administrative officials. They designated sites at which justice might be obtained and granted their support to the man of little resources that he might levy execution on a judgment obtained for breach of an agreement made pursuant to the king's oath. Only when he had accomplished the practical task of reconstituting the immutable order throughout the land might the Mesopotamian ruler claim he had been the Faithful Shepherd and *šar mišarim* of the people.

II. The First Laws Were Born and Observed of Necessity

The life of the law, said Justice Holmes, *has not been logic; it has been experience. The felt necessities of the time, the prevalent moral and political theories, intuitions of public policy, avowed and unconscious, even the prejudices which judges share with their fellow-men, have had a good deal more to do than the syllogism in determining the rules by which men should be governed."*[6]

When, in the earliest days, disputes were brought to the "arbitration people" of Sumer, no theology of divine revelation, matrix of logic, or written rules were there to guide them. Their judgments came from an innate sense of what was "straight," or right, and what "crooked," or wrong. They resolved contested issues with responses thought appropriate to the felt necessities of their time. The first decision makers heard argument and decided issues involving violent offenses, murder, assaults and batteries, robbery, rape, and other major transgressions, adultery, false swearing, and false accusation. The lawmakers of Ur's Third Dynasty dealt with those very offenses in the first law code of its kind. It was essential that the law curb such behavior if society was to hold together.

Even as Ur-Nammu's draftsmen prepared his laws, Sumerian judges in the field were considering a broad range of related legal and social issues: negligence, marital relationships, wills and testaments, conversions, contractual warranties and breaches. Based upon their decisions, carefully preserved in the archives of the courts and the practices developed to manage the courts, subsequent lawmakers formulated and adopted general substantive principles and procedures facilitating the king's administration of justice. It was essential that rules and practices thus established be observed and enforced if the increasingly complex society of the time was to function. Persons entering into adversarial transactions and relationships had to have some idea of how the courts were likely to reconcile their differences. Honest and responsible judges needed the guidance and support of established standards against which their determinations might be measured. If the laws had no binding or even persuasive effect, judges would have been forced to reconsider, as though for the first time, issues that had been argued and resolved many times before—an absurd conclusion.

A civilization dependent for its existence upon an extensive irrigation system, as was ancient Mesopotamia, could not allow a land occupier to place the entire system at risk by his lack of attention to the segment of dyke committed to his care. The riparian owner had of necessity to be held to account. As Bohlen's exhaustive study of English cases clearly indicates (Exhibit B above), English law imposed a positive duty to act when necessity required. The textual sections of early Mesopotamian law codes also reflected the prevalent moral and political theories of their day and imposed similar obligations. Dictated by contemporary exigencies and drafted by able jurists, the codes were as binding upon the subjects of early Mesopotamia as were the laws subsequently enacted by the peoples of Western civilizations. Necessity was truly the mother of convention.

III. The Ancient Law Codes Incorporated General Principles and Procedures Drawn from Experience

The Mesopotamian law codes were more than religious, academic, or aesthetic exercise; their provisions evolved from the study and consideration of an aggregate of individual decisions. The laws were too specific, too mature, too responsive to real and recurring issues to have sprung from the imagination of poet, priest, or theorist, however gifted. Tempered in the furnace of litigated disputes, as the necessity arose, the laws were cast and refined by continuing reexamination and adjustment. When a consensus was finally reached as to how a particular issue, repeatedly argued, might best be resolved and the time came for the laws to be restated, the king's legal experts embodied those conclusions in his code. At times they included hypothetical issues that flowed from the laws they were prescribing; matters that were widely accepted, on the other hand, were not always included. Hammurabi's Code, for instance, contains no general condemnation of the crime of murder. Frequently, issues that were resolved through litigation gave rise to procedures and principles (if not expressed as such) that were later utilized in drafting legal codes.

Reference has been made to the neo-Sumerian cases dealing with the duty of a homeowner to maintain his property so as not to cause harm to others. From such cases the communal authority—crown, temple, or local—adopted a policy and formulated a principle that it would charge an individual when necessary with an affirmative duty to act so as to avoid causing injury to a neighbor. This principle appears later, codified in Eshnunna, when the wall, ox, and dog owners who have been warned take no steps to curb the dangerous instrumentality and are held liable for damages that result.

The "vouching to warranty" procedure utilized in Medieval England to uncover the defective link in a chain of title (especially that of cattle, as was the case in Babylon) was a conventional pleading early in the ancient Near East. So frequently did the Sumerian defendant have occasion to implead his seller when his right of ownership to cattle he possessed was challenged that his plea, *ša iddinu ibašši,* "there is (someone) who sold," was already the usual response in Eshnunna at the opening of the second millenium B.C.[7] Hammurabi ratified this procedure for resolving the contested title dispute in his Laws #9-13.

The courts of Ur's Third Dynasty carefully analyzed and distinguished the numerous acts of conversion its citizens were guilty of and established principles that defined the nature and extent of an individual's right to own personal property. Rules based upon those decisions become apparent in subsequent law codes (Exhibit C above).

It must have been shortly after the concept of individual ownership gained common acceptance that some ancient borrowed a tool or an animal from his neighbor, or placed an item of property with him for safekeeping. He thereby gave rise to the first of the many complex issues addressed by the law of bailments. What responsibility should be imposed upon the bailee if the object is damaged or destroyed while in his possession? Is he to be held an insurer and liable for all damages, whatever the cause? Is it equitable that he should be charged if the cause of the damage was completely beyond his control and if the damage would have been sustained regardless of the change of possession? The policies adopted and the principles formulated by the courts of Sumer and Akkad to cope with these problems, and to recognize force majeure defenses very early, were drawn from experience, not theory. Hammurabi's response, exempting the bailee under circumstances so similar to the approach taken by modern legislators, is set out in sections #263-67 of his Laws and reviewed in Exhibit I below.

IV. The Mesopotamian "Code"

Compilations of ancient laws sometimes called "Codes" only imperfectly satisfy Berman's definition of a code as a "complete, self-contained, internally consistent, systematically arranged set of legal concepts, principles and rules."[8] Nevertheless, the need to clarify a body of law, organize it rationally, restate and make uniform its propositions fully and authoritatively, and, as Hammurabi said, "provide a place where the man who has a cause may turn to have his cause made clear, his mind at ease," is always a challenge to serious lawmakers. It was as much so to jurists of the Near East four thousand years ago as it was to the experts in the United States who recently "codified," more successfully, the entire corpus of commercial law. Particularly is this true when political entities with varying traditions and methods of putting even widely accepted principles into effect are being brought for the first time under a single, central authority.

Such was the situation facing Hammurabi in the last years of his administration, toward the middle of the eighteenth century B.C., when he had subdued neighboring states and was attempting to exert his kingship over all of Mesopotamia. The myriad of related but divergent laws that obtained in Larsa, Mari, the lands of Elam, Eshnunna, and Subartu (Assyria) if allowed to stand would have hampered commerce, restricted social change, frustrated his judges, and posed a threat to his very leadership. It was essential that his restatement of the law be made everywhere applicable if his government was to be stable and effective. For these reasons, the great sovereign of Babylon had little choice but to install a system of uniform laws.

Because a new set of laws may easily be ignored entirely or construed out of existence by a hostile judiciary, Hammurabi replaced local judges who resisted his changes with his own appointees. These men were familiar with and sympathetic to his views, willing to implement his concept of justice. Whether or not Hammurabi's collection of laws may properly be designated a "code" may not be of fundamental importance. Certainly laws demanded by the necessities of real life, remarkable for their sophistication, representing the best legal thinking of the time, and bearing the imprimatur of the "King of the Four Quarters of the World" carried a formidable persuasive weight.

V. Hammurabi's Explicit Direction

Lines rev. xxv 3ff. of the epilogue to Hammurabi's code read:

> *Let any man who has a cause*
> *come into the presence of the statue of me,*
> *the king of justice,*
> *and then read carefully my inscribed stela,*
> *and give heed to my precious words,*
> *and may my stela make the case clear to him;*
> *may he understand the cause;*
> *may he set his mind at ease! (ANET, 178).*

Referring to this passage in "Ammisaduqa's Edict," Finkelstein writes:

Nor is this meant to imply that in individual cases a litigant could not appeal to the provisions of a code (see CH rev. xxv. 3ff.) but such appeal would have carried moral rather than legal force. (This apparently because the "publication" of Hammurabi's code was not commemorated in a date-formula as the *mesharum* acts were; it was not an "event" of any great consequence to the population of the time [103]).

Hammurabi himself would seem to rule out such an assessment when he sternly lectures his successors about the rule of law in lines rev. xxv-60 through rev. xxvi-16 of the epilogue to his Code. Future kings were not to alter the laws he enacted, the ordinances he prescribed, nor rescind his statutes, but were to heed the words he wrote on his stela, words that would show them the way to guide aright the black-headed people. Hammurabi's thunderous warnings to his successors make it difficult to accept the argument that he intended his contemporaries might ignore his choice words.

The corpus of Hammurabi's Code was not poetic or religious embellishment, as were prologue and epilogue. So long as his laws, the most comprehensive and incisive compilation extant, were known, they could not have been disregarded by any responsible authority. Commercial disputes inevitably arise, for instance, from the very nature of the relationships produced by the basic trading transactions of sale, debt, and deposit. The measures advanced by Hammurabi to deal with such issues, whether accepted, rejected, or modified, must have played an important part in the evaluations of subsequent jurists, who would have been fools indeed to despise his wisdom and instruction.

If the publication of Hammurabi's Code was not a significant event to the citizens of Babylon, they were the exception. Peoples of neighboring and subsequent nations placed a high value upon its provisions, for lawmakers of the Assyrian, Hittite, Hebrew, Persian, neo-Babylonian, Greek, and Rhodian nations later adopted and utilized laws that were based upon Hammurabi's.

---

[1] Driver and Miles, The Babylonian Laws, I:311.

[2] Ibid., n. 1.

[3] Gordon, The Ancient Near East, 246 ff.

[4] Oppenheim, Ancient Mesopotamia, 158.

[5] Finkelstein, Ammisaduqa's Edict and the Babylonian Law "Codes," 15 JCS 103 (1961). All quotes by Finkelstein herein are from this publication.

[6] Holmes, The Common Law, 5 (1923).

[7] Reuvon Yaron, The Laws of Eshnunna, 180.

[8] Harold J. Berman, Western Legal Origins, 90 Harv.L.Rev. 904 (1977).

EXHIBIT F

SOME EARLY MESOPOTAMIAN CONTRACTS OF SURETYSHIP

Distinctions between contracts of suretyship, in which the surety's undertaking is deemed to be primary and direct, and contracts of guarantee, as constituting secondary and collateral obligations, have been much criticized and in some jurisdictions eliminated by statute. Civ. Code Cal. sect. 2787:

> *The distinction between sureties and guarantors is hereby abolished. The terms . . . shall have the same meaning as hereafter in this section defined. A surety or guarantor is one who promises to answer for the debt, default or miscarriage of another or hypothecates property as security therefor.*

In 2033 B.C., the fourth year of the reign of Su-Sin, king of Ur, a legal proceeding took place that involved the lease of a ship by Atu to Ata; Luduga was the *lu-gi-na-ab-tum,* or guarantor. When the ship was subsequently wrecked and the wreckage returned to Atu, he denied he had leased the ship to Ata. The testimony of two witnesses and the oaths of Ata and Luduga at the subsequent trial nevertheless established that the lease was valid (NG #62). Falkenstein comments:

> *In denying the existence of a lease agreement, the lessor evidently wanted to obtain a higher amount, damages and fines, than he was entitled to in view of the existence of a lease agreement and on the basis of damage obviously not caused by negligence. In such cases, KH* [CH]*par.238 sets half the purchase price of the ship as compensation.. . . . It is not clear why the document does not mention the indemnification of the lessor. We can hardly assume that he lost his claim because he denied the existence of a lease agreement.*

It is apparent the owner of the ship hoped to recover damages for conversion by denying the existence of the lease. If the damage to the ship was not caused by the lessee's negligence, as Falkenstein says was the case, but rather by a force beyond his control, the question arises, not of greater or lesser damages, but whether any damages at all were due. If a force majeure defense was available to the lessee, upon tender of the wreckage, his obligation would have ceased.[1]

The answer to Falkenstein's query as to why the document does not mention the indemnification of the lessor may be that the guarantor never agreed to hold the lessor harmless from any loss.[2] He merely underwrote the lessee's rental obligation. Such a reading is consistent with the undertakings in four other cases involving guarantors, reported by Falkenstein from the same period. All four dealt with the sale of slaves, and although the tablets' usual brevity of style makes a precise definition of the nature and extent of the guarantor's undertaking difficult, it seems clear these were true contracts of suretyship and not of insurance.

In NG #51, a husband and wife sold a slave with a guarantor participating. Later, the sellers and the guarantor denied the slave had been sold, but, on trial of the matter, the testimony of two witnesses established that a sale had indeed taken place. There is no evidence the sellers withheld delivery of the slave at the time of sale. Presumably, they had completed performance and the only promise left to be guaranteed was that of the buyer to pay the purchase price. The guarantor's undertaking in this case, therefore, was to pay the sellers in the event of the buyer's default.[3] Two persons gave a similar guarantee in NG #61, but the fragmented text adds little except to demonstrate the circumstances of NG #51 were not unique.

The nature of the guarantor's promise in NG #63, which also involved the sale of a slave, differed, however, from the first two cases. In NG #63, the seller retained possession of the slave after the sale, although the full purchase price had been paid. There is no reason to believe the guarantor had the power to compel performance by the seller, which could only have been to deliver the slave. His undertaking must have been to assure the buyer that the rentals (or interest) contracted for were paid as agreed. In fact, when the seller died within a year, the guarantor paid the buyer the *gi-na-tum,* or guaranteed amount. This was the comparatively minor sum due as a rental for the slave's services for the months he was held by the seller and the full measure of the buyer's damages, since, on trial, he was awarded the slave.

NG #70 reported another instance in which the seller retained possession of the slave after sale and receipt of the purchase price. There, the seller resold the slave and was unable to deliver possession when demand was made by the buyer several years later. Upon trial, the guarantor refused to take the oath, in effect admitting liability. The court ordered him to pay damages in the amount of the rental for the period the slave was kept from the buyer. The seller was ordered to replace the slave.

In the first two cases, NG #51 and #61, the *gi-na-tum* appears to have been the purchase price of the slave, and in the latter two, NG #63 and #70, the amount of the lease payments owed by the sellers for the period they retained possession. In all four cases, the guarantor's promise merely supported the obligation of his principal.

Moses Schorr has published a series of related surety contracts from the eighteenth century B.C. The first, AR #64, stated that after Nur-Samas had demanded payment of a debt of forty shekels owed by Anum-gamil and Belizunu, his wife, Idin-Ea seized Belizunu at Malgum, a location near Sippar, as security for another debt. Nur-Samas then summoned Idin-Ea before the court at Babylon, where he was obliged to give assurances (Sinikisam "supported his hand" to the extent of twenty shekels) that he would produce Belizunu on the day appointed.

Allied to this case and more closely resembling the modern bail-bond arrangement, in which the bondsman agrees to pay a specified sum in the event the principal fails to appear at a designated time, are the following. In each instance the principal defaulted on his obligation and a surety came forward to save him from arrest: AR #66: Two brothers failed to deliver three robes for which the temple had advanced one shekel. A guarantor undertook to produce the robes or pay one shekel "when the hands of the [*debtors*] are withdrawn" from execution; AR #67: A creditor demanded payment of a debt of eighty *ka* of grain from two debtors. They produced a guarantor who promised to pay within five days "after the hands of the [*debtors*] have been withdrawn"; AR #68: A Sal Me priestess came forward to support a debtor who owed five and one-sixth of a *kur* of grain to a sister princess. In this case, unlike #66 and #67, the reporter reversed the image and the guarantor "withdrew the hand" of the creditor.

A contract of suretyship negotiable in form appears in AR #105. On the order of Lu-iskurra, Utul-Istar lent a quantity of oil valued at twenty and two-thirds of a shekel of silver to Warad-Marduk, who agreed to bring back a light-colored slave from Gutium, a land in the Zagros range northeast of Babylon. Lu-iskurra agreed that if Warad-Marduk did not return with the slave within one month, he would pay twenty and two-thirds of a shekel of silver to the holder of his document. The parties to this extraordinary agreement apparently anticipated the sale by Utul-Istar of his contractual right to receive the slave from Gutium.

Finally, in AR #157 and #159, two sureties supported the principal's promise to work for the obligee. The penalty for failure to appear was set "pursuant to the laws of the king."

In each of the cases cited, neo-Sumerian and Babylonian, the undertaking of a third person supported a performance promised by the principal to another. The tripartite relationships thus established were contracts of suretyship, a more limited engagement than an indemnity against loss arising from an unknown or contingent event. In these surety contracts, the guarantor understood the nature of the risk and the extent of his possible loss when he entered into the agreement.

A prudent surety may protect himself against loss in such an arrangement by requiring the principal to furnish suitable indemnities or hypothecate collateral as security.[4] The latter course was taken by a guarantor in a case decided in the reign of Amarsu'ena, king of Ur (2046-2038 B.C.). Urse'illa had provided a guarantee of five shekels of silver for Mansina, a herdsman of pregnant cows. In return Mansina "put up" Huhu, his slave, a promise or pledge he later denied. Much of the remainder of the tablet is illegible, but it appears that when Mansina defaulted on his debt, Urse'illa honored his guarantee and brought an action attempting to recover the slave from Mansina. The action was settled, Urse'illa receiving three pregnant cows (NG #95).

The community indemnified victims of certain losses. CH #22-24 provided that if a robber remained unapprehended, the city and governor in whose territory the robbery was committed had to make good any property and provide compensation to his kin if he were slain.[5] A Sumerian case, only partially legible, raises a possibility of some significance, viz., that the community undertook to provide compensation to victims of nonviolent losses. NG #185 records a shortage of four and two-fifths of a *kur* of barley from a deposit made of fifteen *kur*. The tablet reads: "When Atu and his wife make an oath for four and two-fifths of a royal *kur*, the sons of the city will replace it."

Robbery is not a crime usually associated with shortages at grain elevators. The difficulty of eluding pursuit while burdened with a cartload of grain would have deterred all but the most determined culprit. The shortage in the preceding case was more likely due to one or another of the usual reasons, i.e., a conversion by the bailee, spoilage or destruction of the barley, imprecise measurement at deposit or redelivery, improper calibration of the silo, careless record keeping, or thefts by employees. If this shortage occurred at a privately maintained warehouse, the indemnification by city officials of a private, nonviolent loss was more comprehensive than that provided later by Hammurabi, amounting, in effect, to a contract of insurance.

---

[1] CH #238, cited by Falkenstein as KH, follows three sections in which a liability for negligence is more clearly expressed, but the possibility that CH #238 also deals with a lack of care on the part of the lessee and thereby differs from N.G. #62 cannot be dismissed, particularly in light of Driver and Miles' translation of CH #238: *"If a sailor has let the man's ship founder, but then raised it, he shall give half its price in silver (to its owner)."* Babylonian Laws, II:85. More pertinent may be CH #266, in which the bailee bears no responsibility for damage occasioned by a visitation of god. M. Schorr describes a case similar to NG #62 in AR. There the leased ship was returned to the owner after it had been damaged by "enemy action," a common force majeure defense. Unfortunately, the case was settled, and we have no information as to what the court's decision might have been.

[2] Such an undertaking would constitute a contract of insurance, i.e., "a contract whereby one undertakes to indemnify another against loss, damage or liability arising from an unknown or contingent event. " Meyer v. Building & Realty Service Co. Inc. et. al., 196 N.E. 250, 209 Ind. 125, 100 A.L.R. 1442 (1935).

[3] The sellers apparently attempted to invalidate the sale because they valued the slave more highly after the buyer's default than they had when they agreed to the purchase price, or they would have proceeded directly against the guarantor. He, in turn, joined with the sellers in attempting to set aside the sale in order to be relieved of his own obligation.

[4] "A surety is any person who, being liable to pay a debt, is entitled if it is enforced against him, to be indemnified by some other person who ought himself to have paid it before the surety was compelled to do so." Wendlandt v. Sohre, 37 Minn. 162, 33 N.W. 700.

[5] It was not until 1965 that California became the first of the United States to enact legislation providing compensation to the victims of crimes. Its provisions were far less generous than those of Hammurabi. The California program has been called, "parsimonious," "iniquitous," and "weak-kneed." See California's New Crime Victim Compensation Statute, 11 San Diego Law Review 880 (1974).

EXHIBIT G

THE CLAY COMMODITY AND MONEY "PAPER" OF THE ANCIENT NEAR EAST

I. Grain and Silver as Early Mediums of Exchange

The rich soil of ancient Mesopotamia produced great surpluses of grain, and early in its history, barley, its principal crop, became the basic medium of exchange. Silver was highly valued; although not an indigenous resource, "by the time of Manishtusu, king of Kish, (ca. 2400 B.C.), it was a recognized standard of exchange, one mina of silver being equivalent to 60 gur of grain."[1] Later administrations commonly fixed a ratio between the value of silver and other commodities.

Debts were payable in both mediums. In the Laws of Eshnunna, the state set prices for the hire of a wagon with oxen and driver, a boat, a donkey, and the wages due harvesters, winnowers, and hired hands, all payable in barley or silver. Hammurabi provided that wages, hires, damage awards, and other debts might be paid in silver or grain.[2]

The actual handing over of silver and grain to pay debts, however, presented difficulties. Silver was handled in lumps and ingots, which necessitated weighing at each exchange. Coins were unknown; if Herodotus was correct, gold and silver coinage would be introduced in Lydia a thousand years later. Although the state at times sought to regulate the quality of silver by establishing standards and certifying that which met its criteria, the purity of the metal must have been a source of continuing concern. In practice, evidently silver seldom passed in payment.

During the Old Babylonian period, payments for real estate, slaves, goods and services seem to have been only rarely made in silver, although prices as a rule are quoted according to that standard . . . the dowry lists and precious objects mentioned in the wills of that time bespeak clearly the rarity of silver and gold.[3]

Barley and other grains would have served well enough as payment in transactions where the amounts involved were small and could be dealt with conveniently by the recipient. The bailiff of an estate might well have made a single withdrawal of enough grain from a silo or magazine to pay off his work crew at the end of the day or for a short period of time. Workers would not have needed substantial installations to contain the grain until it was consumed.

In a community as populous as Babylon, however, where trade was extensive and large sums expended to purchase valuable properties, the delivery and receipt of quantities of grain upon the closing of each transaction would have been cumbersome, at least, imposing a heavy strain upon the transportation and storage facilities of the city. Every seller would have had to maintain storage units of sufficient capacity to receive his entire sales volume for any given period. Such measures were unnecessary. Surviving forms and statements indicate that transfers of credits were readily effected and debts paid solely by means of documents.

II. The Storage Documents

1. Contemporary Forms

In the United States today, farmers lacking sufficient space to store and care for a harvest until it is sold often deposit surplus grain and other produce in local "country" elevators. The elevator operator provides skilled management and specialized equipment for cleaning, turning, and otherwise safely storing the commodities. He also serves a marketing role, for prospective purchasers may more easily deal with one person or entity than with a large number of individual farmers. Farmers, in turn, may concentrate their energies on producing a crop instead of negotiating terms of sale. Because they are so widely utilized, local elevators at times control a substantial portion of the wealth of a farming community.

When commodities are deposited, the elevator operator issues a warehouse receipt to the depositor.[4] A warehouse receipt is a written acknowledgment by a warehouseman that he holds specified goods in store for the person to whom the writing is issued.[5] Article 7 of the Uniform Commercial Code, which has been adopted by all states except Louisiana, governs the issuance of warehouse receipts and the rights and obligations of the warehouseman. The U.C.C. comprises ten Articles; Article 3 deals with commercial or "money" paper, i.e., drafts and checks, and expressly excludes "documents of title," i.e., warehouse receipts, bills of lading, or "commodity" paper, which are covered by Article 7.

Warehouse receipts are either negotiable or non-negotiable in form. A negotiable warehouse receipt states that the goods received will be delivered to the bearer or to the order of a person named in the document; all other domestic warehouse receipts are non-negotiable.[6] The special incidents the law presently attaches to possession of a negotiable warehouse receipt need not be considered here. There are, however, two attributes of modern negotiable documents that were presumably shared by their ancient counterparts: (i) The document is issued to the bearer in order to facilitate its transfer, and (ii) Delivery of the commodities shown on a negotiable receipt is conditioned upon surrender of the document. The warehouseman of any age who redelivers to his original depositor or anyone else without canceling a negotiable receipt breaches his contract and exposes himself to a double liability if the document is presented subsequently by an innocent purchaser. Today he may face criminal sanctions as well.

2. Storage Documents of Old Babylon

Despite periodic flooding and a salinization problem that resulted from a long period of overcultivation, ancient Mesopotamia for most of its history was an exporter of agricultural products. Barley was its principal cereal grain because it tolerated the alkaline and salty soil, although wheat and other grains were grown as well. In the third millennium B.C., Mesopotamia was already cultivating extensive palm groves and producing dates by artificial pollination; flour and dates provided the principal components of the Mesopotamian diet.[7]

The following tablet, dated during the reign of Samsuiluna, king of Babylon (1749-1712 B.C.), records the deposit of a quantity of dates for storage:

Two kur of dates, one kur of kimru dates, produce of the garden of Sin-mushallim, lessee of Marduk-liwir, secretary of the soothsayers, which have been given over to Idin-lagamal at the warehouse. At the time of the harvest will he measure out two kur of (plain) dates, one kur of kimru dates to the bearer of his document. On the 10th day of Abu, in the year of the Irnina-Canals. Two witnesses (AR #71).

At Sippar, the following undated tablet was unearthed:

180 dates, produce of the garden in the field of the lower meadow, the property of Erišti-Aja, the daughter of Abî-ištamar, which were deposited in the produce warehouse of Tarâm-Ezida. On the day that Erišti-Aja, the daughter of Abî-ištamar orders her to, will she settle the 180 dates. Month . . . Day . . . Three witnesses (AR #73).

In both tablets, the warehouseman acknowledges that quantities of dates have been received at the warehouse and represents that he will deliver them to the bearer or to the person named. Both thus satisfy the definition of a warehouse receipt used today. The first document, which obligates the warehouseman to deliver to the person presenting the receipt, is negotiable in form; the second, requiring delivery to the original depositor, is non-negotiable.[8]

Evidence is scant as to the legal consequences attached by Mesopotamian courts to the form of such documents. What defense, if any, the issuer might assert against the holder of a negotiable warehouse receipt; how, if at all, notice that a non-negotiable warehouse receipt had been transferred to a third party affected his obligation; what other rights and duties the relationship entailed are not known. The following document, executed during Hammurabi's reign (1792-1750 B.C.), dealing with the return of a deposit after loss of the document, offers some illumination:

Concerning the silver which Zikrum and Zabîtum had given to Silli-Ishtar for safekeeping, so have they received it. Their hearts are content. Should a sealed document surface, it will be destroyed. Seal of the witnesses on the 10th day of Tebîtum, year of the goddess Tashmêtum (AR #235).

AR #235 records the acknowledgment by Zikrum and Zabîtum that they have received silver deposited with Silli-Ishtar, although they have not produced his "document," or receipt. By its terms, Silli-Ishtar is protected from another claim by Zikrum and Zabîtum. He was apparently satisfied that he was secure from any claim by a transferee of his document as well, or he would have demanded further assurances.[9] The warehouse receipt issued to Zikrum and Zabîtum, therefore, was probably non-negotiable in form.

III. Delivery Orders

1. Contemporary Forms

The holder of a non-negotiable warehouse receipt need not surrender it to obtain delivery. He may simply instruct the warehouseman by written order to deliver to a named designee. The essentials of a delivery order are simple.[10] A letter, addressed to the warehouseman, stating "You are hereby authorized to deliver the commodities shown hereon to X" and signed by the holder of the receipt will suffice. The warehouseman makes the delivery authorized, obtains a receipt from the person to whom delivery is made, retains the documents, and adjusts his records accordingly.

2. The Sumerian Letters

In *Texts from Cuneiform Sources,* vol. I, Edmond Sollberger has assembled 373 documents of the neo-Sumerian period, all but five in Sumerian. The majority consist of correspondence ("Letters") directed to and received by officials of high standing. "Senders and addressees include the king and high officials (*sukal-mah, ensi, šaduba, šabra,* etc.) as well as private persons." The Letters are terse and follow a form that may comprise:

(a) ***The Address***—the most common is a version of "What S says, say to A," "What S says," or simply, "Say to A."

(b) ***The Message***—is "normally an order, more rarely, a prayer to do something or to give something to a third party."

(c) ***The Exhortation***—employs a phrase, singly or in combination, (i) urging the addressee into immediate action: "He must not argue!" "It is on his neck!" "There is a flood." "The day must not pass!" "quickly," or (ii) invoking a higher authority: "It is an order of the king" (the "palace," the "chancellor," the "governor," the "comptroller," the "captain"); "These are the king's instructions." "In the king's name," "By the king's life," or (iii) appealing to the addressee's good will: "Who is like my mother?" "Who is like my brother?" "In your being, my brother, is my well being." "May he please my heart."

(d) ***The Date***—relatively few Letters are dated; those that are may state (i) place and month, (ii) month only, (iii) year only, or (iv) most commonly, month and year.

(e) ***The Seal Impression***—"Every letter, at least in theory, bore a seal impression either on the tablet itself or on its envelope."[11]

The following letter, 318, is one of three which contain all five parts:

Say to Ummānī: Let him give Sur-Ee 4 gur barley (as) fodder (for the) fattened oxen. It is (an order) of the governor's comptroller! Year Urbilum was sacked. Seal: Irĝu, scribe, son of Sur-Niĝin.ĝara, the equerry.

Addressing a broad range of matters deemed important enough to have caused their highly placed authors to commit their instructions to writing, the Letters may be divided into two, roughly equal, categories; (i) those ordering the addressee to deliver commodities or objects to a third party and (ii) those requiring actions of a different and more diverse nature.

Instructions to the addressees in the second category of Letters anticipate the performance of a full gamut of remedial actions. Directions to arrest, release, enjoin, compel, deny, grant, evict, quiet title, transfer properties, arbitrate cases suggest that the addressees enjoyed an almost unlimited jurisdiction and authority. These Letters provide a detailed and vivid, if kaleidoscopic, view of a community functioning four thousand years ago.

In the first and more prosaic category, the senders order the addressees to deliver the following commodities or objects to third parties:

(1) ***Grains***—barley, emmer, and wheat. Typical is 13:

> *Say to Abī-atī - Let him give Zāriq 1 gur barley. Seal: Lu-bala, son of Bib(b)ī, the general.*

(2)***Woods***—floor timber, siding for boats, old (seasoned) wood, meswood, fir wood, palm wood, fir for the lintels, *u-sar*-wood for door jambs, *mi bu*-wood for doors, "large pieces" of fir, brushwood, stern planks and stem posts, *sir* wood (cut twigs).

(3) ***Oils***—sesame, noble, sweet, cedar, and date.

(4) ***Livestock***—sheep, oxen, donkeys, rams, goats, calves.

(5) ***Foodstuffs***—flour, beer (dida and bread), ewe's milk, dates, cheese, "food for the dogs," butter, figs, fresh figs, small chick peas, apples, pomegranates.

(6) ***Miscellaneous***—bundles of reeds, silver, packets of brooms, bitumen, straw, wool, a basket of tablets, finger rings ("to the farmer"), an account tablet of wool rations, ox hides, sheep carcasses, a beer tablet, *huzza* (linen) and *sagusba*r (woven) garments, cedar perfumes, ax sheaths, copper for door jambs.

Approximately 140 of the orders in this group of documents direct deliveries of barley, in bulk or in rations. The next most commonly delivered commodities are livestock and carcasses (22), flour (7), bundles of reeds (15). Only seven Letters order delivery of silver. The Letters, therefore, indicate barley was by far the most widely utilized medium of exchange in the neo-Sumerian period. Further, it is clear the Letters served as "delivery orders" to the addressees, who maintained and controlled through an actual or constructive possession the commodities delivered in compliance with the sender's order.

IV. Releasing Procedures

The following tablet demonstrates that commodity credits in the form of grain deposits were used to pay routine debts in Babylon during the eighteenth century B.C. Ellil-malik, a grain warehouseman, accounted for deliveries made directly to creditors (or donees) of Damu-idinnam, the warehouse receipt holder, whose account has been charged.

> *(70) ka of grain taken in receipt by Babâ; 100 ka of grain taken in receipt by the whipmaker (?); 100 ka of grain, purchase price for shoes; 60 ka of grain the same; 70 ka of grain as . . . of the publican taken in receipt by Utta-gallu-mansum.*
>
> *Total 1 kur 30 ka of grain is that which Damu-idinnam has taken in receipt from Ellil-malik. In the year in which king Samsu-iluna erected a throne in the great golden chamber which shines like the stars for the goddess Ningal* (AR #227).

Damu-idinnam authorized deliveries in one of the following ways:

1. He took delivery of the grain at the warehouse door, signed a receipt for it, or exchanged his receipt for one reduced by the amount of the delivery. He then delivered the grain to each of his creditors as needed; the quantities being small, he could easily transport the amounts involved, and his creditors could as easily store the grain upon receipt.

2. He obtained a warehouse receipt from Ellil-malik in the name of his creditor for the amount of the debt, exchanged his own receipt for one in a reduced amount and delivered the new receipt to the person named. Internally, Ellil-malik set up a new account for the creditor. His warehouse receipt served as the equivalent of a modern bank note, money order, or gold certificate, except that it was supported by a quantity of grain with an established value per unit set by the crown.[12] The latter procedure facilitated larger transactions where the grain could not have been conveniently transported or stored by the creditors.

The willingness of a creditor to accept such a document depended upon the reputation and integrity of the warehouseman. Starting in a small community where the warehouseman was established and known to his neighbors, the convenient practice of dealing with documents encouraged exchanging credits by delivery of the documents rather than the commodity itself. In time, as the warehouseman's zone of credibility enlarged, his "paper" became acceptable to a wider market. A document issued by palace or temple agencies might have achieved broad circulation.[13]

Damu-idinnam probably followed neither of the above courses, which required him to visit the warehouse. If he had, he would have signed for receipt of the grain, or his original tablet would have been destroyed and it would not have been necessary for Ellil-malik to issue a report listing the amounts and identifying the recipients of each of his deliveries.

3. If Damu-idinnam held a non-negotiable warehouse receipt, he simply issued an order, similar to those in the first category of Letters, instructing the warehouseman to deliver to the creditor, and gave the tablet to the creditor for presentation at the warehouse. Ellil-malik accepted the order, made the delivery as instructed and obtained a receipt for the delivery from the creditor, or retained the grain and issued a new receipt to the creditor for the required amount, at the latter's option. Ellil-malik charged Damu-idinnam's account in either case.

Damu-idinnam's order followed the form of Sollberger's 231:

Say to Sur-Lama: Let him release the barley which has been paid (for) the house of Atu. He must not argue! (Or, perhaps better, which I have paid [for] the house of Atu.)[14]

Ellil-malik retained delivery orders accepted by him to prove that deliveries had been authorized in the event a claim was later asserted under the terms of Damu-idinnam's original receipt. If a large number of transactions made the documentation unwieldy, Ellil-malik could have reached agreement with Damu-idinnam as to the correct outstanding balance and issued a new receipt for that sum, destroying the old receipt and all previous delivery orders.

AR #227 merely represents Ellil-malik's advice to Damu-idinnam that his account had been charged. No starting or closing balance is given. Earlier tablets, from the reign of Rim-Sin (1822-1763 B.C.), king of Larsa, offer more complete summaries of the deposits and withdrawals that characterize an operating account and a continuing relationship. Those tablets record starting balances of commodities in the *edubba,* or storehouse, list subsequent deposits on a line-item basis, strike a balance (*sag-gar-gar-ra,* or "capital sum") for which the warehouseman is responsible, then list deliveries, again on a line-item basis. The total of deliveries is deducted from the capital sum, leaving a closing balance that serves as the opening statement of the next periodic report.[15] The content of such a report is identical in form to modern bank reconciliation statements recording the activity in a checking account.

In *The Business Life of Ancient Athens,* George N. Calhoun describes a state-controlled system of finance that obtained in the closing centuries of the first millennium B.C. under the Ptolemies and Caesars of Egypt:

There is the quaint and curious system of grain finance developed in the royal granaries and probably without parallel in human history. Here we see grain used as money, checked against, transferred on paper from one account to another, or even from city to city—in fact, every transaction that can be carried on with money duplicated in grain.[16]

The Letters and cases above indicate that Mesopotamia had employed a similar system almost two millennia earlier.

V. The Letters in Colonial America

The Sumerian Letters, which allowed a king or high official to transfer commodity credits expeditiously, came to be widely used. Similar documents are frequent in Babylonian literature. At Mari, an order of the late second millennium B.C. anticipated a modern check by directing the addressee to pay the bearer, upon receipt, one talent of silver.[17] In the reign of Darius I, orders were issued for deliveries of commodities and of a standardized coinage. When Ezra led the Jews of Babylon back to Jerusalem, he carried with him Artaxerxes' order on the treasurers "Across the River" for quantities of silver, wine, oil, and salt.

Orders authorizing delivery of commodities similar to the Sumerian Letters were still serviceable in the new settlements of seventeenth-century America. Such documents and the bailee's notes became the immediate ancestors of modern codified negotiable instruments. In the year 1663, in Charles County, Maryland, "hanna Lee Widdow," who had sold a "hous and land" to the county for "12000 lb. tobacco," filed a petition requesting that the "Gouvernour and Councell of Mariland tacke sum Cours" to see that the tobacco owed her "bee speedily payd." The Governor endorsed the back of the petition, ordering ("Thees are thearfor to Requir you to take sum speedy Cours") the Commissioners of Charles County to cause the Sheriff of that county to deliver the tobacco to the petitioner.[18]

The order of the Maryland Governor, payable in tobacco, was not an anomaly. In Colonial America, instruments payable in commodities were common.[19]

These instruments were in wide circulation and appear frequently in the records of the courts. It is particularly important to note that, unlike their English counterparts, these documents were not required to be payable in money. In addition to money paper, there are bonds, bills of exchange . . . and notes . . . all payable in commodities."[20]

In Virginia, the Inspection Act of 1730 attempted to regulate the quality of warehoused tobacco by authorizing licensed inspectors to destroy "trash, bad, unsound and unmerchantable tobacco." Tobacco warehousemen issued negotiable tobacco notes, the only legal tender for payment of public taxes, fees, and rates. These documents were widely circulated. The Assembly compensated owners of tobacco stored in a public warehouse that was destroyed by fire, flood, or other cause.[21]

The Letter Orders of Sumer are ancient precursors of present-day Delivery Orders and Bills of Exchange. Although payable in commodities, amongst the original three parties to the transaction—the Sender-drawer, Addressee-drawee, and Recipient-payee—Letter-Orders performed the same function as contemporary checks drawn on a bank.

VI. A Babylonian Bill of Exchange

What father has not, at some time, received an urgent plea for funds from a son marooned in a distant place? At the nearest office, the worried parent deposits a sum of money with Western Union's agent, who directs his counterpart in an office nearest the anxious offspring to pay over the amount deposited, and an incipient crisis is averted.

In ancient Mesopotamia, a similar procedure enabled a father to ransom a son being held captive in a foreign land. During the reign of Hammurabi, the *tamkārum* was a traveling merchant whose occupation brought him to many foreign lands. When a countryman was captured and held prisoner of war in a foreign country, the *tamkārum,* because of his familiarity with, and access to, foreign markets, was an ideal intermediary to negotiate the release and ransom of the prisoner. Such activities were so much a part of his function that Hammurabi devoted a detailed section to the *tamkārum's* role as ransomer. CH #32 provided that if the *tamkārum* has paid for the prisoner's release, he shall be entitled to reimbursement from the captive, the temple, and the crown, in that order. In a contemporary letter, Hammurabi instructed two officials to take 10 shekels of silver from the temple and give it to the *tamkārum* to obtain the release of a prisoner of war.[22]

In a second case, two men captured by the enemy request the wife of the *rab Amurrim* to intercede with their fathers for their release; the *tamkārum* was to be satisfied so that he would write to his *marum*[23] to release them.[24] In this case, we may presume the *tamkārum* would have been "satisfied" and more disposed to write the letter requested by the captives if their fathers had deposited with him a quantity of silver, grain, or oil equal to the amount he was to order his *marum* to deliver to their captors, plus, perhaps, a small increment for his trouble. Such a letter would have constituted a rudimentary form of a modern bill of exchange; i.e., in general terms, a written order to the addressee to pay a certain sum on a given date to a person designated.[25] This procedure, which surely did not originate with these captives, is essentially the same as that which has contributed to the past success of Western Union.

The earliest form of a bill of exchange noted by Britton in his *Handbook on Bills and Notes* is an Italian bill of the thirteenth century A.D., a "letter addressed by B to C asking C to pay to a third person D a sum of money which A has entrusted to B for this purpose. This letter is handed by B to A who sends it on to D and presents it for payment to C."[26]

The Babylonian procedure set out in the second case above may be distinguished from the Italian, for the *tamkārum* writes to his agent directly; he does not give a document to A for presentation to C; he may, indeed, be the only one with access to C. The procedures of both periods agree essentially, however, in that the Babylonian father (A), the remitter, deposits a sum of money with the *tamkārum* (B), the drawer, who instructs his *marum* (C), the drawee, to pay the money to the captor of the remitter's son (D), the payee.

A modern check is a particular kind of bill of exchange; the order is drawn on a bank and is payable on demand. Hammurabi's letter, through his intermediaries, was a written order to the temple bankers to pay over a sum of silver to the *tamkārum,* a remote ancestor of a very common present-day instrument.[27]

VII. Delivery Orders and Bills of Exchange of the Achaemenid Era

Shortly after Darius ascended the throne of Persia in 522 B.C., he caused a complex of palaces to be erected at Persepolis. Some measure of the city's former grandeur may be gleaned from its broad expanse, its tall columns fluted in Greek style, and the magnificent, finely wrought stone sculpture that remains. To assist his own workers with the construction, Darius hired skilled stonemasons, woodcutters, metalworkers, and goldsmiths from neighboring lands, Ionia, Lydia, Media, Syria, and Egypt. He paid these artisans monthly, in commodities drawn from the royal storehouse and by cash payments from the royal treasury.[28]

Two discrete finds at Persepolis revealed the forms of such payments. In 1933, excavators discovered almost thirty thousand texts within the fortification walls of the site. These "Fortification Texts" relate to (i) the receipt or inventory of commodities—grain, flour, wine, beer, and sheep, or (ii) the distribution of such commodities to workmen and others. Between 1936-38, additional tablets were recovered from the city's treasury building. These dealt exclusively with the payment of cash to workmen, money supplementing the "in kind" distributions from the storerooms.[29] Five of the treasury documents employed the following formula: (i) "To A, the treasurer, speak," (ii) "B says, x karsha, y shekels silver, give to them as wages," (iii) "to workmen at Persepolis under (supervisor) C," (iv) the sum to be paid each workman is then specified.

The treasury tablets were molded around a string that protruded from either side of a flat end, and Cameron says, "we may now be assured" there was a second document, also equipped with a string and tied to the treasury tablets, ordering the chief of the storehouse to release quantities of commodities to the same people as the balance of their pay.[30]

Payment of wages earned by skilled workers of the Near East in the sixth century B.C., therefore, was effected by the use of documents that are ancient equivalents of both the delivery orders ("Commodity Paper" of U.C.C. Art. 7) and bills of exchange ("Money Paper" of U.C.C. Art. 3) of today. It is interesting to note that the Persian physically, if not conceptually, was accustomed to fastening together the commodity and money paper that modern draftsmen have so scrupulously kept separate.

VIII. The Transfer of Intangible Rights in Old Babylon

A long-prevailing notion that because an intangible right could not be delivered a debt could not be assigned impeded development of the law of commercial instruments in England. Thomas Atkins Street writes, "Legal theory begins with the principle that rights of action cannot be assigned at all."[31] Maitland believed that in early law there was a mental incapacity to conceive that a mere right might be transferred from one person to another. Britton offers another explanation: "The debtor-creditor relation was regarded as too personal to permit the first creditor to substitute another in his place."[32]

Ancient Mesopotamian merchants and financiers, however, were not burdened by the legal strictures placed upon, and the intellectual incapacities attributed to, men who lived three millennia after them. They freely substituted parties, debtors and creditors, who were strangers to the original loan transactions.[33]

In a tablet recovered at Sippar, dating from the eighteenth century B.C., the debtor assigned to his son a debt of nine shekels, owed by him to three creditors, a practice that would not have found favor in all cases, with all creditors (AR #61). In fact, another note, also from Sippar, executed by Imgur-rum for three and one-half shekels of "ringing" silver, contained an express prohibition against assignment and provided that Imgur-rum would pay back the silver to the bearer of his document (AR #63).[34]

An unusual tablet from Babylon, executed in 1643 B.C., documents the transfer of a debt at that time:

Concerning the two thirds of a shekel and forty she of silver out of the purchase money of a female slave, which Ali-talimi, the son of Awil-anum and Mudabshu, his brother, owned against Warad-kubi, the son of Ibku-Nikal; this possession has passed from Ali-talimi and Mudab. Warad-kubi in ten days shall pay the money to Sin-rimeni, the son of Ibni-Shamash.[35]

Warad-kubi's debt to the brothers Ali-talimi and Mudabshu represented the balance due on the purchase price of a female slave. Before the debt was transferred to Sin-rimeni, the brothers possessed either a note or an account receivable, i.e., a right to payment of the balance due, with or without a written promise to pay. Because of the strict rule of Babylonian business practice that all such arrangements be in writing, it is likely the brothers held Warad-kubi's note. Unfortunately, we are not told how or by whom the present tablet was executed and it is difficult to understand its true purport. The present perfect form, "has passed," of the operative verb suggests the document represented a written confirmation of a prior transfer as well as Warad-kubi's agreement to accept the assignment and pay Sin-rimeni directly in ten days' time. Executed by the brothers alone, the tablet might also have constituted their direction to Warad-kubi to pay Sin-rimeni—in effect an endorsement of the note—necessarily written on a separate document because of the difficulty, if not impossibility, of writing on the dried tablet they held (an oxymoronic unattachable allonge).

In the unlikely event that Warad-kubi's obligation was not evidenced by a written promise to pay before the transfer, the brothers possessed an "open" account receivable, a right to payment of the balance of the purchase price not evidenced by a writing. If their transfer of that obligation to Sin-rimeni was made for a consideration, the transaction represents early evidence of the sale of an account receivable. Today, such sales and assignments provide the basis of a multibillion-dollar industry.[36]

---

[1] Sir Leonard Woolley, History of Mankind, vol. I, part 2, The Beginnings of Civilization (New York: The New American Library, 1936), 277. (In Babylon, 300 *qu* equalled 1 *kur* [Sum. *gur*] or ca. seven + bushels.)

[2] CH #89: "If a seignior, who (incurred) a debt does not have the money to pay (it) back, but has the grain, (the merchant) shall take grain for his money (with its interest) in accordance with the ratio fixed by the king." ANET, 169.

[3] Oppenheim, Ancient Mesopotamia, 87.

[4] Frequently in the form of a "scale ticket" printed automatically when the truck bearing the produce is weighed, tare and net.

[5] N.D. Vannett v. Reilly - Hertz Automobile Co. 173 NW 466, 42 N.S. 607 (1919).

[6] U.C.C. 7-104 (1): "A warehouse receipt, bill of lading or other document of title is negotiable (a) if by its terms the goods are to be delivered to bearer or to the order of a named person; or (b) where recognized in overseas trade, if it runs to a named person or

assignee. (2) Any other document is non-negotiable." Standard forms of negotiable and non-negotiable warehouse receipts approved by the American Warehousemen's Association are attached to Exhibit H herein.

[7] Lloyd, The Archeology of Mesopotamia, 19 (1978).

[8] The original parties to the negotiable document understood that it might ultimately be presented by a stranger to the original transaction. Today, it is common practice to sell grain stored in elevators merely by endorsing and delivering warehouse receipts if they are negotiable in form.

[9] In AR #236, a priest-bailee, delivering papers entrusted to him, to a person other than the original bailor, requires that the recipient "settle further claims with respect to it."

[10] U.C.C. 7-102 (1) (d): "'Delivery Order' means a written order to deliver goods directed to a warehouseman, carrier or other person who, in the ordinary course of business, issues warehouse receipts or bills of lading."

[11] Sollberger, Texts From Cuneiform Sources, Vol. I, The Business and Administrative Correspondence Under the Kings of Ur, (Locust Valley, New York: J.J. Augustin Publisher, 1966), 5.

[12] Gold Certificates, a form of paper money, "were issued as mere certificates of ownership of gold held in Treasury, dollar for dollar, for their redemption. They are issued against gold and bullion deposited in the United States treasury. They are something like warehouse receipts for gold." Whitney, The Law of Modern Commercial Practices, 17 (2nd. ed., 1958).

[13] The Mesopotamian authenticated his tablets by seal, witnesses, and by impressing his fingernails or the hem of his garment into the wet clay, or by a combination of these methods. The use of bearer documents suggests the authentication thus achieved was sufficiently persuasive to enable a person not a party to the original transaction to part with a consideration, confident of the document's enforceability. As the warehouseman's own "paper" gained wider acceptance, he might have developed an equal confidence in the authenticity of the orders addressed to him.

[14] Tablet 231 is interesting because it specifies the consideration for which the order was issued, although it lacks the usual designation of the third party to whom delivery is to be made, as in 13:

Say to Abi-ati: - Let him give Zariq 1 gur barley,
Seal: Lu-bala.sa, son of Bib(b)i, the general.

[15] Leemans, Legal and Economic Records from the Kingdom of Larsa, 50 (1954).

[16] Calhoun, The Business Life of Ancient Athens, 130 (1926).

[17] Astour, New Evidence on the Last Days of Ugarit, 69 AJA 255 (1965).

[18] 53 Archives of Maryland 414 (1936).

[19] Because of the instability of the Colonial monetary system, payment in commodities was often preferred. In early eighteenth-century Virginia, the clergy was compensated in pounds of tobacco, and a parish was deemed more desirable if it produced the more highly valued, "sweet scented" type.

[20] Beutel on Brannon, The Negotiable Instruments Law, 37. Tobacco, wampum and beaver skins, corn and many other commodities were used "either de facto or with approval of colonial legislatures as mediums of exchange or legal tender" (a Virginia statute authorized payment in twenty-two different commodities).

[21] In a neo-Sumerian *dinutilla* text, the "sons of the city" provide compensation for a shortage of barley. The cause of the shortage is not given. NG 185.

[22] Yale Oriental Series, Babylonian Texts, II 32.

[23] Lit. "son," possibly "agent," "apprentice."

[24] King, The Letters and Inscriptions of Hammurabi.

[25] More precisely: "A written order of one party upon another for the absolute payment of money to a third or designated person, or to his order or bearer, upon demand, or at a specified or determinable time." Bull v. First Nat'l. Bank, 123 U.S. 105, 31 L.ed. 97, 8 S.Ct. 62 (1887). See U.C.C. 3-104.

[26] Britton, Handbook on the Law of Bills and Notes, 4 (1943).

[27] A check is a "draft (bill of exchange) drawn on a bank and payable on demand. " U.C.C. 3-104 (2) (b).

[28] Cameron, Persepolis Treasury Tablets Old and New, 17 JNES 161 (1958).

[29] The right to coin money was an exclusive prerogative of the Persian Great King. "Money" is a defined term under the Uniform Commercial Code: " . . . .a medium of exchange authorized or adopted by a domestic or foreign government as part of its currency." U.C.C. 1-201.

[30] These are comparable to the "Letter Orders" addressed to grain warehousemen used fifteen hundred years before by Sumerian officials.

[31] 3 Street, Foundations of Legal Liability, 76.

[32] Britton, Handbook, 3.

[33] In The Old Babylonian Merchant, 53 (1950), Leemans notes a tablet, TCL X,108, from the time of Rim-Sin at Larsa (1822-1763 B.C.), which records that Nammu-tukulti ordered Mannia to pay to Hurasatum one-third of a shekel of silver, the balance of an account which Mannia owed to Nammu-tukulti, and that this was done.

[34] Other bearer documents are set out in AR #58, 59, 60, and 105.

[35] Chiera, Old Babylonian Contracts, 151 (1922).

[36] Toward the end of the eighteenth century, British textile mills utilized "factors" as sales and marketing representatives to exploit the rapidly expanding American market. Eventually the factors assumed the credit risk on the sales and bought the account they had generated, the debtor being notified to pay the factor directly. Today factoring has developed into a great commercial banking business, as has the practice of financing accounts receivable, either by sale or by assignment as security. See Whitney, The Law of Modern Commercial Practices, 938.

EXHIBIT H

AN ANCIENT DISCLAIMER

Phoenician ports of the early sixth century B.C. teemed with a commerce described graphically by Ezekiel. There, the merchants of Tyre imported "all kinds of riches," from everywhere in the Mediterranean: fir, cedar, oak, and boxwood trees for ship building, Egyptian linens for sails, silver, iron, tin, and lead, men, pilots and mariners, vessels of bronze, horses, war horses and mules, horns of ivory and ebony, Syrian emeralds, coral, rubies, and food, wheat, olives, and early figs, honey, oil, and balm. In exchange, they gave manufactured goods, the wares, the multitude of handiworks produced by their craftsmen and builders.[1] Documents that traced the generation and movement of these commodities achieved a high level of sophistication.

Two tablets recovered at Uruk, an ancient and historic city in southern Babylonia, attest to the accuracy of Ezekiel's description of the numerous commodities received during the sixth century in port cities of the eastern Mediterranean and transported into the interior of Asia Minor.[2] (Handsomely painted Athenian vases of this period have been recovered there, indicating that Greek merchants were no strangers to the extensive commercial distribution of the East.) The Uruk documents contain substantial entries: six hundred *minas* of copper from Yamana, two hundred and thirty-three *minas* of alum from Egypt, two hundred and fifty-seven *minas* of iron from Lebanon, and other items of metals, dyes, wines, and foodstuffs. One of the tablets bears a legend that could only have been inserted by a bailee experienced in the storage and transportation of merchandise.

All reasonable men will agree that if A deposits a sealed box with B, telling him it contains silver plate, and B, in good faith, issues a receipt to A for a box of silver plate, B should have no responsibility if he returns the box, unopened, to A, and it proves to contain plate made of a material less valuable than silver. If A, however, passes the receipt on to C, who gives value, relying upon the representation that the box contains silver plate, and A absconds, the question of whether B or C is to bear the loss must be addressed.

Today's statutes provide that B, the bailee, will have no responsibility for a misdescription if the description of the box's contents provided by A is set out under a legend that reads, "'contents, condition and quality unknown,' 'said to contain' or the like, if such indication be true, or the party or purchaser otherwise had notice."[3] All modern professionally prepared warehouse receipts and bills of lading contain such a legend, conspicuously displayed, above the description of the goods.[4]

Oppenheim describes the Uruk documents as "typical for the Mesopotamian trade that was concerned with distribution of large-scale imports furnished by overland trade." In the earlier of the documents, an entry lists eight boxes, each reinforced with copper, a "sort of strongbox transported under lock and seal." The entry bears an admonitory legend, "whose content has not been established," thereby anticipating the very language recommended by today's statutes and alerting a possible purchaser of the document, as well as the bailor himself, that the bailee assumed no responsibility for the contents of the boxes.

This may seem an obvious course, and although we may presume the Mesopotamian bailee had reason to believe he might so exculpate himself, we do not know what effect the courts of the time accorded the provision. The law in the United States on this issue was settled by state statutes only in the opening decades of the twentieth century. The Commissioner's note to Sect. 20 of the Uniform Warehouse Receipts Act, the predecessor of Sect. 7-203 of the Uniform Commercial Code, read:

> *This section imposes upon the warehouseman a stricter rule than that generally in force in this country in that it makes a warehouseman liable for an innocent misdescription of the goods. . . . But as the warehouseman can readily protect himself by inserting in the receipt only what he knows, namely, the marks on the goods or the statements of the depositer regarding them, it seems best to make the warehouseman responsible for what he asserts.*

The second of the two documents published by Oppenheim was issued in 550 B.C., a year and two days after the first. Each document lists quantities of merchandise received from Egypt, Yamana, and Lebanon by the same consignee. The second document contains seven entries for major amounts, identical to seven on the first, leading Oppenheim to conclude that shipments were made on a "recurrent, in fact, an annual basis."

It is possible, however, that the identical entries on the two documents represent merchandise that, in fact, never moved. When the first document was issued, it contained twelve entries. If the depositor had occasion to withdraw part of the merchandise listed, the withdrawals could not have been posted on the dry clay tablets held by the parties. Even if not contained in an envelope (frequently used), the need to moisten the tablet, restate the amounts remaining, and authenticate the changes, more than once, would presumably have been impracticable. Two courses were then open to the storer. First, he could destroy the original document and issue another reflecting the withdrawal. But this would necessitate reissuing the entire, and somewhat lengthy, text. A simpler course would be for the depositor to execute a document acknowledging receipt of the partial withdrawal and for both parties to maintain copies, filed with the original document, a balance to be struck at a convenient time in the future. As partial withdrawals are made and new documents issued for subsequent deposits by the same depositor, the documentation becomes unwieldy or inaccurate, for mistakes inevitably creep into the "clay work." Then it becomes expedient for the parties to recount the inventory, make whatever adjustments are necessary, and issue a new, accurate tablet for the items actually on hand. All documents previously issued are then destroyed. Such a procedure is common in the modern field warehousing industry.

It seems more likely that Oppenheim's second document was such a "consolidating," or "superseding," document than that the same consignee received substantial shipments of the same commodities in identical amounts in consecutive years from the same distant sources. The Uruk tablets suggest the formalization of a transportation and distribution system in western Asia during the sixth century B.C. that resulted from a commercial practice of many years duration. Highly developed commercial forms, procedures, and laws do not proceed from the occasional transaction. They achieve clarity and precision through repetition, reconsideration, and adjustment, and depend, in the last analysis, upon a community in which trading activity flourishes. The Uruk documents represent a stage in the continuing refinement and clarification of the bailor-bailee relationship, an issue that written law had first addressed in the boatman-carrier provision of the Laws of Eshnunna fourteen centuries before, and amplified thereafter in #236-38 of the Laws of Hammurabi. (LE #36 and #37, and CH #120-26 addressed the storer's liability.)

---

[1] Ezekiel, 27:1-36.

[2] Oppenheim, Essay on Overland Trade in the First Millennium B.C., 21 JCS 236 (1967).

[3] Uniform Commercial Code (U.L.A.) Sect.7-203 - warehouse receipts, Sect. 7-301 (1)- bills of lading. The phrase is of critical importance in the issuance of a document of title.

[4] Attached to this exhibit are forms of negotiable and non-negotiable warehouse receipts bearing the prominent "Said to Be or Contain" legend above the column in which the goods are described. The forms are today standard for the warehousing industry. Published with permission of The American Warehousemen's Association, Chicago, Illinois.

AWA Seal of Security

AMERICAN WAREHOUSE COMPANY

A PUBLIC WAREHOUSE

2121 AMERICAN AVENUE • AMERICA

Date of Issue__________________ Consecutive No.__________________

THIS IS TO CERTIFY that we have received in Storage Warehouse__________________

situated at__________________

for the account of__________________

in apparent good order, except as noted hereon (contents, condition and quality unknown) the following described property, subject to all the terms and conditions contained herein and on the reverse hereof, such property to be delivered to (His) (Their) (Its) order, upon payment of all storage, handling and other charges and the surrender of this Warehouse Receipt properly endorsed,

LOT NO.	QUANTITY	SAID TO BE OR CONTAIN	STORAGE PER MONTH		HANDLING IN AND OUT	
			RATE	PER	RATE	PER
		NEGOTIABLE Quantities subject to deliveries noted below.				

Advances have been made and liability incurred on such goods, as follows:

____

____

American Warehouse Company claims a lien for all lawful charges for storage and preservation of the goods; also for all lawful claims for money advanced, interest, insurance, transportation, labor, weighing, coopering and other charges and expenses in relation to such goods.

The property covered by this receipt has NOT been insured by this company for the benefit of the depositor against fire or any other casualty.

(This clause to be omitted from forms used in those states where warehousemen are required by law to insure goods.)

AMERICAN WAREHOUSE COMPANY

By__________________

This Receipt Is Valid Only When Signed by an Officer of the Company.

THE GOODS MENTIONED BELOW ARE HEREBY RELEASED FROM THIS RECEIPT FOR DELIVERY FROM WAREHOUSE. ANY UNRELEASED BALANCE OF THE GOODS IS SUBJECT TO A LIEN FOR UNPAID CHARGES AND ADVANCES ON THE RELEASED PORTION.

DELIVERIES

DATE	LOT NUMBER	QUANTITY RELEASED		SIGNATURE	QUANTITY DUE ON RECEIPT

AMERICAN WAREHOUSE COMPANY
STREET ADDRESS • CITY & AMERICA 00000
TELEPHONE: (312) – 123-4567

ORIGINAL
NON-NEGOTIABLE WAREHOUSE RECEIPT

AMERICAN WAREHOUSE COMPANY claims a lien for all lawful charges for storage and preservation of the goods; also for all lawful claims for money advanced, interest, insurance, transportation, labor, weighing, coopering and other charges and expenses in relation to such goods, and for the balance on any other accounts that may be due. The property covered by this receipt has NOT been insured by this Company for the benefit of the depositor against fire or any other casualty.

DOCUMENT NUMBER
DATE
CUSTOMER NUMBER
CUSTOMER ORDER NO.
WAREHOUSE NO.

RECEIVED FROM

THIS IS TO CERTIFY THAT WE HAVE RECEIVED the goods listed hereon in apparent good order, except as noted herein (contents, condition and quality unknown), SUBJECT TO ALL TERMS AND CONDITIONS INCLUDING LIMITATION OF LIABILITY HEREIN AND ON THE REVERSE HEREOF. Such property to be delivered to THE DEPOSITOR upon the payment of all storage, handling and other charges. Advances have been made and liability incurred on these goods as follows:

FOR ACCOUNT OF

DELIVERING CARRIER	CARRIER NUMBER	PREPAID/COLLECT	SHIPPERS NUMBER

QUANTITY	SAID TO BE OR CONTAIN (CUSTOMER ITEM NO., WAREHOUSE ITEM NO., LOT NUMBER, DESCRIPTION, ETC.)	WEIGHT	RATE CODE	STORAGE RATE / HANDLING RATE	DAMAGE & EXCEPTIONS
	TOTALS				

NO DELIVERY WILL BE MADE ON THIS RECEIPT EXCEPT ON WRITTEN ORDER.

AMERICAN WAREHOUSE COMPANY
BY
AUTHORIZED SIGNATURE

FORM 2 3/70

EXHIBIT I

THE BABYLONIAN BAILEE'S OBLIGATION TO REDELIVER

It may be another rule of logic rather than law that if A, the "bailor," deposits an item of property with B, the "bailee," and no superseding event occurs, A should have an absolute right to the return of his property when he asks for it. Lawmakers addressing the bailor-bailee relationship are likely to begin with an affirmation of this unsurprising rule. They are then apt to enumerate events that will excuse nondelivery by the bailee when demand is made. So, the able lawyers who drafted the Uniform Commercial Code, presently the law in the United States, except Louisiana, began Article 7-403(1) of that Code, the "Obligation of Warehouseman or Carrier to Deliver; Excuse," as follows:

*The bailee must deliver the goods to a person entitled under the document [*Warehouse Receipt or Bill of Lading*] . . . unless and to the extent that the bailee establishes . . . (b) damage to or delay, loss or destruction of the goods for which the bailee is not liable [but the burden of establishing negligence in such cases is on the person entitled under the document].*[1]

The compilation of laws promulgated by Hammurabi may be the outstanding jurisprudential achievement of the pre-Christian era. CH #263-267, describing the obligation of a bailee to deliver and the lawful excuses justifying nondelivery, demonstrate the cogency of its reasoning. Hammurabi's legal scribes began, as the draftsmen of Article 7 of the Uniform Commercial Code did, by setting out an unconditional obligation of the bailee-shepherd in CH #263 to return the animals deposited with him:

If he [the shepherd] has lost [the ox] or sheep which was committed to him, he shall make good, ox for [ox], sheep for [sheep] to their owner (ANET, 177).

CH #266 describes exculpating circumstances that relieved the shepherd of his obligation:

> *If a visitation of god has occurred in a sheepfold or a lion has made a kill, the shepherd shall prove himself innocent in the presence of god, but the owner of the sheepfold shall receive from him the animal stricken in the fold* (ANET, 177).

In the latter section, the shepherd who wishes to be relieved of his obligation for a lost animal must swear an oath explaining the loss and produce the animal's remains. Babylonian legislators were unwilling to accept the shepherd's unsupported representation, even under oath, and required him to produce evidence of the missing animal's fate.

The requirement that a bailee explain why commodities deposited with him were missing was the focus of recent major litigation in the United States. In the infamous "Salad Oil" scandal of the early 1960's, a warehousing company in New Jersey found itself in the unenviable position of being unable to account for nearly $140 million dollars of oil for which it had issued warehouse receipts. For several years, every major law firm in New York City was involved in attempting to resolve the host of legal problems engendered by this debacle.

A critical question raised in the litigation was whether the warehousing company could defend by showing that although it was unable to account for a large quantity of the missing oil, it had exercised the reasonable care required by Article 7-204 and should therefore not be held responsible. Article 7-204 (1) of the U.C.C. reads:

> *A warehouseman is liable for damages for loss of or injury to the goods caused by his failure to exercise such care in regard to them as a reasonably careful man would exercise under like circumstances but unless otherwise agreed he is not liable for damages which could not have been avoided by the exercise of such care.*

In rejecting the defendant's argument, the Court of Appeals of New York relied upon a rationale founded in simple logic and public policy concerns that the framers of Hammurabi's laws would undoubtedly have found persuasive. The Court noted that notwithstanding the provisions of Article 7-204 cited by the defense, the issue of due care could not be considered until the warehouseman had provided some explanation for what had happened to the missing oil.

> *It would establish an unwise rule to place a bailee in better position to be excused if he knew less about the disappearance of the goods than if he knew more. That is the underlying reason for the time-*

honored law of New York and New Jersey requiring a warehouseman to make an explanation of injury or loss in the case of bailed merchandise.[2]

In *The Babylonian Laws,* Driver and Miles raise a question about CH #263 and #267.

The man in 263 is liable without proof of negligence if he loses an ox or a sheep in his charge, but . . . why should he be liable absolutely in 263 but only if negligence is proved in 267?[3]

CH #267 reads:

If the shepherd was careless and has let lameness develop in the fold, the shepherd shall make good in cattle and sheep the loss through the lameness which he let develop in the fold and give [them] to their owner (ANET, 177).

It is submitted that the man in CH #263 was not liable absolutely. His liability was conditioned by CH #266 which afforded force majeure defenses and CH #267 which made him liable only for his negligence, defenses available to the bailee today under Article 7-403 (1) (b).

Driver and Miles also express doubt that the shepherd of CH #267 could excuse himself by proving he had taken reasonable care to prevent disease. They argue:

If a herdsman loses any of the flock entrusted to him he is excused only if the loss is caused by a "stroke of god," or by a lion; in all other cases he is liable as in 266 [sic].[4]

Such an analysis, however, holds the non-negligent shepherd who has lost an animal to disease to a standard of strict liability, a result difficult to sustain when CH #267 is read literally. Moreover, however carefully tended, animals will die. The range of fearsome diseases likely to ravage a herd of cattle or a flock of sheep virtually assures a loss of at least part of any herd or flock held for a prolonged period.[5]

To hold a herdsman liable for any but a CH #266 loss, therefore, would make him responsible for an event over which he had no control and transfer the entire burden of economic loss to him without any showing he was better able to bear the loss or that the rewards to be earned from his occupation would have enabled him to accept such a responsibility.

It might be closer to Hammurabi's intent to give literal effect to CH #267 and conclude that section was intended to provide a defense to a diligent herdsman against the demand of an owner whose animal was lost to disease. Such a reading would bring CH #263, #266 and #267 of

Hammurabi's laws into substantial agreement with the treatment of the bailee's obligation to redeliver envisioned by Article 7 of the Uniform Commercial Code.

---

[1] Section 7-403 is a recasting of section 8 of the Uniform Warehouse Receipts Act, which it superseded. Section 8 had read: "A warehouseman, in the absence of some lawful excuse . . . is bound to deliver the goods upon a demand made either by the holder of the receipt for the goods or by the depositor. . . . In case the warehouseman refuses or fails to deliver the goods in compliance with a demand by the holder or depositor . . . the burden shall be upon the warehouseman to establish the existence of a lawful excuse for such refusal."

[2] Procter & Gamble v. Lawrence American Field Warehousing Corp., 16 N.Y.2d. 344, 213 N.E.2d. 873 (1965).

[3] Driver and Miles, Babylonian Laws, 1:463, n. 2.

[4] Ibid., 463.

[5] A partial listing of diseases to which animals alive today are susceptible, according to information made available by the United States Department of Agriculture, includes anthrax, black quarter, brucellosis, foot and mouth disease (See Department of Agriculture pamphlet, "When will foot and mouth disease wipe you out?"), leukemia, plague, pleuro-pneumonia, rinderpest, tuberculosis. Even in modern well-run feed lots, when disease and parasitic infections are better understood, where high-quality stock is selected, inoculated against disease, fed rations formulated by computer under the supervision of nutritionists and veterinarians, death loss is anticipated and charged, within an agreed-upon range, to the owner as a normal risk.

EXHIBIT J

THE COMMITTEE OF STYLE AND ARRANGEMENT

The following are the distinguished members of the Committee of Style and Arrangement as seen through the eyes of a fellow delegate to the Federal Convention of 1787, Major William Pierce of Georgia.[1]

William Samuel Johnson (1727-1819)

Son of the first President of King's College (Columbia) and a graduate of Yale, Johnson received a Master's degree from Harvard, practiced law in Connecticut and New York, served in the Connecticut legislature and as judge of the Superior Court. Opposed to the Revolution, he retired to private life during its course. President of Columbia College, 1781-1800, Johnson was also the first United States senator from Connecticut. Of him, Pierce reports:

Dr. Johnson is a character much celebrated for his legal knowledge; he is said to be one of the first classics in America, and certainly possesses a very strong and enlightened understanding.

As an Orator in my opinion, there is nothing in him that warrants the high reputation which he has for public speaking. There is something in the tone of his voice not pleasant to the Ear—but he is eloquent and clear—always abounding with information and instruction. He was once employed as an Agent for the State of Connecticut to state her claims to certain landed territory before the British House of Commons; this Office he discharged with so much dignity, and made such an ingenious display of his powers, that he laid the foundation of a reputation which will probably last much longer than his own life. Dr. Johnson is about sixty years of age, possesses the manners of a Gentleman, and engages the Hearts of Men by the sweetness of his temper, and that affectionate style of address with which he accosts his acquaintance.

Gouverneur Morris (1752-1816)

Morris's family, of distinguished Welsh lineage, owned almost 2,000 acres on the western shore of the Hudson. A graduate of King's College in 1768 and licensed to practice law in 1771, Morris helped draft the New York State Constitution and served as delegate to the Convention from Pennsylvania, an honor he did not seek. Pierce:

Mr. Governeur Morris is one of those Genius's in whom every species of talents combine to render him conspicuous and flourishing in public debate: He winds through all the mazes of rhetoric, and throws around him such a glare that he charms, captivates and leads away the senses of all who hear him. With an infinite stretch of fancy he brings to view things when he is engaged in deep argumentation, that render all the labor of reasoning easy and pleasing. But with all these powers, he is fickle and inconsistent—never pursuing one train of thinking—nor ever regular. He has gone through a very extensive course of reading, and is acquainted with all the sciences. No man has more wit—nor can anyone engage the attention more than Mr. Morris. He was bred to the law, but I am told he disliked the profession, and turned merchant. He is engaged in some great mercantile matters with his namesake Mr. Robert Morris. This Gentlemen is about 38 years old, he has been unfortunate in losing one of his Legs, and getting all the flesh burned off his right arm by a scald, when a youth.

Rufus King (1755-1827)

A graduate of Harvard in 1777 and admitted to the Bar in 1778, King served on the General Court of Massachusetts and in the Continental Congress. He later became United States Minister to Great Britain (1796-1803). Of King, Pierce says:

Mr. King is a Man much distinguished for his eloquence and great parliamentary talents. He was educated in Massachusetts, and is said to have good classical as well as legal knowledge. He has served for three years in the Congress of the United States with great and deserved applause, and is at this time high in the confidence and approbation of his Countrymen. This gentleman is about thirty three years of age, about five feet ten inches high, well formed, an handsome face, with a strong expressive Eye, and a sweet high toned voice. In his public speaking there is something peculiarly strong and rich in his expression, clear and convincing in his arguments, rapid and irresistible at times in his eloquence but he is not always equal. His action is natural, swimming, and graceful, but there is a rudeness of manner sometimes accompanying it.

But take him tout en semble, he may with propriety be ranked among the Luminaries of the present Age.

James Madison (1751-1836)

After graduating from Princeton in 1771, Madison remained another year in order to study Hebrew. At home he read systematically in theology, philosophy, and the law. Madison served on the Committee that framed the Virginia Constitution and Declaration of Rights, was a member of the Continental Congress, "Father" of the United States Constitution, and fourth President of the United States. According to Pierce:

Mr. Maddison is a character who has long been in public life; and what is very remarkable every Person seems to acknowledge his greatness. He blends together the profound Politician, with the Scholar. In the management of every great question he evidently took the lead in the Convention, and tho' he cannot be called an Orator, he is a most agreeable, eloquent and convincing Speaker. From a spirit of industry and application which he possesses in a most eminent degree, he always comes forward the best informed Man of any point in debate. The affairs of the United States, he perhaps, has the most correct knowledge of, of any Man in the Union. He has twice been a Member of Congress, and was always thought one of the Ablest Members that ever sat in that Council. Mr. Maddison is about 37 years of age, a Gentleman of great modesty—with a remarkable sweet temper. He is easy and unreserved among his acquaintances, and has a most agreeable style of conversation.

Alexander Hamilton (1757-1804)

Although Hamilton was a brilliant student at King's College, his studies were interrupted by the Revolution. He served courageously as a Captain of Artillery, and as a Lt. Colonel and aide-de-camp to General Washington during that conflict. He later served in the Continental Congress and New York legislature. Pierce's portrait of Hamilton:

Colo Hamilton is deservedly celebrated for his talents. He is a practitioner of the Law, and reputed to be a finished Scholar. To a clear and strong judgment, he unites the ornaments of fancy, and whilst he is able, convincing and engaging in his eloquence the Heart and Head sympathize in approving him. Yet there is something too feeble in his voice to be equal to the strains of oratory—it is my opinion that he is rather a convincing Speaker, than a blazing Orator. Colo Hamilton requires time to think—he enquires into every part of his subject with the searchings of philosophy, and when he comes forward he comes highly charged with interesting matter, there is no skimming over the surface of a subject with him, he must sink to the bottom to see what foundation it rests on. His language is not always equal, sometimes didactic like Bolingbroke's at others light and tripping as Stern's. His eloquence is not so defusive as to trifle with the senses, but he rambles just enough to strike and keep up the attention. He is about 33 years old, of small stature and lean. His manners are tinctured with stiffness, and sometimes with a degree of vanity that is highly disagreeable.

As to his own character, Pierce was willing to allow those who chose to speculate on it to consider it "in any light that their fancy or imagination may depict." His best intention in rendering his services in Congress and the Convention was towards the interest of Georgia, and "the general welfare" of the Confederacy.

---

[1] "The Records of the Federal Convention of 1787," edited by Max Farrand, Copyright Yale University Press. Used by permission.

CHRONOLOGICAL TABLE

MESOPOTAMIANS, HITTITES, and PERSIANS

B.C.	
4000	Sumer—Irrigation, extensive agriculture, domestication of animals, use of copper, early city-states.
3000	Cuneiform Writing—wheeled vehicles, pottery wheel, sail boats.
2800-2400	First Dynasty of Ur—legal documents in use.
ca. 2350	"Reform Document" of Urukagina—*amargi* "freedom," of the people.
2334-2279	Sargon of Akkad—First Mesopotamian Empire.
2112-2004	Third Dynasty of Ur.
2112-2095	Ur-Nammu—First Written Law Code. "If a man" protasis throughout.
2094-2047	Shulgi—Prologue's purposes evident in hymnology.
ca. 2000	Laws of Eshnunna. Assyrian merchant colony in Cappadocia.
1934-1924	Lipit-Ishtar—Law Code and Prologue. "If a man" form frequent.
1894-1595	First Dynasty of Babylon.
1792-1750	Hammurabi—Law Code—wide dissemination and imitation. "If a man" form usual. Advanced commercial practice.
1680-1650	Labarnas founds Hittite empire. King answers to *pankus,* council of nobles.
1650-1620	Hittite expansion under Hattusilis I.
1620-1590	Mursilis I conquers Babylon (1595), withdraws. Hittites leading power in Near East.
1550-1150	Kassites rule in Babylon.

1525-1500	Hittite Telipinus's reforms—democratic leanings—*pankus* or *nagbāti,* council of nobility, and *kabtūti* or *tuliyas*, lesser nobility, check on royal power.
ca. 1500	Alphabetic writing in Syria.
1380-1346	Hittite power consolidated under Suppiluliumas I, XIV century—Hittite Code of Laws, written in cuneiform on clay tablets—close resemblance to Mesopotamian law codes. "If a man" form common.
1300-1000	Assyrian hegemony—Middle Assyrian Laws—"If a man" form common.
1250-1200	Hittite decline. Capital at Hattusas burned.
1000-625	Assyrian Empire.
745-727	Tiglath-Pileser III—Expansion of Assyrian Empire.
705-681	Sennacherib—destroys Babylon (689).
680-669	Esarhaddon.
668-625	Assurbanipal.
625-539	Neo-Babylonian Dynasty.
604-562	Nebuchadnezzar II.
559-331	Persian Empire.
559-529	Cyrus—takes Babylon (539).
529-522	Cambyses—conquers Egypt.
522-486	Darius I—"Ordinance of Good Regulations"—"If a man" form probable, as indicated by exclusive use in second century Iranian law.

GREEKS

ca.1800	First Speakers of Greek in Greece.
1500-1200	Mycenaean Civilization dominant in eastern Mediterranean.
1194-1184	Trojan War.
ca. 1130	Mycenae destroyed.
ca. 1000	Early Greek colonies in Asia Minor.
ca. 780	Greek writing—Phoenician letters.
ca. 725	Homer—*Iliad* and *Odyssey*.
ca. 725	Hesiod—*Works and Days, Theogony*.
ca. 621	Laws of Dracon.
640-560	Solon—Reforms (593)—"If a man" form to Solon's laws imputed by later Greeks.
570-500	Pythagoras.

500-430	Protagoras.
499-479	Persian Wars.
495-406	Sophocles—*Antigone* (ca. 442).
490	Marathon.
480	Thermopylae—Salamis.
485-425	Herodotus—*The Histories* (ca. 450).
470(?)-380(?)	Democritus.
461-429	Pericles.
436-338	Isocrates—*Panegyricus, To Nicocles.*
430-354	Xenophon—*Anabasis, Oeconomicus, Cyropaedia.*
401	Battle of Cunaxa.
399	Trial and execution of Socrates.
427(?)-347	Plato—*The Laws*—"If a man" form frequent throughout Bks. VIII-XII.
384-322	Aristotle—*The Politics, Athenian Constitution.*
383-322	Demosthenes—Use of "If a man" form frequent in private orations.
ca.300	Rhodian Sea-Law—"If a man" use apparent.

HEBREWS

2000-1600	Patriarchs.
1600-1300	Sojourn, servitude in Egypt.
1290-1250	Moses—Exodus —Ten Commandments. "If a man" form in Covenant Code, *Ex.* 20:22-23:33, esp. Chap. 22.
1250	Conquest of Canaan.
1200-1000	Judges.
1020-1000	Saul.
1000-961	David.
961-925	Solomon.
925-721	Tribes divide—Israel and Judah.
721	Assyria destroys kingdom of Israel.
720	Isaiah.
621	Earliest Scripture—Book of the Law.
586	Nebuchadnezzar conquers Judah—leading families taken to Babylon.
586-538	Exile.
538-333	Persian rule—Cyrus allows Jews to return to Jerusalem.
458	Ezra's return from Babylon—Book of the Law of Moses.

INDEX

ACKNOWLEDGMENTS

I am most grateful for the characteristically generous assistance of Professor Ingrid Cunninghame-Blank. Betty Gardiner's rare intelligence, skill, and unfailing good humor made editing the book a pleasure. My thanks to my wife, Patricia, for her forebearance, insights, and good counsel; to my daughter, Cecilia, who found the images of the ancient Near East intriguing and volunteered to do the illustrations, and to my son, Michael, who more than once put aside his bass and cheerfully extricated me from the implacable logic of the computer.

This book grew out of a decade-long correspondence between the writer and Professor Samuel Noah Kramer. From the very first fifteen-page draft, Professor Kramer and Milly, his thoroughly admirable wife, offered encouragement and support which I deeply appreciate. From time to time Milly also urged me to call the Professor "Sam," as many of his friends did, but I could not bring myself to do so. If I had, I would have felt very much as Gouverneur Morris did when once on a dare he threw an arm over George Washington's shoulder and later swore that having once done it he would never do it again. My regard for the Professor, founded in affection rather than awe, was nevertheless no less; he was truly, as Plato said of Socrates, "Of all men of his time that I have known . . . the wisest and justest and best."

It was a grievous loss when Professor Kramer, still active and productive at the age of ninety three, passed away. At the time, this book was not yet finished; its faults and frailties are all my own.

James T. McGuire